EVIDENCE

&

ADVOCACY

EVIDENCE
&
ADVOCACY

Fifth Edition

Peter Murphy

BLACKSTONE PRESS LIMITED

This edition published in Great Britain 1998 by Blackstone Press
Limited, Aldine Place, London W12 8AA.
Telephone 0181-740 2277

First Edition 1984
Second Edition 1986
Third Edition 1990
Fourth Edition, 1994
Fifth Edition, 1998

Chapters 3, 9 and 12 (the chapters on civil hearsay, expert evidence
and preparing and presenting a civil case) of this edition are based on
lectures given by David Barnard for the Temple Lectures course, The
Advocate in Evidence, during 1981 and 1982.

ISBN: 1 85431 767 9

Typeset by Style Photosetting Ltd, Mayfield, East Sussex
Printed by Bell & Bain Limited, Glasgow

Contents

Preface ix

Preface to the First Edition x

1 Fundamentals of Evidence 1

Introduction — Burden of proof — Standard of proof —
Relevance, admissibility and weight — Making and refuting
objections to admissibility — Judicial discretion to admit or
exclude evidence — Evidence illegally or unfairly obtained
— Personal knowledge of the court — Further reading —
Notes

2 The Rule against Hearsay at Common Law 24

Introduction — What hearsay is — The crucial question:
direct evidence or hearsay? — Distinguishing direct
evidence from hearsay: some useful examples — Exceptions
to the rule against hearsay — The excited utterance rule —
Further reading — Notes

3 The Rule against Hearsay in Civil Cases 39

Introduction: the Civil Evidence Act 1995 — Abolition of
the rule against hearsay in civil proceedings — Proceedings
to which the Act applies — Procedural safeguards —
Matters affecting weight — Use of copies — Statements
made by persons called as witnesses — Impeachment of the
maker of an admissible hearsay statement — Preservation of
common law exceptions — Proof of business and public
authority records — Admissions — Further reading — Notes

4   The Rule against Hearsay in Criminal Cases   53

Introduction — Admissible hearsay statements: Criminal
Justice Act 1988, section 23 — Admissible hearsay statements contained in documents created or received in the
course of a trade, business, profession etc.: Criminal Justice
Act 1988, section 24 — Discretion of the court to exclude
evidence otherwise admissible under sections 23 and 24:
Criminal Justice Act 1988, section 25 — Documents prepared for the purposes of criminal proceedings or the
investigation of crime: Criminal Justice Act 1988, sections
26 and 24(4) — Documents produced by computers: Police
and Criminal Evidence Act 1984, section 69 — General
considerations — Further reading — Notes

5   Confessions and the Codes of Practice   63

Introduction — Being there — Taking instructions about
confessions — Admissibility of confessions — Confessions
and the Codes of Practice — Recognising breaches of the
Codes — Challenging the weight of confessions — Confessions implicating co-defendants — Confessions made in
response to confessions of co-defendants — Confessions
which reveal previous bad character — Further reading —
Notes

**6   The Defendant's Denials, Mixed Statements, and
Silence**   89

Denials — Mixed statements — The defendant's silence —
The defendant's silence when questioned — The defendant's
failure to give evidence at trial — General provisions
affecting sections 34 to 37 — The defendant's failure to
comply with disclosure provisions — Civil cases — Further
reading — Notes

7   Evidence of Character   107

Introduction — Good character — Bad character — Cross-
examination about bad character — Defences involving
imputations on character — Discretionary exclusion of character — Giving evidence against co-defendants — Improper
references to character — Further reading — Notes

8 Witnesses 127

Introduction — What witnesses can I call to give evidence?
— What witnesses can I compel to attend to give evidence?
— How many witnesses should I call to give evidence? —
What kinds of witnesses should I call to give evidence? —
Further reading — Notes

9 Expert Evidence 146

Introduction — Preparation of expert evidence — Disclosure
of expert evidence before trial — Admissibility of expert
reports — Presentation of expert evidence at trial — Summary — Further reading — Notes

10 Privileges 156

Introduction — General principles — Legal professional
privilege — Privilege against self-incrimination — Without-
prejudice communications — Further reading — Notes

11 Presentation of Evidence at Trial 167

Introduction — Examination-in-chief — Evidence of
children in youth courts — Evidence given by written
witness statement in civil cases: CCR Ord. 20, r. 12A —
Cross-examination — Impeachment of the maker of an
admissible hearsay statement — Re-examination and
evidence in rebuttal— Presentation of documentary and real
evidence — Further reading — Notes

12 Preparing and Presenting a Civil Case 198

Introduction — Before the hearing — Preparing for trial —
At the hearing — Brown's rules — During your opponent's
cross-examination — Your own cross-examination — Final
speech — Further reading — Note

13 Preparing and Presenting a Criminal Case   212

Introduction — The concept of the ideal closing speech — Gathering the evidence — Preparation of cross–examination — Preparing the defendant's evidence-in-chief — Preparing and delivering your speech — Further reading

Appendix: Extracts from Statutes, Codes of Practice and Rules of Court   229

Criminal Evidence Act 1898, section 1, as amended — Police and Criminal Evidence Act 1984, sections 58 and 76–80 — Code of Practice (C) for the Detention, Treatment and Questioning of Persons by Police Officers — Code of Practice (E) on Tape Recording of Interviews with Suspects — Criminal Justice Act 1988, sections 23 to 26, 32 and 32A, Schedule 2 — Civil Evidence Act 1995 (1995, c. 38) — County Court Rules 1981, Order 20, rules 27 and 28 — Rules of the Supreme Court 1965, Order 38, rules 36 to 44

Index   312

Preface

This fifth edition is intended to bring *Evidence & Advocacy* up to date as at the beginning of March 1998. As in previous editions, I have made every effort to preserve something of the spirit of the lectures originally given by David Barnard and myself under the auspices of Temple Lectures. The book is still intended primarily as a simple guide to the everyday techniques of advocacy in the magistrates' and county courts. It should be emphasised that it is not and is not intended to be a complete text on the law of evidence. In this edition, I have included suggestions for more detailed reading at the end of each chapter.

This edition includes coverage of many new statutory provisions, including those of the Criminal Justice and Public Order Act 1994, the Civil Evidence Act 1995 (and the rules made pursuant to that Act) and the Criminal Procedure and Investigations Act 1996. It also includes the many important cases decided by the House of Lords and Court of Appeal since publication of the last edition. A separate chapter is now devoted to the question of the defendant's silence during investigation and at trial in the light of the Criminal Justice and Public Order Act 1994, and a new chapter has been added dealing with the basics of the law of privilege.

As always, my thanks go to the publishing team at Blackstone Press Limited, especially Alistair MacQueen and Heather Saward, and my editor Derek French, for their unfailing support and excellence in all they do.

Peter Murphy
Houston, Texas

Preface to the First Edition

This book is based upon a course for solicitor advocates devised and organised by 'Temple Lectures', which was presented at six centres in England and in Hong Kong during 1982. The authors are grateful to Mr Rowland Ellis for permission to reproduce the material originally delivered at the course.

The idea of the lectures and of this book is to provide a guide to advocates practising in county courts and magistrates' courts as to how the rules of evidence are applied in practice.

The authors are separated by six thousand miles of land and water. For that reason each has taken the responsibility of providing part of the book. The major part, which deals in particular with criminal advocacy has been written by Peter Murphy. The chapters on civil evidence and on the presentation of a case at a county court are by David Barnard.

The authors wish to express their gratitude to their publishers for all their help and forbearance. Thanks are also due to Arlene Nabours and Sherry M. Fries who typed the manuscript.

Peter Murphy, San Francisco
David Barnard, London
June 1984

One

Fundamentals of Evidence

Introduction

This being a book concerned primarily with evidence, and with the relationship of evidence to successful advocacy in the magistrates' and county courts, it must begin by considering what evidence is, and what its function is.

You will not need too much experience as an advocate in any court before you learn an important fact of life, namely that there is a world of difference between having a good case and proving it to a court. A prosecution, defence or civil action may be supported by the facts in every respect, but unless the facts necessary to demonstrate this are both available and properly presented to the court, how is the court to appreciate and act on them? The answer is, of course, that the court can be informed and persuaded only by the presentation of evidence. Evidence may, therefore, be defined as any material which tends to persuade the court of the truth or probability of the facts necessary to sustain the case asserted by the party presenting it. Note the use of the word 'tends'. It serves as a reminder of the sad, but inescapable reality that evidence will succeed in persuading a court only if that evidence appears as truthful, reliable and cogent. Even if a party is in possession of evidence, as it has just been defined, it does not follow that the case will be proved to the satisfaction of the court. Moreover, because the law imposes restrictions on the kinds of evidence that may be adduced, in the interests of fairness to the parties, the evidence must be such that the court is empowered to receive it: it must be both relevant and admissible, when judged by reference to the legal rules of evidence.

Although, therefore, the gulf between having a good case and proving it may be described in terms of having the necessary evidence of the relevant facts, that description raises at least as many problems as it solves. Which of the parties has the burden of proving particular facts to the court, and will therefore fail if those facts cannot be proved? Is there any minimum standard of persuasiveness which that party's evidence must attain, and does that standard vary from case to case? What is meant by relevance? What rules govern the admissibility of evidence? Who has the function of deciding whether evidence is, or is not admissible? Can a party be permitted to adduce admissible evidence which has been obtained in an illegal or unfair manner?

The object of this introductory chapter is to offer some basic answers to such questions, with particular emphasis on the ways in which they are likely to arise in the magistrates' and county courts. An understanding of these basic answers will enable the advocate not only to deal successfully with evidential problems that arise in these courts, but also to develop an organised method of trial preparation based upon the actual evidential demands of the case at hand. This is particularly important for the advocate who has never received a formal course in the law of evidence, or whose training in that subject has been obscured by the mists of time. It is a serious error to try to launch into the detailed rules of evidence without first understanding the fundamental principles upon which they all depend.

It should never be forgotten that evidence has one built-in trap for the advocate which the rules of substantive law or of procedure do not, or at any rate should not, set for him. Almost always, points of law and procedure can be anticipated and researched before going into court. Points of evidence, on the other hand, have a habit of arising quite unexpectedly, because of some unforeseen and often unforeseeable question asked or document produced. An objection must be taken swiftly, or the court will be exposed to evidence which it should not see or hear. Your opponent's objections to your evidence may be equally unanticipated, and if unfounded, must be promptly refuted before the court rules that some vital piece of evidence is inadmissible. A sound working knowledge of the rules of evidence is therefore essential to successful advocacy; you cannot rely entirely on trial preparation, although preparation is certainly necessary to deal properly with all problems which can be foreseen.

Evidence may be presented to a court in various forms. It may be oral evidence given by a witness in court (or the equivalent presented in an affidavit or hearsay statement when permitted), documentary evidence, in which the contents of a document are admitted as evidence in their own right, or so-called real evidence. Real evidence means any material from which the court can draw conclusions by using its own senses, such as the appearance of an object, the demeanour of witnesses, or a photograph, tape recording or film, or a view of the *locus in quo*.

Burden of proof

In both civil and criminal cases, a party who must prove an issue to the court is said to bear the burden of proof on that issue.

Criminal Cases

In criminal cases, it is a fundamental rule of English law that the prosecution bear the burden of proving the guilt of the defendant. In almost all cases, this means proving all essential elements of the offence charged. This was emphasised by the House of Lords in the landmark decision in *Woolmington* v *DPP* [1]. The defendant was charged with the murder of his wife. His defence was that the gun had gone off accidentally. The jury were directed that, once the prosecution proved that the deceased was killed by the defendant, it was then for the defendant to show that the killing did not amount to murder. Holding this direction to be improper, Viscount Sankey LC said:

> Throughout the web of the English criminal law one golden thread is always to be seen, that it is the duty of the prosecution to prove the prisoner's guilt. . . . If, at the end of and on the whole of the case, there is a reasonable doubt . . . as to whether the prisoner killed the deceased with a malicious intention, the prosecution has not made out the case and the prisoner is entitled to an acquittal. No matter what the charge or where the trial, the principle that the prosecution must prove the guilt of the prisoner is part of the common law of England and no attempt to whittle it down can be entertained.

An essential, if elementary, part of your trial preparation will therefore be to ascertain what the essential elements of a charge are, for this will ordinarily fix the parameters of the burden of proof that lies on the prosecution in your case. Once you have established that the essential elements of a charge of theft are that the defendant (a) dishonestly (b) appropriated (c) property (d) belonging to another (e) with the intention of depriving the other of it permanently, you have identified the facts which the prosecution must prove in order to obtain a conviction. And whether you are prosecuting or defending, you have incidentally focused your mind on the facts to which the evidence must be directed.

The burden of proof described above, the burden of proving to the required standard all the facts legally necessary to prevail, is known technically as the 'legal' burden of proof. There is also an 'evidential' burden of proof. This evidential burden requires the prosecution to prove facts sufficient to prevent the bench from dismissing the charge on the ground that there is no case to answer. The defence may also bear an evidential burden to 'raise an issue' in certain cases, where the defendant wishes to raise a defence involving facts which do not form part of the prosecution's case. Obviously, if these facts are not part of the prosecution case, there is no way for the court to hear them, unless they are raised by the defence. This does not mean that the defence have to prove these facts, merely that they must adduce some evidence of them. This may be done either by eliciting them during cross-examination, or by calling evidence for the defence. If the defence does so then the prosecution must disprove the facts, insofar as they are relevant, beyond reasonable doubt. A good example is where the defendant asserts an alibi. Although it is often described loosely as a 'defence', an alibi is actually no more than a denial that the defendant was at the scene of the crime (a fact which the prosecution must prove beyond reasonable doubt to obtain a conviction). For obvious reasons, the defendant must adduce some evidence of his or her whereabouts if the court is to consider the alibi, even though the defendant bears no legal burden of proof. Therefore, the defendant may be considered to have an evidential burden with respect to an alibi.

It is important to appreciate that the proper time for the bench to assess whether the prosecution have discharged their burden of proof is at the conclusion of the entire case. If the prosecution close their case without adducing any evidence capable of proving an essential element of the offence charged, i.e., without discharging the evidential burden, the bench will uphold a submission of no case to answer, because the burden cannot be discharged. However, provided that the prosecution adduce, with respect to each essential element of the charge, evidence on which the court would be entitled to find such element proved, the case will survive the submission. This is often known as making out a *prima facie* case.

Establishing a *prima facie* case may not be enough to secure a conviction, because the defence are entitled to argue that the overall burden of proof has not been discharged. The fact that the court may be entitled to find the case proved does not mean that it must do so. Nonetheless, once the prosecution have established a *prima facie* case, the defence run a serious tactical risk in not calling evidence to rebut it, not because the defendant is called upon to prove his innocence (which would be contrary to the rule in *Woolmington's* case) but because the court may exercise its entitlement to accept the uncontradicted prosecution evidence.

Despite the rule set forth above, and although the prosecution must in all cases prove the guilt of the defendant, there is no rule that the defence cannot be required to bear the legal burden of proof on individual issues. A number of statutory provisions in fact contain such requirements, which are specifically expressed. For example, the Prevention of Crime Act 1953, s. 1, which deals with offensive weapons, provides that: 'Any person who without lawful authority or reasonable excuse, *the proof whereof shall lie on him,* has with him in any public place any offensive weapon shall be guilty of an offence' (emphasis added).

This does not require a defendant charged with unlawful possession of an offensive weapon to prove his innocence, but only that he had lawful authority or reasonable excuse for the possession, and, of course, the defendant need not prove even this unless and until the prosecution establish a *prima facie* case that the defendant in fact had such a weapon with him in a public place.

The section cited above is a good illustration of the kinds of case in which a limited burden of proof is placed on the defence. Where the prosecution would otherwise have to prove a negative (for example that the defendant lacked lawful authority or reasonable excuse) or where the burden of proof would be very onerous for the prosecution, but relatively light for the defence (for example that the defendant was a member of an excepted class such as licence-holders) the burden of proof may fairly be placed on the defence on such an issue. In summary cases, this has been elevated into a general principle by what is now s. 101 of the Magistrates' Courts Act 1980, which provides:

Where the defendant to an information or complaint relies for his defence on any exception, exemption, proviso, excuse or qualification, whether or not it accompanies the description of the offence or matter of complaint in the enactment creating the offence or on which the complaint is founded, the burden of proving the exception, exemption, proviso, excuse or qualification shall be on him; and this notwithstanding that the information or complaint contains an allegation negativing the exception, exemption, proviso, excuse or qualification.

The predecessor of this section was held to reflect and to have enacted a common-law rule, and the principle enshrined in it applies equally to non-statutory offences and to cases tried on indictment: *Edwards* [2]. However, the rule is of particular importance in relation to regulatory offences in the magistrates' courts, which frequently involve questions of licences or authorisation to perform otherwise proscribed acts. Common examples are a licence to drive a motor vehicle on a road, and authority to possess a dangerous drug.

In *Hunt* [3] the House of Lords held that, in addition to cases in which a statute expressly imposes the burden of proof on an issue on the defendant, there may be cases in which the wording of a particular statutory provision imposes such a burden of proof by necessary implication. The House held that this principle would in general be confined to cases broadly analogous to those provided for by s. 101, and that the courts should be slow to construe any penal statute against the defendant. However, each case must be decided on its own merits, and the court must scrutinise the language of the statutory provision concerned, wherever there is doubt as to the intention of Parliament with regard to the burden of proof on the issue under consideration.

Civil Cases

In civil cases, the party who must prove an issue in order to succeed in establishing his claim or defence bears the burden of proof on that issue. This is a question of law and should be reflected in the pleadings. The plaintiff must prove all the essential elements of his cause of action, and if the defence is confined to a straightforward denial, the plaintiff will bear the burden of proof throughout. However, where the defendant raises an affirmative defence which goes beyond a mere denial, the defendant bears the burden of proving such defence. Thus, in an action for breach of contract, the plaintiff bears the burden of proving both the contract and the breach, and the defendant bears no burden of disproving these; but where the defendant asserts an accord and satisfaction, the defendant bears the burden of proving that defence. Similarly, in an action for negligence, the burden of proving the existence and breach of a duty of care lies on the plaintiff, and the defendant need not disprove them; but where the defendant raises the defence of contributory negligence, he bears the burden of proving such defence. If the pleadings are in order, each party will be found to bear the burden of proof on each positive issue raised for the first time by his pleading, though the true test is the legal composition of the cause of action or defence and not the manner of pleading.

It is very important to note that there are no 'draws' in litigation. If, at the end of and on the whole of the evidence, the court is, in good conscience, unable to decide between the competing allegations of the parties, the result is not a 'draw'. The result is that the party who has the burden of proof loses. For example, in *Rhesa Shipping Co. SA v Edmunds* [4] the plaintiff shipowners sought to recover from the defendant underwriters in respect of the loss of its vessel, the *Popi M,* which had sunk in the Mediterranean in calm seas and good weather. The plaintiffs alleged that she had struck a submerged submarine, which, if true, would have amounted to loss by the perils of the seas, a loss covered by the defendants' policy. The defendants argued that the ship had been lost because of wear and tear, a loss that would not be covered. The trial judge found that the plaintiffs' explanation of the loss was extremely improbable, but he also found that the defendants' explanation was entirely inconsistent with the known facts (which suggested a sudden holing of the vessel). Effectively, therefore, the judge was unable to decide how the ship had been lost. He gave judgment for the plaintiffs, in which he was supported by the Court of Appeal. However, the defendants prevailed in the House of Lords. The plaintiffs bore the burden of proving how the loss had occurred. Since the judge had found the plaintiffs' case to be extremely improbable, it was not open to him to find that the plaintiffs had discharged their burden of proof on that issue. The burden was to prove that loss due to perils of the seas was more probable than not, not that it was more probable than the explanation advanced by the defendants. It was true that the judge had rejected the defendants' explanation entirely. But because the defendants bore no burden of proof, it was not incumbent on them to advance any explanation, and because the rejection of the defendants' evidence did not strengthen the plaintiffs' explanation of events, this was of no avail to the plaintiffs.

Standard of proof

The standard of proof defines the degree of persuasiveness which a case must attain before a court may convict a defendant or grant relief in respect of a cause of action, as the case may be.

In civil cases, the standard is that of proof on a preponderance of probabilities, which means simply that the party bearing the burden of proof must prove that his case is more likely than not to be true. Any tipping of the scales in his favour, however slight, is enough; but if the probabilities are equal, so that the court is unable to decide between the parties, the asserting party has failed to discharge his burden of proof to the required standard [5]. Where a civil court is considering allegations of fraud or other criminal or quasi-criminal conduct, or of conduct involving a high degree of moral turpitude, the court still applies the standard of the preponderance of probabilities, though in such cases the court may require more cogent evidence (often called 'clear and convincing evidence'), the cogency required increasing with the gravity of the charges, before finding that the scales have been tipped in favour of the asserting party [6].

The question of the standard of proof in matrimonial cases has long been uncertain. In some older cases [7] it had been held that the criminal standard of proof should be applied to allegations of adultery, cruelty, and desertion, which were then the grounds for divorce. However, at that time, these 'matrimonial offences' were considered to carry a quasi-criminal stigma. At least since the coming into force of the Divorce Reform Act 1969, this view has rightly been seen as inconsistent with the modern approach to matrimonial disputes, which favours the protection of children and the making of proper provision for affected members of the family, rather than the allocation of blame for the breakdown of the marriage. It is now generally thought that the usual civil standard of proof should apply to such cases. However, in *Re H (Minors) (Sexual Abuse: Standard of Proof)* [8], a case involving the making of a care order under s. 31(2) of the Children Act 1989, in the light of the alleged sexual abuse of a child, the majority of the House of Lords held that, although the civil standard should be applied, the court should require evidence of a cogency commensurate with the gravity of the allegations. Thus, it may be that the clear and convincing gloss is appropriate in such cases. Lord Lloyd of Berwick, dissenting on this point, would have preferred the ordinary civil standard without that gloss, but no member of the House favoured any higher standard. It is almost certain that in any matrimonial case not involving such grave allegations, the ordinary civil standard will apply.

In criminal cases, the law imposes a higher standard on the prosecution with respect to the issue of guilt. Here, the invariable rule is that the prosecution must prove the guilt of the defendant beyond reasonable doubt, or, to put the same concept in another way, so that the court is sure of guilt. These formulations are merely expressions of the high standard required, which was defined by Denning J in *Miller v Minister of Pensions* [9] as follows:

> It need not reach certainty, but it must carry a high degree of probability. Proof beyond reasonable doubt does not mean proof beyond the shadow of a doubt. . . . If the evidence is so strong against a man as to leave only a remote possibility in his favour which can be dismissed with the sentence 'of course it is possible, but not in the least probable', the case is proved beyond reasonable doubt, but nothing short of that will suffice.

The law therefore precludes a conviction based on suspicion, mere 'satisfaction' (which implies the civil standard) or even a feeling of being 'fairly sure'. Note, however, that this standard of proof is applicable to the burden on the prosecution of proving the guilt of the defendant. In the cases where the defence bear a limited burden of proof on a specific defence or issue, the standard required of the defence on such limited issue is that of a preponderance of probabilities, and the standard of proof beyond reasonable doubt on the issue of the defendant's guilt is still required of the prosecution in such a case.

Where the admissibility of evidence is an issue, the party asserting admissibility bears the burden of proof. The standard of proof is the same as that on the main issue, and accordingly varies as between civil and criminal cases in the same way.

Relevance, admissibility and weight

The terms 'relevance', 'admissibility' and 'weight' are fundamental to an understanding of evidence. The first two refer to qualities which evidence must possess, as a matter of law, before the court will admit and consider it. The third refers to qualities which the court will consider in assessing the cogency of evidence, assuming that it has been found to be admissible.

It is far easier to identify relevant (or irrelevant) evidence than to define it. In *DPP v Kilbourne* [10], Lord Simon of Glaisdale said:

> Evidence is relevant if it is logically probative or disprobative of some matter which requires proof. . . . It is sufficient to say . . . that

relevant (i.e., logically probative or disprobative) evidence is evidence which makes the matter which requires proof more or less probable.

Obviously, there may be degrees of relevance, and there may be cases in which the same piece of evidence is relevant to more than one fact which requires proof. But at a minimum, evidence must in some way be probative of at least one fact which requires proof. On a charge of exceeding the speed limit, evidence that the defendant's car had defective lights would not be relevant, whereas on a charge of driving with defective lights, its relevance would be obvious. On a charge of driving with excess alcohol, the fact that building tools were found in the defendant's car would be unlikely to be relevant, whereas on a charge of going equipped for burglary, the same evidence might be highly relevant. On either charge, the same evidence might be relevant to the defence. On the first, the defendant might wish to show that he was on his way from work, high above the ground, and had not been drinking. On the second, the defendant's occupation as a builder might offer some reasonable explanation of his possession of the tools which might otherwise appear suspicious.

It not infrequently happens that the relevance of evidence which you wish to adduce is not readily apparent to the court at the moment when you propose to adduce it. This may be because you have not yet called some further evidence, or raised some issue which will make the evidence relevant. The proper course in such a case is to invite the court to admit the evidence conditionally upon your demonstrating its relevance at a later stage. This is sometimes known as admitting the evidence '*de bene esse*'. Be sure, however, that you can fulfil the condition. Failure to do so may result in a successful application by the other side for a retrial, since the court has been exposed to irrelevant and possibly prejudicial evidence.

Although evidence will not be admitted unless it is relevant, it does not follow that all relevant evidence is admissible. In fact, relevant evidence is often excluded because of the rules of law governing admissibility. These rules occupy a substantial part of what follows in this book. They have grown up over some two hundred years in a haphazard and often illogical fashion, and it cannot be pretended that they are either consistent or desirable in all cases. Nonetheless, it is necessary for every advocate to be familiar with them, since they control his or her conduct of every case. The rules are by no means necessarily the same for civil and criminal cases, particularly in the case of the rule against hearsay, which is accorded three separate chapters in this book in order to deal with the now very different rules which must be applied in the magistrates' and county courts respectively.

As with relevance, there are cases where the admissibility of evidence has not been demonstrated at the time when you wish to adduce it, for example when cross-examining on a document whose authorship has not been proved. In such a case, the court may admit the evidence *de bene esse,* on the condition that the admissibility of the evidence is later demonstrated. The consequences of failing to comply with the condition are the same.

One of the hazards of the law of evidence is the rule that evidence may be admissible for one purpose, but not for another. There are examples of the rule in this book. Thus, a previous consistent statement admitted for the purpose of rebutting an allegation of recent fabrication is, in a criminal case, admissible evidence that there was no recent fabrication, but it is not admissible to prove that what was previously stated was true. And where the prosecution are permitted to cross-examine the defendant about his previous bad character, because the defendant has made imputations on the character of the prosecution witnesses, the evidence of bad character is evidence of the defendant's credit in making the imputations, but cannot be used as evidence of his guilt. It is important for an advocate to make clear to the court what uses can and cannot legitimately be made of evidence, since practical realities dictate that the court should receive the evidence for the limited purpose for which it is admissible. The court must be prevented, as far as possible, from being prejudiced with respect to issues on which the evidence is inadmissible.

Relevance and admissibility are questions of law, or of mixed law and fact, to be decided by the court before any assessment of the persuasive value of the evidence can arise. This assumes, of course, that the admissibility of the evidence is disputed. In many cases, all parties agree what evidence is admissible or inadmissible, and there is no issue of admissibility for the court to decide, unless the court of its own motion raises such an issue; of course, the court is the final arbiter on any matter of law, and the parties cannot compel the court to accept inadmissible evidence, whatever their agreement.

Assuming that evidence is found to be relevant and admissible, the question of its weight can then be considered. Some advocates make the mistake of considering only whether evidence can be placed before the court at all, and fail to consider its likely persuasive value or lack thereof. Of course, some relevant and admissible evidence is better than none at all and there are cases in which beggars cannot be choosers. But frequently, an advocate can exercise some judgment about evidence, based on its weight, or likely persuasive value.

Evidence which lacks weight is not inadmissible, but the tactical effect of placing it before the court (assuming you have the luxury of choice) can be very serious. The court may well assume that if you are reduced to calling such evidence, your case can have little substance. This is an entirely natural reaction, even if misconceived. If you have one piece of good evidence, of considerable weight, it is generally a sound rule not to dilute it with weak evidence to the same effect. If evidence is weak and unconvincing in your own eyes, it will almost certainly be so in the eyes of the court; if possible, dispense with it and prove the case by other means. The weight of evidence is not always apparent at the outset of a case, and you should always be prepared to re-evaluate it. If the court exhibits great interest in some piece of evidence which you had considered weak, or if some unexpected evidence on the other side demolishes evidence which you had considered to be irrefutable, you must be flexible enough to rethink your approach to the case.

Making and refuting objections to admissibility

Questions of admissibility of evidence are questions of law for the court. This means that in the county court, all such questions are decided by the judge (or district judge if hearing a case as a judge) and that in the magistrates' court, all such questions are decided by the bench, after taking advice from their clerk. The burden of proving that any proffered evidence is admissible lies upon the party tendering that evidence. All decisions on the admissibility of evidence must be made by the court of trial, and not by a tribunal hearing preliminary or interlocutory matters, such as a master, district judge, or magistrates sitting as committing justices [11]. Only the tribunal which has responsibility for the conduct of the trial, and the advantage of hearing the case as a whole, should make such basic decisions. Part II of sch. 1 to the Criminal Procedure and Investigations Act 1996 expressly denies to committing justices the power to decide questions of the admissibility of confessions or hearsay evidence, or the exercise of any discretionary power to exclude evidence. Of course, when sitting as a trial court, the magistrates (or, in the county court, the district judge) can and must adjudicate on matters of admissibility.

In most cases, questions of admissibility can be resolved solely by legal argument. However, in some instances, a question of admissibility may depend upon the court's finding of preliminary facts. Such facts are said to constitute a secondary issue. One example is that of tape recordings. In order for a tape recording to be admissible as a piece of real evidence, it must be shown that the recording is, on the face of it, genuine and original [12]. This can be done by introducing evidence on the secondary issue which shows that the recording is the original, that it has remained in safe custody and has not been tampered with since it was made. Unless the court is satisfied by such secondary evidence, it will hold that the tape recording is inadmissible.

Cases in which secondary evidence is required present some problems both in the magistrates' and county courts. All courts have one or more persons whose function it is to decide questions of law or fact, and who may be referred to as 'tribunals of law' and 'tribunals of fact' respectively. The functions of deciding questions of law and questions of fact may or may not be vested in the same person. In the Crown Court, the tribunals of law and fact are conveniently separated in the persons of the judge and jury, questions of law being for the judge and questions of fact for the jury. Since the judge has the function of deciding questions of admissibility, he also hears the secondary evidence on which such questions depend. The hearing of secondary evidence takes place in the absence of the jury, so that, if the judge rules that the evidence is inadmissible, the jury are not exposed to it and cannot be prejudiced by it. This is known as a 'trial within a trial', and is an invaluable procedure.

Unfortunately, it cannot be duplicated exactly in the county or magistrates' court, because the county court judge, or the magistrates must act both as the tribunal of law and the tribunal of fact. If the court must rule on the question of admissibility, it must in many cases be exposed to the evidence before ruling on its admissibility. If the court then rules the evidence to be inadmissible, it must put the evidence out of its mind. Even in the case of a trained lawyer such as a county court judge or a stipendiary magistrate, this is an extremely difficult process, and advocates tend to be understandably sceptical that it can be done effectively. In the case of a lay bench, it can be said, without in any way criticising lay justices, that the problem is particularly acute.

By far the most critical and by far the most common problems arise in relation to confessions in criminal cases. As will be seen in Chapter 5, the admissibility of a confession depends upon proof by the prosecution that it has been made in the absence of oppression and of circumstances likely to render unreliable any confession which might have been made by the defendant. These considerations give rise to substantial secondary issues and often hotly contested conflicts of secondary evidence. In many cases, the nature of the confession is such that, if it is held to be inadmissible, an advocate would probably apply to the bench for a retrial before a differently constituted bench because of the likelihood of prejudice arising from the exposure of the bench to it. This is a highly inconvenient and expensive step to take, and is also of doubtful effectiveness, since the bench hearing the retrial would not be bound by the decision of their predecessors.

So formidable do these difficulties appear that many advocates resign themselves to abandoning questions of admissibility, and confine themselves to attacking the weight of the evidence in question. However, like any failure to take advantage of legitimate arguments, this is not good advocacy. Not only does a strongly worded argument carry the potential for persuading the bench to exclude, but it also plants a doubt in the mind of the bench as to the weight that ought to be attached to the evidence, even if they decide to admit it. You can follow up on the question of weight in your closing speech, being careful of course to avoid alienating the court by giving the impression of reopening a decided question of admissibility.

Although the separation of judge and jury cannot be reproduced in the magistrates' court, the magistrates may exercise their discretion as to the proper time to consider questions of admissibility, and may deal with them as part and parcel of the trial itself. The only case in which they must hold a trial within a trial is when, before the close of the prosecution case, the defence raise the issue of the admissibility of a confession: *Liverpool Juvenile Court, ex parte R* [13]. In *Sat-Bhambra* [14] the Court of Appeal held that a defendant who wishes to exclude a confession must make a representation to the court before the confession is admitted, and seek the court's ruling at that time. This decision was based on the apparently mandatory wording of s. 76. If the defence fail to do so, the bench may consider the matter at any later time when it may arise. The judgment of Russell LJ in the *Liverpool Juvenile Court* case contains some valuable guidelines both for advocates and the courts on how to deal with this situation. In all other cases, the court may consider questions of admissibility at any appropriate time, including during their deliberations. Therefore, advocates must be flexible enough to deal with such questions either as a separate issue, or by cross-examining and adducing evidence in the usual course of the trial, and dealing with them in the closing speech. In all cases, the court should be asked to make a specific ruling on the issue of admissibility which is not lost in a general finding of guilt, and which can be reopened or challenged on appeal.

I suggest the following general approach to arguing questions of admissibility based on secondary evidence in front of a lay bench.

Firstly, always warn the prosecutor in advance that a question of admissibility will arise, and tell him what that question is. In a surprising number of cases, this resolves the problem in itself, because the prosecutor (who may not have considered the point) may agree with you, or at least feel that he can prove the case with other evidence anyway. But apart from this, it is vital to ask the prosecutor not to refer to the disputed evidence in his opening speech, since if he does, your argument about admissibility will lack conviction and may well become wholly academic. No prosecutor should open evidence which he has been told is disputed, and if this occurs, an application for a retrial may succeed.

Secondly, inform the clerk of the general nature of the argument to be presented, and the secondary evidence involved. Try to arrange the presentation of the evidence, in conjunction with the prosecutor and the clerk, in such a way that the detailed substance of the disputed evidence is not revealed to the bench in advance of their ruling, unless absolutely necessary. In some cases, this will be impracticable, since the court's evaluation of the secondary evidence may require a consideration of the disputed evidence itself. For example, you may have to argue that the appearance of a written statement under caution betrays the fact that it was obtained by oppression. But in many other cases, the bench can decide the matter in the abstract. For example, if the objection is to hearsay, you may be able to say to the bench, 'I apprehend that the witness is about to relate what someone else said to him, and I object that such evidence would be inadmissible as hearsay'. A document may be described to the bench in general terms, sufficiently for them to decide whether it is admissible or inadmissible, and no bench should baulk at this approach if the prosecutor and their clerk have no objection.

Thirdly, make sure you tell the bench that you would prefer a specific trial within a trial on the issue of admissibility. The procedure is that the prosecution call whatever witnesses they wish (usually the police officers who obtained the confession) but confine their evidence to the subject of the confession. The defence may cross-examine these witnesses, and call the defendant and any other witnesses, again confining the evidence to the same issue. The advocates may address the bench on the issue of admissibility. The bench should then reach a decision on that issue before continuing with the trial. If the bench decide to admit the confession, it would seem unnecessary to repeat the evidence given during the trial within a trial. (Of course, this is necessary in a trial on indictment in the Crown Court, because otherwise the jury would not hear the evidence.)

Remember that, when considering the admissibility of a confession, the bench may not concern themselves with the question of whether or not the confession is true. The only issue is whether it may have been obtained by oppression, or in circumstances which would have rendered any confession made by the defendant in the circumstances unreliable: see the Police and Criminal Evidence Act 1984, s. 76(2), and *Liverpool Juvenile Court, ex parte R* [15]. It is crucial to make this point, to remind the bench to take the difficult step of distinguishing the question of admissibility from that of the weight which may be accorded to the confession if (and only if) it is held to be admissible.

Lastly, as with all legal argument, be familiar with the rules of evidence, and have the current edition of *Blackstone's Criminal Practice* available to support your submissions. You never know when some point will arise which requires you to object, or to resist an objection, without warning.

The procedure recommended above assumes that the objection to the disputed evidence is taken at the usual and natural stage of the trial, that is to say, at the stage when the evidence is about to be given or introduced in the normal course of events. Almost always, this is the correct time for an objection to be made. However, where the evidence is so fundamental to the prosecution case that an opening speech cannot coherently be made, or the case cannot coherently be presented without the disputed evidence, the objection should be resolved at the earliest possible moment. Such a case may arise where the only, or only significant evidence against the defendant consists of a confession whose admissibility is disputed. Where appropriate, it is proper and responsible for the prosecution to make clear to the bench that, if the evidence is held to be inadmissible, the prosecution case is effectively at an end, and that the prosecution would no longer seek a conviction.

Despite the inherent problems, evidential objections do make for good advocacy in the magistrates' court, inasmuch as any point well taken implies some weakness in the case against you, which will not be overlooked by the court. Often, the seeds of a successful argument on weight are sown in the course of an ostensibly unsuccessful argument on admissibility. Do not throw this weapon away.

Judicial discretion to admit or exclude evidence

The next question is whether the court has any discretion to admit evidence which is technically inadmissible, or to exclude evidence which is technically admissible, in the interests of securing a fair trial. Authority suggests that there is no discretion to admit inadmissible evidence (inclusionary discretion) either in civil or criminal cases. In *Sparks* v *R* [16], the defendant was charged with indecent assault on a small girl, who, because of her age, was not called to give evidence. The defendant wished to elicit evidence from the girl's mother that the girl had described her attacker as being coloured, the defendant being white. The Privy Council rejected the argument that the evidence, which was plainly hearsay, should have been admitted despite this. Lord Morris of Borth-y-Gest said:

It was said that it was 'manifestly unjust for the jury to be left throughout the whole trial with the impression that the child could not give any clue to the identity of her assailant'. The cause of justice is, however, best served by adherence to rules which have long been recognised and settled.

At common law, however, it was established that the trial judge had a discretion to exclude technically admissible prosecution evidence in a criminal case (exclusionary discretion) on the ground that the prejudicial nature of the evidence outweighed its probative value as evidence. The exercise of this discretion was essentially a process of balancing the legitimate persuasive value of the evidence against its potential for inflaming the court or diverting the court from the true issues in the case. This process has been described in a number of leading cases [17]. The discretion has now been given statutory effect for criminal cases (including summary trials in a magistrates' court) by s. 78 of the Police and Criminal Evidence Act 1984, which provides:

(1)   In any proceedings the court may refuse to allow evidence
on which the prosecution proposes to rely to be given if it appears
to the court that, having regard to all the circumstances, including
the circumstances in which the evidence was obtained, the admission
of the evidence would have such an adverse effect on the fairness of
the proceedings that the court ought not to admit it.

(2)   Nothing in this section shall prejudice any rule of law
requiring a court to exclude evidence.

It should be noted that the discretion applies only to evidence
tendered by the prosecution and cannot be employed to exclude
admissible evidence tendered by a defendant which may affect adversely the case for a co-defendant. It seems probable that in deciding
whether to exercise this discretion, courts will continue to balance the
probative value of the evidence (its legitimate persuasive effect)
against its potential for prejudice which may produce an adverse effect
on the fairness of the trial. The section applies, for example, to
unnecessarily graphic exhibits.

Section 78(1) may be used to exclude prosecution evidence of any
kind. Examples include depositions (*O'Loughlin* [18]) evidence of
identification parades (*Beveridge* [19]) and Intoximeter readings
(*McGrath* v *Field* [20]). A common subject is character evidence. Even
where the defendant has become liable to be cross-examined about his
character, for example, because he has made an imputation on the
character of a prosecution witness, the court may either exclude or
restrict the cross-examination in the interests of securing a fair trial
(*Selvey* v *DPP* [21]; *Burke* [22]). The most important case, however,
is probably the use of discretion to exclude confessions, even when
they are technically admissible.

A good example of this is *Mason* [23]. On their own admission,
police officers 'set about conning' the defendant and his solicitor by
falsely representing to both that they had incriminating evidence
against the defendant in the form of fingerprints. No such evidence
existed. In response to the misinformation, the defendant made a
confession. The trial judge admitted the confession, and the defendant
was convicted. The Court of Appeal quashed the conviction, and held
that the confession should have been excluded. Although there was no
oppression and although the confession may have been reliable, the
method by which it had been obtained (deception of a kind which the
Court of Appeal hoped would never occur again) had an unacceptably

adverse effect on the fairness of the proceedings. The discretionary exclusion of confessions will be considered in more detail in Chapter 5. In civil cases, the position is unclear. Although s. 18(5) of the Civil Evidence Act 1968 (which is unaffected by the Civil Evidence Act 1995) provides that nothing in the Act shall prejudice 'any power of a court, in any legal proceedings, to exclude evidence (whether by preventing questions from being put or otherwise) at its discretion', it is uncertain whether any such power exists. As a matter of common sense, the answer is (as it so often is in civil cases tried by a judge) that if a county court judge is minded to exclude evidence in his discretion, he will give it little or no weight anyway, and is therefore likely, if pressed, to admit but then disregard it. To press the judge in such circumstances, when he has made his views on the subject clear, is bad advocacy.

Evidence illegally or unfairly obtained

It is by no means uncommon in criminal cases, and occasionally happens in civil cases, that it will be alleged that evidence, though apparently relevant and admissible, has been obtained by means which are either unlawful or unfair. Such means may range from outright theft to deception, from entrapment to searches made without warrant. In many cases in the past, it was argued that evidence so obtained should be held to be inadmissible for reasons of public policy, or alternatively should be capable of being excluded in the discretion of the court. It is now firmly established that evidence is not rendered inadmissible, save perhaps in one kind of case, merely because it has been obtained by unlawful or unfair means, even though those means may subject the party who indulged in them to some other criminal or civil sanction. If the evidence is otherwise relevant and admissible, it will be admitted regardless of the manner in which it was obtained [24]. There is, therefore, no objection to evidence obtained by the police by means of a subterfuge, such as deliberately leaving attractive goods in a position in which they might well be stolen (*Williams* v *DPP* [25]), operating a sham business purporting to 'fence' stolen goods (*Christou* [26]) or obtaining information by 'bugging' a cell in which suspects were being held (*Bailey* [27]) or even a private home (*Khan* [28]).

However, the discretion under s. 78 of the Police and Criminal Evidence Act 1984 applies equally to cases in which the illegality or unfairness of the method by which the evidence was obtained adversely affects the fairness of the trial. Such was the case in *Mason* referred to above. The most important application of the discretion is in cases in which the police obtain evidence, especially confessions, by means of breaches of the Codes of Practice. This is considered further in Chapter 5. In theory, the discretion may apply to any illegal or unfair obtaining of evidence, but the decisions referred to in the previous paragraph indicate that the courts have little interest in the discretion except in the area of confessions. Nonetheless, an appropriate submission should always be made to the bench. Sometimes the bench may be outraged enough to exclude, and, even if they are not, you will at least preserve the point for appeal.

This does not affect the rule that confessions must have been obtained in the absence of oppression and of circumstances likely to render unreliable any confession made by a defendant, since the issue there is one of admissibility, not of the means by which the confession was obtained, as such.

However, s. 78 of the Police and Criminal Evidence Act 1984, which is set out in full above, makes it clear that the manner in which evidence is obtained is one factor which the court may consider in deciding whether to exclude evidence tendered by the prosecution in the exercise of its discretion, and to that limited extent, it may be said that the court has power, in a criminal case, to exclude prosecution evidence on the ground that it has been obtained illegally or unfairly. It appears that the court has no wider power to exclude either in civil or criminal cases [29].

The exceptional case referred to above was adumbrated by Warner J in *ITC Film Distributors Ltd* v *Video Exchange Ltd* [30], in which the defendant, who was acting in person during the trial of a suit against him, obtained by a trick papers belonging to the plaintiffs and their solicitors, which had been brought into court for the purposes of the trial. The judge held that the public interest in the administration of justice and the fact that the defendant's conduct probably amounted to a contempt of court, outweighed the defendant's apparent right to introduce into evidence the copies of the documents which he had obtained.

Personal knowledge of the court

Every advocate who appears regularly in a local magistrates' or county court is familiar with the flash of recognition that often sweeps across the face of the judge or of a magistrate at the mention of some notorious street or establishment. No magistrate who sits frequently to adjudicate upon road traffic cases or acts of petty theft or violence, and no judge who decides landlord-and-tenant cases and disputes about used cars, can fail to be aware of significant local conditions within his jurisdiction. Moreover, since justices are drawn from many different walks of life, it would be remarkable if, in some cases, magistrates did not possess some personal or professional knowledge of some relevant facts or some speciality such as medicine which in some way bears upon the issues in the case. The question is to what extent the court may make use of such knowledge.

It would obviously be wrong for the court to act on fortuitous personal knowledge to decide a case, instead of relying upon the evidence tendered by the parties. But the court may 'properly and within reasonable limits' make use of such personal knowledge, not as a substitute for the evidence, but to aid it in understanding and evaluating the evidence. In *Ingram* v *Percival* [31], it was held that justices had acted properly in making use of their local knowledge of tidal conditions, and in *Wetherall* v *Harrison* [32] the Divisional Court held that the bench had been entitled to take into account the professional knowledge of one of their number, and to draw on their wartime experience of inoculations, in evaluating medical evidence called for the prosecution.

A good advocate will always sense when a bench is making use of local knowledge, and will try to make that knowledge work for his own case. Such knowledge often aids meritorious arguments, and shortens cases. The bench will often indicate that they are familiar with a relevant geographic area, and this adds a new dimension to a plan or map, or to evidence about the *locus in quo*.

Quite apart from personal knowledge, the court may take judicial notice of any fact which is notorious or beyond reasonable dispute. The taking of judicial notice is a useful device for dispensing with evidence of facts which require no evidence, because they are universally accepted, or nearly so. The device is used by courts more often than the casual observer would suspect. Whenever a court explicitly or tacitly acknowledges that Christmas Day is celebrated on 25 December, or that it is possible to travel from King's Cross to Victoria by Underground, or that the FA Cup Final is played at Wembley Stadium, it is taking judicial notice of those facts, and no evidence is required of them. It is often worth inviting the court expressly to take judicial

notice, even where the notoriety of the facts concerned is less obvious
than in the examples given.

Further reading

Murphy on Evidence, 6th ed., ch. 1, 3 and 4: *Blackstone's Criminal
Practice 1998*, F1—F3.

Notes

1. [1935] AC 462.
2. [1975] QB 27. See also *John* v *Humphreys* [1955] 1 WLR 325.
3. [1987] AC 352.
4. [1985] 1 WLR 948.
5. *Miller* v *Minister of Pensions* [1947] 2 All ER 372; *Rhesa Shipping Co. SA* v *Edmunds* [1985] 1 WLR 948.
6. *Hornal* v *Neuberger Products Ltd* [1957] 1 QB 247; *Re Dellow's Will Trusts* [1964] 1 WLR 451, 454–5.
7. See, e.g. *Bater* v *Bater* [1951] P 35.
8. [1996] AC 563.
9. [1947] 2 All ER 372, 373.
10. [1973] AC 729, 756.
11. *Sullivan* v *West Yorkshire Passenger Transport Executive* [1985] 2 All ER 134.
12. *Robson* [1972] 1 WLR 651.
13. [1988] QB 1.
14. (1988) 88 Cr App R 55.
15. [1988] QB 1.
16. [1964] AC 964.
17. For example, *Christie* [1914] AC 545; *List* [1966] 1 WLR 9; *Sang* [1980] AC 402.
18. [1988] 3 All ER 431.
19. (1987) 85 Cr App R 255.
20. [1987] RTR 349.
21. [1970] AC 304.
22. (1985) 82 Cr App R 156
23. [1988] 1 WLR 139.
24. *Kuruma, Son of Kaniu* v *R* [1955] AC 197, 203 per Lord Goddard CJ; *Sang* [1980] AC 402.
25. [1993] 3 All ER 365.

26. [1992] QB 979.
27. [1993] 3 All ER 513; *Roberts* [1997] 1 Cr App R 217.
28. [1997] AC 558.
29. *Sang* [1980] AC 402; *Universal City Studios Inc.* v *Hubbard* [1983] Ch 241.
30. [1982] Ch 431.
31. [1969] 1 QB 548.
32. [1976] QB 773.

Two

The Rule against Hearsay at Common Law

Introduction

There should probably be an organisation called 'Hearsay Anonymous'. Membership would be open to those judges, practitioners and students (not to mention occasional law teachers) to whom the rule against hearsay has always been an awesome and terrifying mystery. Like its partner in terror, the rule against perpetuities, the rule against hearsay ranks as one of the law's most celebrated nightmares. To many practitioners, it is a dimly remembered vision, which conjures up confused images of complex exceptions and incomprehensible and antiquated cases. When Dickens's Mr Justice Stareleigh refused to permit Sam Weller to relate to the court what the soldier had said, he was merely demonstrating a familiar reflex which had, by Dickens's time, already afflicted lawyers for a century or more and which even today seems to be an integral part of the lawyer's psyche.

'We can't have what Mr X said to you' is one of the most frequently recurring injunctions given to witnesses. It is probably the least understood by witnesses, particularly those witnesses who know Mr X to be an honest and reliable person. It is also, not infrequently, wrong. In fact, you often can, and should have what Mr X said to the witness. If you are conducting a suit for slander or a prosecution for threatening words, and the words spoken by Mr X to the witness happen to be those complained of, you will not get very far unless the witness relates to the court what Mr X told him, and common sense suggests that the words will not be excluded in such a case by a technical rule of evidence. In this instance, common sense is a true guide. Nonetheless, there are many cases where the rule does preclude evidence of what

Mr X said to the witness, and there are even more cases where lawyers wrongly believe it to do so. Never was Professor Cross so perceptive as in his identification of the 'superstitious awe . . . about having any truck with evidence which involves A's telling the court what B said' [1].

It is one of the most abiding and pervasive fallacies to suppose that the rule against hearsay forbids a witness ever to relate what somebody else told him. Close in its scope is the related fallacy that true (inadmissible) hearsay somehow becomes admissible if contained in a document, instead of being imparted by word of mouth. To the destruction of these and other fallacies this chapter is devoted. It should perhaps be entitled 'Everything you always wanted to know about hearsay but were afraid to ask'.

Starting from first principles, the rule against hearsay will be examined in as much detail as is appropriate to practice in the magistrates' and county courts. I hope to make clear that the rule is by no means as difficult as you might have supposed. In fact, if you keep an open mind, you may well end by wondering why you ever thought it was difficult in the first place. The rule is really not that difficult, provided — and it is an important proviso — that you begin by grasping, and never thereafter lose sight of, the definition of hearsay which is considered below.

Before reading any further, please note that in both civil and criminal cases, the common law hearsay rules have been modified substantially by statute. In civil cases, the Civil Evidence Act 1995 has abolished the rule against hearsay, though hearsay must still be dealt with in special ways. In criminal cases, the Police and Criminal Evidence Act 1984 and the Criminal Justice Act 1988, which in turn superseded the Criminal Evidence Act 1965, have laid down important statutory rules governing the admissibility of hearsay evidence. However, these statutory rules cannot be properly understood without a thorough understanding of what hearsay is. Moreover, by no means all kinds of hearsay evidence are covered by these provisions in criminal cases. So, while you must make a careful study of the detailed provisions dealt with in Chapters 3 and 4, relating to civil and criminal cases respectively, make sure that you first read and digest the basic principles dealt with in this chapter.

What hearsay is

Hearsay is a kind of evidence which has, since the 18th century, been held to be inadmissible at common law. The rule against hearsay may be stated as follows:

Evidence by a witness of what another person stated (whether verbally, in writing or otherwise) on a prior occasion is inadmissible for the purpose of proving that any fact stated by that person on such prior occasion is true, but is admissible for any other relevant purpose.

This definition is longer, and intended to be slightly more descriptive, than others which may be offered. A generally accepted common law definition is that adopted by Lord Havers in *Sharp* [2] from the 6th edition of *Cross on Evidence*:

An assertion other than one made by a person other than while giving oral evidence in the proceedings is inadmissible as evidence of any fact asserted.

Curiously, there was no statutory definition of hearsay until the coming into force of the Civil Evidence Act 1995. Section 1(2) of that Act defines hearsay as follows:

In this Act—
(a) 'hearsay' means a statement made otherwise than by a person while giving oral evidence in the proceedings which is tendered as evidence of the matters stated; and
(b) references to hearsay include hearsay of whatever degree.

This remains the only statutory definition, and it applies only for the purposes of the 1995 Act. However, it will be seen that it comports well with the common law definitions offered above.

The same rule applies to statements made on prior occasions by the witness himself, which are generally known as previous consistent, or self-serving statements. However, special rules apply to self-serving statements, which are considered in Chapter 11.

Although our first definition would probably not satisfy all academic criticisms that might be made of it, it is a sound one for all practical purposes. Read it a number of times, until you digest and begin to feel comfortable with it. Notice the following essential points; they will be discussed in more detail, but it is worth drawing attention to them straight away:

(a) The rule excludes evidence of what the witness was told only as evidence of the truth of any fact stated. The rule does not prevent that evidence being given for any other relevant purpose, for example to prove that the words were in fact spoken, or were spoken in a certain way or on a certain occasion. That is why, in a suit for slander or a prosecution for threatening words, it is permissible to introduce evidence of what Mr X said to a witness, in order to show what words Mr X did, in fact, speak.

(b)   A statement was made on a prior occasion if the maker made the statement other than in the course of giving evidence in the proceedings now before the court.

(c)   It is irrelevant whether the statement was made verbally, or in writing or by gesture or by any other medium of communication. The rule is designed to prevent a party from trying to prove the truth or falsity of a fact through the mouth of someone who is not before the court to give evidence and to be cross-examined. It is logical that the rule would also prevent attempts to prove the truth or falsity of the fact by that someone's pen, his camera, his computer, his body or any other means by which he may have expressed himself.

The rule has been explained and justified in a number of ways, some of them related to the historical development of the law. Two simple considerations will suffice here to illustrate the dangers which the rule is perceived to avoid. Firstly, it is impossible to cross-examine a witness effectively on the subject of whether what somebody else stated is true or false. Only when the maker of the statement is before the court as a witness in the instant case will the other side have an opportunity to test what he has stated. Secondly, evidence consisting of a repetition of what someone else has said carries an obvious risk of distortion or inaccuracy (even assuming that the statement is not actually dishonest) which increases in proportion to the number and circumstances of the repetitions made before the statement is relayed to the court. Where a witness tries to repeat a statement which he himself has made on a prior occasion, the basis for the rule is that a 'self-serving' statement has no value when compared to his sworn evidence before the court.

The crucial question: direct evidence or hearsay?

Evidence consisting of the speaking of words or the making of a document, or any other means of communication, may be either direct evidence or hearsay, depending upon the purpose for which a party seeks to introduce it, or in other words, depending upon what the party contends the evidence proves. This concept becomes easier to understand with the aid of a diagram.

Figure 1

FACT:

D ROBBED THE BANK. . . . . PW. . . . . HW

Figure 1 illustrates the formation of hearsay. A witness, PW, perceives a fact which will later become relevant to a case, in this instance that D took part in the robbery of a bank. We have called this witness PW as shorthand for 'percipient witness'. Obviously, PW's evidence of what he perceived (in this case, saw) would be admissible, 'direct' evidence of the truth of the fact that D robbed the bank.

But now suppose that PW described to another person, whom we shall call HW as shorthand for 'hearsay witness', what he perceived. It may be that PW did this verbally, by giving HW, a police officer, a description of D at the scene, or it may be that he made a formal written witness statement; it does not matter for present purposes. HW did not perceive the robbery of the bank. He has no knowledge of whether D is the culprit, except in terms of what he has been told by PW.

Next, suppose that because of death, illness, absence abroad or some other cause, PW's admirable direct evidence is not available to the prosecution on the trial of D on a charge of robbery of the bank. Now, the question is: can the prosecution call HW to give evidence that D robbed the bank, based on the information supplied to him by PW? To answer this question, it is necessary to refer to the definition. Was PW's statement made on a prior occasion, i.e., other than while giving evidence in this case? Obviously, yes; it was made at the scene or shortly after the event, and certainly not while PW was a witness at D's trial. Then, what do the prosecution intend to prove by calling HW to give evidence? Again, obviously, there is no relevance in the mere fact that PW made a statement, or in how the statement came to be made. The intent of the prosecution is to prove that what PW told HW is true, that is that D robbed the bank. HW's evidence is, for this purpose, hearsay and inadmissible.

This does not mean that HW could not in any circumstances be permitted to give evidence of what PW told him. It means only that, in any situation where the intent of the party calling HW is to invite the court to infer from HW's evidence that D robbed the bank, HW's evidence cannot be used for that purpose. The party calling HW may not be concerned with the truth or falsehood of what PW said; in fact, whether or not what PW said is true or false may be irrelevant to the case. Obviously, in the prosecution of D for robbing the bank, it is of relevance. But consider now a different set of facts. Suppose it has been established that D was not, in fact, involved in the robbery. D has brought an action for defamation against PW for falsely stating to HW that D robbed the bank. The only issue is whether PW did in fact make the statement, or perhaps whether or not he did so under circumstances of qualified privilege. Can D call HW to give evidence of what PW told him? The simplest way to answer this question is to expand Figure 1 into Figure 2.

Figure 2
>   FACT 1:
>   D ROBBED THE BANK . . . . PW . . . . HW
>
>   [FACT 1]. . . . . FACT 2:
>   PW TOLD HW THAT
>   D ROBBED THE BANK . . . . . HW

From Figure 2 it will be seen that we have not taken an inconsistent position that PW's statement is admissible in one case, but not in another, to prove the same fact. Rather, we have changed the fact proposed to be proved. Fact 1 involves the truth or falsity of what PW said. Fact 2, however, involves only the issue of whether or not PW did in fact make that statement, or, if the issue is qualified privilege, whether or not PW made the statement in circumstances entitling him to the benefit of that privilege. Whereas, in the prosecution of D for robbery of the bank, the prosecution set out to prove fact 1, in D's action for defamation, D sets out only to prove fact 2.

Note that we are not saying that hearsay is admissible in one case but not in another. We are saying that PW's statement is hearsay for the purpose of proving fact 1, but not for the purpose of proving fact 2. Why? Simply because the making of a statement may be a fact to be proved, just as robbing a bank may. HW is a percipient witness of the fact that PW made a statement. In order to illustrate this point, consider Figure 3, which shows that, as to the fact that PW made the statement, there is no reason why there should not be a hearsay witness, as well as a percipient witness.

Figure 3
      FACT 1:
      D ROBBED THE BANK . . . . PW . . . . HW

      [FACT 1] . . . . FACT 2:
      PW TOLD HW THAT
      D ROBBED THE BANK . . . . HW HW2
                                        (ALIAS PW2)

In Figure 3, you will observe that HW, alias PW2, is a percipient witness of the fact that PW made the statement to HW (fact 2). HW2, a person to whom HW (alias PW2) relates what PW told him, is a hearsay witness of both fact 1 and fact 2.

If you now return to our definition of hearsay, which is always the starting-point in considering whether evidence is, or is not, hearsay, you will find that the analysis contained in Figures 1 to 3 satisfies the questions posed when discussing Figure 1. Ask yourself first whether the evidence of HW or HW2 would consist of the repetition of a statement made by PW on a prior occasion, as we have defined that term. Then ask for what purpose the prosecution, or D, propose to tender that evidence to the court.

These hearsay problems are by no means as tricky as they at first appear, especially if you take the trouble to sketch your own diagram as we have done above. A diagram, combined with an application of both questions raised by our definition of hearsay will almost certainly produce the answer. In time, you will find that you no longer need the diagram; indeed, the problem-solving process will probably become automatic.

Distinguishing direct evidence from hearsay: some useful examples

There is no doubt that examples do make the rule against hearsay easier to understand. Now that you have studied the definition of hearsay, you will probably already be recalling examples from your own experience of practice. These will almost certainly include instances where the justices refused to allow you to present some piece of evidence which, at the time, seemed to you to be both relevant and cogent. You may by now have concluded that all concerned were right: you were right to believe that the evidence was relevant and cogent, and the justices were right to rule that it was nonetheless inadmissible.

Analysing one or two situations which arise frequently may enable you to foresee such problems in future cases, and perhaps to find alternative ways of proving the same facts.

The following paragraphs discuss five examples, based on frequently recurring fact patterns. Examples 1 and 2 will be examples of pure hearsay, inadmissible on any view. Examples 3 and 4 will be cases where the making of the statement is direct evidence of a relevant fact, and where evidence of the statement is therefore admissible, despite a superficial appearance of hearsay. The fifth example will illustrate a situation in which the same piece of evidence may be admissible for one purpose, in relation to which it is direct evidence, and inadmissible for another purpose, in relation to which it is hearsay.

Example 1: adapted from Jones v Metcalfe [3] PW, an eyewitness to a road traffic accident, sees the registration number of a vehicle which leaves the scene without stopping, and the bad driving of which is alleged to have caused the accident. PW writes down the number, ABC 123V, on a cigarette packet. Later, he makes a verbal statement to a police officer, HW, and HW writes down PW's statement, including the number, in his notebook. At trial, the issue is the identity of the vehicle, since the defendant, D, while admitting that he is the owner of ABC 123V, states that he was driving elsewhere at the time of the accident. PW is called as a witness for the prosecution. He is asked to state the number of the vehicle in question. By now, some months after the event, PW has forgotten the number, and, since no one asked him to keep it, he has thrown away the cigarette packet. The prosecution wish, therefore, to salvage their case by calling officer HW to state the number as recorded in his notebook. HW's evidence is hearsay and inadmissible, because it consists of a statement made to him by PW other than while giving evidence at the trial, and because the purpose of tendering the evidence is obviously to prove the truth of a relevant fact stated by PW, namely that ABC 123V is in fact the identity of the offending vehicle. The result of all this is that the prosecution are unable to prove the identity of the offending vehicle, and D will leave the court without a stain on his character, a surprised but happy man.

Before leaving this example, consider how easily the prosecution could have avoided this débâcle. If officer HW had ensured that the cigarette packet was preserved, PW would have been permitted to refresh his memory from it while giving evidence, since it is unquestionably a contemporaneous document. Moreover, if officer HW had taken the trouble to have PW read and sign his notebook immediately after it was made, PW could have refreshed his memory from the notebook, since he would have verified it contemporaneously. In these circumstances, there is no question of the cigarette packet or the notebook being introduced into evidence in defiance of the rule against hearsay. All that is happening is that the witness, PW, is refreshing his memory while giving direct, oral evidence of the facts he perceived. This is permissible and usual, and is a courtesy extended to all witnesses. A more detailed treatment of this subject is to be found in Chapter 11.

Example 2: adapted from R v Gibson [4]   D is alleged to have wounded V by throwing a stone at him. At the scene of the offence, an eyewitness, PW, says to the investigating officer, HW: 'The man who threw the stone went into that building'. HW then enters the building indicated by PW, finds D, who is the only occupant, and arrests him. Meanwhile, PW, who has not been asked to remain at the scene, has disappeared and is not available to give evidence at the trial. Again, the prosecution wish to call HW to prove the identity of the offender. Unfortunately, the only way in which HW can do this is to relate to the court what PW said to him. In the absence of evidence of PW's identification, the finding of D in the building is meaningless. HW's evidence of what he was told by PW is, however, hearsay and inadmissible for the same reason as HW's evidence was hearsay and inadmissible in Example 1. Unless D is good enough to admit enough facts to implicate himself, the prosecution are likely to regret their failure to ensure that PW was made available for trial.

Example 3: adapted from R v Chapman [5]   D is charged with driving while the amount of alcohol in his blood exceeded the prescribed limit. The arrest of D for this offence resulted from an accident, in which D was injured. While D was at a hospital being treated for his injuries, a police officer, W, arrived, intending to require D to take a breath test. In order to satisfy a statutory requirement, W asked Dr Z, the physician in charge of the treatment of D, whether he (Dr Z) had any objection to W's taking a sample of D's breath. Dr Z indicated that he had no objection. W thereupon administered the test, which proved positive. It has now been established that D's blood-alcohol level exceeded the prescribed limit. At trial, the prosecution wish to prove that the statutory procedure was fully complied with, and call W to state that

Dr Z said he had no objection to the administration of the breath test. The defence make the objection that whatever Dr Z may have said to the officer is hearsay and inadmissible. In fact, the evidence is entirely unobjectionable. Of course, it consists of a statement made by Dr Z other than while giving evidence at the trial. But there is no issue of whether or not anything Dr Z said was or was not true. The only issue is: did Dr Z in fact state that he had no objection or not? In other words, the making of the statement is the issue, not the truth or falsehood of any fact stated. As to the issue of whether or not Dr Z did in fact make the statement, W is a percipient witness, since he heard the statement being made. His evidence of the making of the statement is direct evidence, and is admissible to prove that the statutory requirement was complied with.

Example 4: adapted from Subramaniam v Public Prosecutor [6]   D is charged with the unlawful possession of a firearm. He contends that his only reason for possessing the firearm was that he had been threatened with loss of his life by certain criminals, unless he agreed to hide the weapon for them. D relies upon these facts to assert the defence of duress. D wishes to state in evidence that the criminals told him that he would be killed, unless he agreed to hide the firearm. The prosecution object, contending that whatever the criminals may have said to D is hearsay and inadmissible. In fact, the evidence is perfectly admissible. Although it consists of statements made by the criminals on prior occasions, D is not tendering the evidence in order to prove that anything stated by the criminals was true or false, but for the purpose of establishing his state of mind at the time he took possession of the firearm, and thereby also establishing his defence of duress. The issue is whether or not the criminals did, in fact, make the statements attributed to them. As to this issue, D is obviously a percipient witness, having heard the statements being made, and he may therefore give direct, oral evidence of the making of the statements.

Example 5: adapted from R v Willis [7]   D is charged with handling stolen goods. D admits that he received the goods, but contends that (a) the goods in question were not stolen goods, and that (b) even if the goods were stolen, he neither knew nor believed them to be so at the time when he received them. D wishes to give evidence that the person from whom he received the goods had assured him that the goods were not stolen. Is this evidence admissible? These simple facts provide an excellent illustration of the distinction between direct evidence and hearsay, which repays study. The answer is that the evidence of what the supplier of the goods said to D is admissible for one purpose, but not for the other. This means, as a practical matter, that the evidence may be given, but may be considered by the bench only for a limited purpose.

The first question is whether the evidence of what the supplier said on the prior occasion is admissible to prove the first of D's proposed defences, namely that the goods were not stolen. In this case, D is clearly trying to prove that what the supplier said to him was true, i.e., that the goods were not stolen. D is not a percipient witness on the issue of whether the goods were or were not stolen, but is merely relating what the supplier told him. For this purpose, his evidence is hearsay and inadmissible. But for the purposes of D's second defence, the analysis will yield a different result. In order to establish that he was not dishonest, D need not show that the goods were not stolen, merely that he neither knew nor believed that they were stolen, at the time he received them. In other words, just as in example 4, D is seeking to establish his state of mind. His state of mind was governed, at least in part, by what he was told by the supplier of the goods. The supplier's statement is accordingly direct evidence of D's state of mind, and is admissible for that limited purpose, even though it is not admissible on the issue of whether the goods were stolen. D should be permitted to relate what the supplier told him, with a view to showing that he (D) neither knew nor believed the goods to be stolen at the time he received them from the supplier.

When you encounter a hearsay problem you may find it useful to review this part of this chapter, at least until you become more comfortable with the rule. A helpful technique may be to turn first to the definition of hearsay (always the starting-point), secondly to the diagrams (make your own to correspond to the facts of your case) and lastly to the examples, to find one that offers guidance. With experience, you will find that these steps will become routine. As in all fields of study and application, practice makes perfect.

Exceptions to the rule against hearsay

The rule against hearsay at common law was developed over a period of about two hundred years. During this time, various exceptional cases emerged in which hearsay evidence of different kinds was admitted, either because it was thought to enjoy a reliability lacking in hearsay generally (for example, statements contained in public documents) or because of sheer necessity (for example, statements made by persons since deceased). In more recent times, however, the House of Lords in *Myers* v *DPP* [8] held that any further development of exceptions to the rule should be undertaken by Parliament rather than the courts. Since then, as we have noted, Parliament has responded by first altering substantially and then abolishing the rule in civil cases, and introducing major statutory exceptions in the Criminal Evidence Act 1965, the Police and Criminal Evidence Act 1984 and the Criminal Justice Act 1988, for criminal cases. These statutory rules will be dealt with in detail in Chapters 3 and 4.

Despite the newer statutory rules, it remains important to consider the vestiges of the common-law exceptions to the rule against hearsay. For present purposes, this may be done quite briefly. Three common-law exceptions only remained generally significant after the coming into force of the Police and Criminal Evidence Act 1984, from which time it could be said with justification that reasonably comprehensive rules governing the admissibility of hearsay evidence existed in both civil and criminal cases. Of these, only one, the *res gestae* rule (or, as we shall call it, the excited utterance rule) is still significant as a common-law exception.

The other two exceptions, namely statements contained in public documents and statements made by persons since deceased, have effectively been swallowed up by the Civil Evidence Act 1995 and the Criminal Justice Act 1988, by virtue of which such statements would now almost always be admissible. The only situation in which either is likely to enjoy any separate identity is that in which an oral statement by a person since deceased is tendered in a criminal case (usually in the form of a dying declaration). This is a comparatively rare occurrence, probably almost unknown in the magistrates' court, and need not detain us here [9].

The *res gestae* or excited utterance rule, however, has retained much of its vitality.

The excited utterance rule

The name which we have adopted for this exception is the American usage. It is vivid and descriptive of the scope of the exception, and is generally more helpful than the traditional common-law appellation of

res gestae. But to mutilate Shakespeare a little, an exception by any
other name would be just as effective. This exception needs no
complex description. The exception is simply this: where a person who
is involved in or witnesses an event makes an uncalculated, spontaneous statement in the nature of an outburst in the heat of the moment,
referring to the event, the statement may be admissible as evidence of
the truth of what was stated. The reason for the exception is that such
statements explain the event, or lend a significance to it of such
magnitude that the true nature and circumstances of the event become
clearer.

The statement may be admitted only if it is shown that it was truly
spontaneous. The importance of this is that spontaneity tends to negate
the possibility of a calculated self-serving declaration by the witness.
Almost three centuries of jurisprudence have failed to improve on the
formulation of the exception made by Holt CJ in *Thompson* v
Trevanion in 1693. The plaintiff had sued for an assault on his wife,
and the Chief Justice said, 'that what the wife said immediately upon
the hurt received, and before that she had time to devise or contrive
any thing for her own advantage, might be given in evidence' [10]. A
good modern statement of the rule is to be found in the speech of Lord
Wilberforce in *Ratten* v *R* [11]. Although in *Thompson* v *Trevanion,*
Holt CJ clearly pointed out the importance of the immediacy of the
statement as the best guarantee that it is not calculated and self-serving,
the courts for a time lost sight of the true principle underlying the rule.
During the 19th century, there were a number of cases which took the
concept of contemporaneity to extremes, and insisted that the statement
must be literally contemporaneous with the event. The result of this
was to make the law extremely artificial, and to hedge the exception
about with technicalities to the point of rendering it virtually useless.
Lord Wilberforce in *Ratten* pointed out the error of this narrow
approach, but it was left to the House of Lords in *Andrews* [12] to
overrule the older cases and to restate the law in modern terms.

In *Andrews,* the victim of a robbery was seriously wounded. He told
police officers that he had been robbed by two men, and identified the
defendant as one of them. The victim then became unconscious, and
was taken to hospital, where he died some two months later. On appeal
to the House of Lords, the question was whether the victim's statement
to the police should have been admitted. It was conceded that it was
not admissible as a dying declaration, because there was no showing
that the victim had been under a 'settled, hopeless expectation of death'

when the statement was made. However, the House held that it had been rightly admitted under the excited utterance rule. Lord Ackner said that in order for a statement to be sufficiently spontaneous, it must have been so closely associated with the event which excited it, that it could fairly be said that the mind of the maker of the statement was still dominated by the event. He added: 'Thus, the judge must be satisfied that the event which provided the trigger mechanism for the statement was still operative'.

Hence, the modern law recognises that a gap in time between the event and the statement need not be fatal to admissibility. A gap in time before the event ('Look out! That car is going to hit her.') or after the event ('That driver made no attempt to stop at the red light.') may very well be acceptable. In *Nye* [13] a statement made by the victim of an assault, identifying his assailants to the police, was likewise held to be admissible, even though several minutes had elapsed since the assault.

But you must demonstrate to the bench that the statement was both spontaneous and uncalculated. This may be done by asking the witness to describe how the statement came to be made, and his state of mind at the time. Of course, you should do this before allowing the witness to relate what he said, so that the bench are not exposed to inadmissible evidence, if they decide against you.

Used in the right way, the excited utterance rule can often be employed to put before the court very cogent, contemporaneous statements. It is particularly useful in giving evidence of dramatic incidents, such as a fight or an accident, in which it is likely to be easier to persuade the court that the statement was made in the heat and excitement of the moment. If such a statement is tendered against you, ask the court for permission to cross-examine the witness about its spontaneity, before the detail of the statement is revealed. Ask about the timing, and challenge it, if there is any possibility of concoction.

Further reading

Murphy on Evidence, 6th ed., chapter 7; *Blackstone's Criminal Practice 1998*, F15–F16.

Notes

1.   [1965] Crim LR 68, 82.

2. [1988] 1 WLR 7.
3. [1967] 1 WLR 1286.
4. (1887) 18 QBD 537.
5. [1969] 2 QB 436.
6. [1956] 1 WLR 965.
7. [1960] 1 WLR 55.
8. [1965] AC 1001.
9. For more detail, see *Murphy on Evidence*, 6th ed., p. 219 et seq.
10. (1693) Skin 402.
11. [1972] AC 378.
12. [1987] AC 281.
13. (1977) 66 Cr App R 252; cf. *Tobi* v *Nicholas* [1988] RTR 343.

Three

The Rule against Hearsay in Civil Cases*

Introduction: the Civil Evidence Act 1995

The rule against hearsay at common law, as described in Chapter 2, owed much to the supposed inability of juries and, to a lesser degree, magistrates, to evaluate hearsay evidence responsibly. Modern studies have cast doubt on this older assumption, and suggest that juries are probably quite capable of understanding that hearsay evidence, being untested by cross-examination, should be treated with some caution. In civil cases, which in modern practice are almost always tried by a judge sitting alone, the justification for excluding hearsay lost its force. Some statutory incursions into the rule were made as early as the Evidence Act 1938, though these were very limited. A more general inclusive code was enacted in Part I of the Civil Evidence Act 1968.

The 1968 Act did not abolish the rule against hearsay, but made sweeping provisions for the admission of hearsay evidence in civil cases tried in the High Court and county courts. The admission of this evidence was, however, circumscribed by an elaborate system of procedural safeguards, consisting of the serving of notices of intention to adduce such evidence, and, in some cases, counter-notices designed to require that the maker of an admissible hearsay statement be called as a witness, if available. The Act successfully shifted the focus from the issue of admissibility to that of weight. In cases tried by a judge sitting alone, the professional judgment of the parties' legal advisers proved to be just as effective in keeping out unreliable evidence as any rule of admissibility. The Civil Evidence Act 1968 applied only to

---

*The original version of this chapter, based on the Civil Evidence Acts 1968 and 1972, was written by David Barnard.

statements of fact, but the Civil Evidence Act 1972 extended the operation of the 1968 Act to statements of opinion also.

In view of the success of these provisions, the Law Commission recommended the total abolition of the rule against hearsay in civil cases. This was achieved by the Civil Evidence Act 1995, which, with a fairly minor exception, relating to the admissibility of the 'Ogden' actuarial tables issued by the Government's Actuarial Department, and used in personal injury and fatal accident cases, came into effect on 31 January 1997. The Act repeals Part I (only) of the 1968 Act. The result is that, in civil cases in the county court, you no longer have to concern yourself with the admissibility of hearsay evidence. However, you must still recognise it and be prepared to treat it in special ways. The Act contains a number of important provisions dealing with the presentation of hearsay evidence, the calling of the maker of a hearsay statement as a witness, matters affecting the credibility of the maker, and matters affecting the weight to be attached to the evidence. In addition, there are some rules of court which must be followed, though these are, mercifully, a great deal simpler than those applicable under the 1968 Act. All these matters are dealt with below.

In common with other statutes which have provided for the admission of hearsay evidence, the Civil Evidence Act 1995 does not cure any defect of evidence other than its hearsay quality. Section 14 specifically provides that nothing in the Act affects the exclusion of evidence on a ground other than hearsay, 'whether the evidence falls to be excluded in pursuance of any enactment or rule of law, for failure to comply with rules of court or an order of the court or otherwise'. Section 18(5) of the Civil Evidence Act 1968, which remains in effect, provided expressly that nothing in that Act precluded the court from excluding evidence in the exercise of its discretion. The Civil Evidence Act 1995 is silent on that issue, unless it is implicitly included in the phrase 'rule of law'. But the existence and extent of any general exclusionary discretion has always been uncertain in civil cases. What usually happens is that the judge simply assigns no weight to evidence he would be minded to exclude in his discretion.

Section 5(1) of the Act excludes statements made by those who would be regarded as incompetent as witnesses. The section provides:

(1) Hearsay evidence shall not be admitted in civil proceedings if or to the extent that it is shown to consist of, or to be proved by means of, a statement made by a person who at the time he made the statement was not competent as a witness.

For this purpose 'not competent as a witness' means suffering from such mental or physical infirmity, or lack of understanding, as would render a person incompetent as a witness in civil proceedings; but a child shall be treated as competent as a witness if he satisfies the requirements of section 96(2)(a) and (b) of the Children Act 1989 (conditions for reception of unsworn evidence of child).

The question of the competence of witnesses, including children, is dealt with in Chapter 8. Section 13 of the Act confirms that a witness is not incompetent merely because a defect of speech or hearing compels him to communicate by means of writing or signs.

Abolition of the rule against hearsay in civil proceedings

It is provided by the Civil Evidence Act 1995, s. 1(1) and (2) that:

(1)   In civil proceedings evidence shall not be excluded on the ground that it is hearsay.
(2)   In this Act—
(a)   'hearsay' means a statement made otherwise than by a person while giving oral evidence in the proceedings which is tendered as evidence of the matters stated; and
(b)   references to hearsay include hearsay of whatever degree.

Section 13 provides, *inter alia*:

'statement' means any representation of fact or opinion, however made;
'oral evidence', includes evidence which, by reason of a defect of speech or hearing, a person called as a witness gives in writing or by signs.

As we saw in Chapter 2, the definition of hearsay provided by the section is the first statutory definition to be enacted. It corresponds well with the common law definitions which we explored in that chapter. By virtue of the definition of 'statement' in s. 13, the Act applies alike to statements of fact and statements of opinion, and accordingly supersedes the corresponding provisions of the Civil Evidence Act 1972.

Unlike the Civil Evidence Act 1968, the 1995 Act does not distinguish between statements made orally and statements made in documents (whereas, as we shall see in Chapter 4, there continues to be a significant difference in criminal cases). Nor does it distinguish between different levels of hearsay, i.e., it recognises no difference, with respect to admissibility, between a statement made by A to B which B then relates, and a statement made by A to B and then repeated to C, which C then relates. However, the presence of such 'multiple' hearsay may adversely affect the weight of a statement (see s. 4(2)(c) of the Act). In evaluating multiple hearsay, it may be important to have regard to the original statement, i.e., the source of the facts or opinion in question. Section 13 defines 'original statement' as follows:

'the original statement', in relation to hearsay evidence, means the underlying statement (if any) by—
(a) in the case of evidence of fact, a person having personal knowledge of that fact, or
(b) in the case of evidence of opinion, the person whose opinion it is.

Proceedings to which the Act applies

The Civil Evidence Act 1995 applies only to civil proceedings. Section 11 of the Act provides:

In this Act 'civil proceedings' means civil proceedings, before any tribunal, in relation to which the strict rules of evidence apply, whether as a matter of law or by agreement of the parties.
References to 'the court' and 'rules of court' shall be construed accordingly.

The Civil Evidence Acts 1938 and 1968 did not apply to civil proceedings in the magistrates' courts, though there were some specific provisions, such as rules made pursuant to s. 96 of the Children Act 1989, which did. Section 11 of the 1995 Act is wide enough to cover any civil proceedings in magistrates' courts. Of course, the Act has no application to criminal proceedings in any court.

Procedural safeguards

Like the Civil Evidence Act 1968, the 1995 Act contains procedural provisions designed to reduce the disadvantage which accrues to an opponent whenever a party is permitted to adduce hearsay evidence. The provisions are, however, notably simpler than those of the 1968 Act, and reflect the experience of the courts under that Act that the disadvantages are rather less serious than had initially been anticipated. Section 2 of the Civil Evidence Act 1995, provides:

(1) A party proposing to adduce hearsay evidence in civil proceedings shall, subject to the following provisions of this section, give to the other party or parties to the proceedings—
    (a) such notice (if any) of that fact, and
    (b) on request, such particulars of or relating to the evidence, as is reasonable and practicable in the circumstances for the purpose of enabling him or them to deal with any matters arising from its being hearsay.

(2) Provision may be made by rules of court—
    (a) specifying classes of proceedings or evidence in relation to which subsection (1) does not apply, and
    (b) as to the manner in which (including the time within which) the duties imposed by that subsection are to be complied with in the cases where it does apply.

(3) Subsection (1) may also be excluded by agreement of the parties; and compliance with the duty to give notice may in any case be waived by the person to whom notice is required to be given.

(4) A failure to comply with subsection (1), or with rules under subsection (2)(b), does not affect the admissibility of the evidence but may be taken into account by the court—
    (a) in considering the exercise of its powers with respect to the course of proceedings and costs, and
    (b) as a matter adversely affecting the weight to be given to the evidence in accordance with section 4.

Section 3 provides:

Rules of court may provide that where a party to civil proceedings adduces hearsay evidence of a statement made by a person and does not call that person as a witness, any other party to the proceedings may, with the leave of the court, call that person as a witness and cross-examine him on the statement as if he had been called by the first-mentioned party and as if the hearsay statement were his evidence in chief.

Pursuant to these sections, virtually identical rules of court have been promulgated for use in the High Court and county courts. In the High Court, the rules are to be found in RSC, Ord. 38, rr. 20 to 24, and in the county courts, in CCR, Ord. 20, rr. 14 to 17. These rules, using the county court rule numbers, are as follows:

Application and interpretation
14.—(1) In this Part of this Order the '1995 Act' means the Civil Evidence Act 1995 and any expressions used in this Part of this Order and in the 1995 Act have the same meanings in this Part of this Order as they have in the Act.

(2) In this Part of this Order:

'hearsay evidence' means evidence consisting of hearsay within the meaning of section 1(2) of the 1995 Act;

'hearsay notice' means a notice under section 2 of the 1995 Act.

(3) This Part of this Order applies in relation to the trial or hearing of an issue arising in an action or matter and to a reference under section 65 of the Act (Power of judge to refer to district judge or referee) as it applies to the hearing of an action or matter.

(4) Nothing in this Part of this Order shall apply in relation to proceedings which have been referred to arbitration under section 64 of the Act.

Hearsay notices
15.—(1) A hearsay notice must

(a) state that it is a hearsay notice;

(b) identify the hearsay evidence;

(c) identify the person who made the statement which is to be given in evidence;

(d) state why that person will (or may) not be called to give oral evidence, and

(e) if the hearsay evidence is contained in a witness statement, refer to the part of the witness statement where it is set out.

(2) A single hearsay notice may deal with the hearsay evidence of more than one witness.

(3) The requirement to give a hearsay notice does not apply to

(a) evidence which is authorised to be given by or in an affidavit; or

(b) a statement which a party to a probate action desires to give in evidence and which is alleged to have been made by the person whose estate is the subject of the action.

(4)   Subject to paragraphs (5) and (6), a party who desires to give in evidence at the trial or hearing of an action or matter hearsay evidence shall, not less than 28 days before the day fixed for the trial or hearing, serve a hearsay notice on every party and file a copy in the court.

(5)   Unless the court otherwise directs, paragraph (4) shall not apply to an action or matter in which no defence or answer has been filed and, where a defence or answer is filed less than 28 days before the day fixed for the trial or hearing, any party who is required to give a hearsay notice shall apply to the court for an adjournment or for such other directions as may be appropriate.

(6)   Where witness statements are served under rule 12A of this Order (or under that rule as it is applied by Order 17, rule 11), any hearsay notice served under this rule shall be served at the same time as the witness statements.

Power to call witness for cross-examination on hearsay evidence
16.—(1)   Where a party tenders as hearsay evidence a statement made by a person but does not propose to call the person who made the statement to give evidence, the court may, on application, allow another party to call and cross-examine the person who made the statement on its contents.

(2)   An application under paragraph (1) shall be made on notice to all other parties not later than 28 days after service of the hearsay notice.

(3)   Where the court allows another party to call and cross-examine the person who made the statement, it may give such directions as it thinks fit to secure the attendance of that person and as to the procedure to be followed.

Credibility
17.—(1)   If
  (a)   a party tenders as hearsay evidence a statement made by a person but does not call the person who made the statement to give oral evidence, and
  (b)   another party wishes to attack the credibility of the person who made the statement;
that other party shall notify the party tendering the hearsay evidence of his intention.

(2)   A notice under paragraph (1) shall be given not later than 28 days after service of the hearsay notice.

These rules replace the former RSC, Ord. 38, rr. 20 to 34, and CCR, Ord. 20, rr. 14 to 24, with effect from 31 January 1997. However, they have no application to proceedings commenced before that date (see *Bairstow* v *Queens Moat Houses plc* [1]). The former rules apply to such cases, so you may want to preserve your copy of the 4th edition of this book for some time.

Evidence admissible other than by virtue of the Civil Evidence Act 1995 is excepted from the procedural safeguards by s. 1(4). However, unlike the position under the Civil Evidence Act 1968, which made similar provision, it is difficult to think of evidence which would not be admissible under the Civil Evidence Act 1995. Further provision for the making of rules for carrying the provisions of the 1995 Act into effect, and for the application of the Act to arbitration proceedings is made by s. 12.

Matters affecting weight

Section 4 of the Civil Evidence Act 1995 provides:

(1)   In estimating the weight (if any) to be given to hearsay evidence in civil proceedings the court shall have regard to any circumstances from which any inference can reasonably be drawn as to the reliability or otherwise of the evidence.

(2)   Regard may be had, in particular, to the following—

(a)   whether it would have been reasonable and practicable for the party by whom the evidence was adduced to have produced the maker of the original statement as a witness;

(b)   whether the original statement was made contemporaneously with the occurrence or existence of the matters stated;

(c)   whether the evidence involves multiple hearsay;

(d)   whether any person involved had any motive to conceal or misrepresent matters;

(e)   whether the original statement was an edited account, or was made in collaboration with another or for a particular purpose;

(f)   whether the circumstances in which the evidence is adduced as hearsay are such as to suggest an attempt to prevent proper evaluation of its weight.

In common with earlier statutes, the 1995 Act lays down specific matters to be taken into account in assessing the weight of the evidence admitted. As weight, rather than admissibility, is now the focus, the provision is understandable. But it may be observed that s. 4(2) suggests factors which any experienced judge would automatically take into account. The list of factors is not intended to be exhaustive. Section 4(2)(a) is a welcome indication that live oral evidence is to be preferred, and that it will be unwise to use the Act to protect potential witnesses from having to undergo cross-examination. Ordinarily, the weight of a hearsay statement must be considerably less where it is clear that the maker could have been called as a witness without undue difficulty.

Use of copies

Section 8 of the Civil Evidence Act 1995 provides:

(1) Where a statement contained in a document is admissible as evidence in civil proceedings, it may be proved—
(a) by the production of that document, or
(b) whether or not that document is still in existence, by the production of a copy of that document or of the material part of it, authenticated in such manner as the court may approve.
(2) It is immaterial for this purpose how many removes there are between a copy and the original.

Section 13 provides:

'document' means anything in which information of any description is recorded, and 'copy', in relation to a document, means anything onto which information recorded in the document has been copied, by whatever means and whether directly or indirectly.

Section 8 reproduces provisions to the same effect in the Civil Evidence Act 1968 and the Criminal Justice Act 1988, with the sensible addition that a copy need not be a direct copy of the original. If it is not, and if there is reason to suspect that the copy may not be a completely true copy of the original, the weight of the statement may be adversely affected. The definitions of 'document' and 'copy' provided by s. 13 are incorporated by reference into the Police and Criminal Evidence Act 1984 and the Criminal Justice Act 1988 (see Civil Evidence Act 1995, sch. 1, paras 9 and 12) and so apply equally in criminal proceedings for the purposes of those Acts. Section 8 applies only for the purposes of proving admissible hearsay statements contained in documents. Where a document is tendered as substantive evidence of its contents, the best evidence rule applies, and the original must be produced unless one of the exceptions to that rule applies. This rule is dealt with in Chapter 11.

Statements made by persons called as witnesses

Section 6 of the Civil Evidence Act 1995 makes specific provisions for cases in which a previous statement made by a person called as a witness may be admitted. These statements involve other principles with respect to evidence in chief and cross-examination, which will be considered in detail in Chapter 11. Here it may be noted that, although the Act abolishes the rule against hearsay, it recognises that previous statements made by persons who are called as witnesses, and give oral evidence in the proceedings, bring those other principles into play, and should be treated somewhat differently from other kinds of hearsay evidence. These cases arise where the witness uses the statement to refresh his memory while testifying, where the statement is tendered to rebut a suggestion of recent fabrication, or where the statement is used to attack the credibility of the maker. With respect to these cases, s. 6 of the Act provides as follows:

(1)   Subject as follows, the provisions of this Act as to hearsay evidence in civil proceedings apply equally (but with any necessary modifications) in relation to a previous statement made by a person called as a witness in the proceedings.

(2)   A party who has called or intends to call a person as a witness in civil proceedings may not in those proceedings adduce evidence of a previous statement made by that person, except—
    (a)   with the leave of the court, or
    (b)   for the purpose of rebutting a suggestion that his evidence has been fabricated.
This shall not be construed as preventing a witness statement (that is, a written statement of oral evidence which a party to the proceedings intends to lead) from being adopted by a witness in giving evidence or treated as his evidence. . . .
    (4)   Nothing in this Act affects any of the rules of law as to the circumstances in which, where a person called as a witness in civil

proceedings is cross-examined on a document used by him to refresh his memory, that document may be made evidence in the proceedings.

(5) Nothing in this section shall be construed as preventing a statement of any description referred to above from being admissible by virtue of section 1 as evidence of the matters stated.

The effect of s. 6 may be summarised in two propositions:

(a) subject to the overriding power of the judge to grant leave in any particular case in which he deems it appropriate, the section leaves essentially unaffected the common law rules as to the circumstances in which a previous statement of a witness should be admitted (these circumstances are dealt with in Chapter 11); but

(b) it provides that, if admitted, instead of being of limited evidential value as at common law, the statement will be admissible as evidence of the truth of matters stated in it.

Impeachment of the maker of an admissible hearsay statement

Where a hearsay statement is admissible by virtue of the Civil Evidence Act 1995, s. 5(2) provides that certain evidence may be adduced to attack or support the credibility of the maker, akin to the evidence which might have been adduced had the maker been called as a witness. This evidence is subject to other rules, and is considered in Chapter 11.

Preservation of common law exceptions

Continuing provisions contained in s. 9 of the Civil Evidence Act 1968, s. 7 of the Civil Evidence Act 1995, preserves without altering in substance certain common law exceptions to the rule against hearsay, relating to public records, published works, and evidence of reputation and family tradition. These exceptions are not dealt with in detail in this book, because they are encountered rarely in everyday practice. Section 7 also supersedes the common law exception relating to adverse admissions in civil cases, which is of far more importance, and is considered briefly at the end of this chapter. For more detail, reference should be made to *Murphy on Evidence*, 6th ed., ch. 8, 11 and 12.

Proof of business and public authority records

The Civil Evidence Act 1995 introduced special rules for the admissibility and proof of records of a business or public authority. These documents are generally a highly reliable form of hearsay, and may be of importance in many forms of litigation. Section 9 of the Act provides:

(1)   A document which is shown to form part of the records of a business or public authority may be received in evidence in civil proceedings without further proof.

(2)   A document shall be taken to form part of the records of a business or public authority if there is produced to the court a certificate to that effect signed by an officer of the business or authority to which the records belong.

For this purpose—

(a)   a document purporting to be a certificate signed by an officer of a business or public authority shall be deemed to have been duly given by such officer and signed by him; and

(b)   a certificate shall be treated as signed by a person if it purports to bear a facsimile of his signature.

(3)   The absence of an entry in the records of a business or public authority may be proved in civil proceedings by affidavit of an officer of the business or authority to which the record belongs.

(4)   In this section—

'records' means records in whatever form;

'business' includes any activity regularly carried on over a period of time, whether for profit or not, by any body (whether corporate or not) or by an individual;

'officer' includes any person occupying a responsible position in relation to the relevant activities of the business or public authority or in relation to its records; and

'public authority' includes any public or statutory undertaking, any government department and any person holding office under Her Majesty.

(5)   The court may, having regard to the circumstances of the case, direct that all or any of the above provisions of this section do not apply in relation to a particular document or record, or description of documents or records.

Admissions

An admission is a statement made by a party adverse to that party's case, which is tendered against him by an opposing party. At common law, admissions were admitted as an exception to the rule against hearsay in both civil and criminal cases. In criminal cases, adverse admissions made by the defendant are known as confessions, and because of the special protections afforded the defendant in criminal cases, are the subject of specialised rules of very great importance. These rules occupy the entirety of Chapter 5.

In civil cases, admissions operate without the special protective rules conferred on the defendant in criminal cases. In particular, a party cannot insist on any right of silence in a civil case, unless the admission is such as to attract the privilege against self-incrimination (as to which see Chapter 10). The admissions to which we are referring are properly known as informal admissions, to distinguish them from formal admissions which may be made (both in civil and criminal cases) for the purpose of proceedings. Formal admissions are the equivalent of evidence of the facts admitted, and, once made, are generally binding on a party in the sense of constituting sufficient proof of those facts. Conversely, an informal admission is simply a piece of evidence, which may be denied or explained away, and whose weight is always open to attack. An admission may be made in various ways, by means of a written or oral statement, or incriminating conduct such as suborning perjury, destroying evidence, failing to answer serious allegations, refusing to undergo a test which would establish paternity, or running away from the scene, from which an adverse inference may be drawn against the party concerned [2].

As noted above, admissions are now admissible by virtue of s. 7 of the Civil Evidence Act, 1995, which supersedes the common law principles of admissibility. The one difference of consequence which seems to flow from this change is that, unlike confessions in criminal cases, which are admissible only against the maker of the confession and not against any other person implicated by them (the common law rule) admissions in civil cases, which are now to be considered without reference to the rule against hearsay, may be evidence in the case for any purpose, i.e., against any party. However, the weight of an admission will clearly not always be great against a person who did not make or assent to a statement, and had no opportunity to challenge or influence the content of the statement when made. The weight of an admission must be judged by its overall content and effect, taking into account the impact of any passages which may be favourable to the case for the maker of the admission. For this reason, an admission should be presented to the court in its entirety and in its original, unedited form.

In addition to admissions which he makes himself, a party may also be bound by admissions made by his authorised agent, acting within the scope of express or apparent authority [3]. The existence of the agency may be proved by any admissible evidence, including the admissible hearsay statement of the agent. A very important form of agency for our purposes is that of the legal representative. A solicitor, by virtue even of his general instructions, has the authority to make admissions binding on his client. This may be done, e.g., by filing pleadings, writing letters, giving notices, drafting and exchanging documents, or making statements in court [4]. In criminal cases, a solicitor can make an admission binding on the client only pursuant to express instructions. A good example is the disclosure, on the client's instructions, of the client's alibi, as required by s. 5 of the Criminal Procedure and Investigations Act 1996. Barristers also have some authority to bind the lay client, though it is limited to the specific matter for the purposes of which they have been instructed. Within this authority, they may make admissions binding on the lay client by means of statements in court or endorsements on their opponents' briefs [5]. Clearly, these principles must be borne in mind at all times when representing a client — an ill advised admission can have a devastating effect on a case.

Further reading

Murphy on Evidence, 6th ed., ch. 8 and 10 (part A).

Notes

1 [1998] 1 All ER 343.
2. *Moriarty* v *London, Chatham and Dover Railway Co.* (1870) LR 5 QB 314; *Re H (A Minor) (Blood Tests: Parental Rights)* [1997] Fam 89; *Wiedemann* v *Walpole* [1891] 2 QB 534.
3. *Edwards* v *Brookes (Milk) Ltd* [1963] 1 WLR 795.
4. *Ellis* v *Allen* [1914] 1 Ch 904.
5. *Turner* (1975) 61 Cr App R 67; *Wu Chun-Piu* v *R* [1996] 1 WLR 1113.

Four

The Rule against Hearsay in Criminal Cases

Introduction

In criminal cases, the rule against hearsay continues in force, so, in the magistrates' court, we must contend with the rule and its exceptions, instead of simply concentrating on giving notice and assessing the weight of hearsay evidence, as we may now do in the county court. In addition to the common law exceptions outlined in Chapter 2, there are important statutory exceptions, which are the subject of this chapter. These exceptions are contained in ss. 23 to 26 of and sch. 2 to the Criminal Justice Act 1988 and s. 69 of the Police and Criminal Evidence Act 1984. Perhaps the most obvious difference between civil and criminal cases is that, in criminal cases, none of the statutory exceptions permits the admission of oral hearsay statements — admissibility is confined to statements contained in documents. Moreover, there are conditions of admissibility which must be strictly observed, and an express judicial discretion to exclude otherwise admissible hearsay evidence, in addition to the general discretion to exclude prosecution evidence (for which see Chapter 1). The preference for live oral evidence given by witnesses who are available for cross-examination remains strong in criminal cases. This most important principle necessarily restricts, in criminal cases, the free admissibility of hearsay which we now have in civil cases.

Admissible hearsay statements: Criminal Justice Act 1988, section 23

This section provides:

(1)   Subject [to provisions dealing with confessions, computers etc.] a statement made by a person in a document shall be admissible in criminal proceedings as evidence of any fact of which direct oral evidence by him would be admissible if—

(i)   the requirements of one of the paragraphs of subsection (2) below are satisfied; or

(ii)   the requirements of subsection (3) below are satisfied.

(2)   the requirements mentioned in subsection (1)(i) above are—

(a)   that the person who made the statement is dead or by reason of his bodily or mental condition unfit to attend as a witness;

(b)   that—

(i)   the person who made the statement is outside the United Kingdom; and

(ii)   it is not reasonably practicable to secure his attendance; or

(c)   that all reasonable steps have been taken to find the person who made the statement, but that he cannot be found.

(3)   The requirements mentioned in subsection (1)(ii) above are—

(a)   that the statement was made to a police officer or some other person charged with the duty of investigating offences or charging offenders; and

(b)   that the person who made it does not give oral evidence through fear or because he is kept out of the way.

(4)   [deals with confessions].

There are two most important points to be made about this section. Firstly, in a criminal case, we cannot admit oral hearsay statements into evidence. Only statements contained in documents are admissible. Secondly, in a criminal case, a hearsay statement can be admitted under s. 23 of the 1988 Act only where the party seeking to adduce it can demonstrate to the court, in effect, that it would be impossible, impracticable or pointless to call the maker of the statement as a witness, for one of the reasons given in subsection (2) or subsection (3). Therefore, the party wishing to adduce the evidence must show that either one of the conditions set out in subsection (2) or those set out in subsection (3) are satisfied.

Where a party relies on one of the subsection (2) reasons, reasonable steps must be taken to secure his attendance or to find him. The Act does not specify what is reasonable in this respect, but it would be foolish for a prosecutor to go to court without at least some evidence of enquiries by mail and/or telephone made in ample time before trial. What is reasonable probably depends on the time and expense that would be involved in bringing the witness to court, the gravity of the charge and the availability of other evidence to prove the case. It is certainly unacceptable for the prosecution to take no steps to secure the attendance of a witness. For example, in *Bray* [1], a prosecution witness had been abroad, in Korea, for seven months leading up to the date of trial, and nothing had been done during that time to try to make him available, despite the fact that the prosecution had had access to information of his whereabouts. The Court of Appeal held that the prosecution had failed to satisfy the requirement of the section, because it was clear that means existed at least to make the effort to bring the witness before the trial court.

In a more serious case, you may sometimes have to consider whether a witness is afraid to give evidence, or is being kept out of the way, in which case you may be able to rely on subsection (3). In order to do this, you must adduce admissible evidence to show that the witness is either afraid or is being kept out of the way. At a minimum, it is necessary to call a witness, for example, a police officer, to give evidence that the fear has been expressed to him. In this case, the statement by the witness who is afraid would be admissible as a present state of mind, a common law exception to the hearsay rule [2]. The fear need not be based on reasonable grounds [3], though the reasonableness or otherwise of the fear may be relevant in persuading the court that it does or does not exist. Curiously, the section does not specify that the witness must have been intimidated or kept out of the way by or on behalf of the defendant. However, although the point has not yet been decided, it would seem highly undesirable that the prosecution should be permitted to adduce hearsay evidence from a witness whom the police have kept out of the way, albeit for reasons they consider valid, such as the witness's own protection.

Admissible hearsay statements contained in documents created or received in the course of a trade, business, profession etc.: Criminal Justice Act 1988, section 24

Section 24 of the Criminal Justice Act 1988 dispenses with the requirement that the maker of the statement not be called as a witness for one of the reasons given in s. 23, in cases where the hearsay statement is made, not only in writing but also as part of a commercial, professional or official transaction. This is a provision equivalent, broadly speaking, to the former s. 4 of the Civil Evidence Act 1968. Although the 1988 Act does not employ the words 'record' and 'duty', the idea that statements made deliberately for such purposes are likely to be reliable is the same as that underlying s. 4 of the 1968 Act, and the conditions of admissibility are very similar.

Section 24 provides:

(1)   Subject [to provisions dealing with confessions, computers etc.] a statement in a document shall be admissible in criminal proceedings as evidence of any fact of which direct oral evidence would be admissible, if the following conditions are satisfied—

(i)   the document was created or received by a person in the course of a trade, business, profession or other occupation, or as the holder of a paid or unpaid office; and

(ii)   the information contained in the document was supplied by a person (whether or not the maker of the statement) who had, or may reasonably be supposed to have had, personal knowledge of the matters dealt with.

(2)   Subsection (1) above applies whether the information contained in the document was supplied directly or indirectly but, if it was supplied indirectly, only if each person through whom it was supplied received it—

(a)   in the course of a trade, business, profession or other occupation; or

(b)   as the holder of a paid or unpaid office.

(3)   [deals with confessions].

(4)   [dealt with below].

This provision is wider and more satisfactory than earlier attempts to make commercial and organisational records admissible. There is no restriction of evidence to records of a 'trade or business' as there had been in the Criminal Evidence Act 1965, so the section applies not only to commercial records, but also to the records of a governmental, voluntary or charitable organisation. The safeguard of the reliability of the evidence lies in the fact that it was created in the course of a routine organisational operation, which minimises the possibility that anyone had a motive to conceal, falsify or exaggerate the facts stated. It is curious that s. 24(1)(i) adds that it should be enough that the document should have been 'received' in the course of such activities, because this is no guarantee of the reliability of the document as created. Nonetheless, the section is welcome as admitting a broad category of documents which, in general, are highly reliable. If the magistrates have doubts about the reliability of a particular document tendered under s. 24, it is always open to them to exclude it in the exercise of their discretion.

Discretion of the court to exclude evidence otherwise admissible under sections 23 and 24: Criminal Justice Act 1988, section 25

Because of the importance of ensuring that criminal cases are tried primarily on the basis of oral evidence, s. 25(1) of the Criminal Justice Act 1988 gives the Court power to direct that any evidence technically admissible under s. 23 or s. 24 shall not be admitted if, in the opinion of the court, it should not be admitted in the interests of justice. This gives the court a general discretion to exclude, not dissimilar to that provided by s. 78 of the Police and Criminal Evidence Act 1984, which we discussed in Chapter 1, except that, unlike the provision in the 1984 Act, s. 25(1) of the 1988 Act seems to apply to evidence tendered by the defence as well as the prosecution. Although the court is given a general discretion, subsection (2) sets out the following matters to which the court must have regard when exercising it, that is to say:

(a) to the nature and source of the document containing the statement and to whether or not, having regard to its nature and source and to any other circumstances that appear to the court to be relevant, it is likely that the document is authentic;

(b) to the extent to which the statement appears to supply evidence which would otherwise not be readily available;

(c) to the relevance of the evidence that it appears to supply to any issue which is likely to have to be determined in the proceedings; and

(d) to any risk, having regard in particular to whether it is likely to be possible to controvert the statement if the person making it does not attend to give oral evidence in the proceedings, that its admission or exclusion will result in unfairness to the accused or, if there is more than one, to any of them.

In considering whether it would be possible for the defendant to 'controvert' prosecution evidence, the court may consider the availability for cross-examination of other prosecution witnesses, the availability of defence witnesses, and the fact that the defendant is entitled to give evidence. There is no rule that s. 25 should be applied merely because the defendant may effectively be compelled to give evidence in order to controvert the prosecution evidence [4].

Documents prepared for the purposes of criminal proceedings or the investigation of crime: Criminal Justice Act 1988, sections 26 and 24(4)

Of particular concern in criminal proceedings is the possibility that hearsay statements made for the purposes of criminal proceedings or criminal investigation may be admissible under s. 23 or s. 24 of the Criminal Justice Act 1988. Such statements, for example, witness statements, police notebooks or logs of police activity, are compiled by police officers or others with experience of their likely effect, and even if they are compiled with scrupulous objectivity, their language is apt to be more suggestive and partisan than would be the oral evidence of the maker of the statement [5]. They clearly lack the neutrality, for example, of statements made in business or official documents created before any prospect of proceedings or an investigation could have been foreseen. Sections 26 and 24(4) of the Act, therefore, provide some limitation on the admissibility of such statements. The joint effect of these provisions may be summarised as follows:

(a) A statement which has been prepared for the purpose of pending or contemplated criminal proceedings, or of a criminal investigation, and which is otherwise admissible under s. 23 or s. 24, is admissible only with the leave of the court.

(b) The court shall not give leave unless if finds that to do so would be in the interests of justice.

(c) In considering this question, the court must have regard to the contents of the statement; to whether or not it will be possible to controvert it if the maker does not give evidence; to any possibility of unfairness resulting from its admission or exclusion to any accused person; and to any other relevant circumstances.

(d) In a case where the statement is admissible under s. 24, it must further be shown that it is, in effect, either impossible or impracticable to call the maker of the statement as a witness; or that the maker is not being called because he is afraid to give evidence, or is being kept out of the way; or that he cannot reasonably be expected (having regard to the time which has elapsed since he made the statement, and any other circumstances) to have any recollection of the matters dealt with.

(e) The only cases in which the above rules do not apply are: expert reports admissible under s. 30 of the Criminal Justice Act 1988; glossaries and similar forms of evidence permitted under s. 31 of the Act [6]; and certain statements made pursuant to letters of request issued to foreign courts or tribunals to obtain evidence for use in criminal proceedings in the United Kingdom.

Sections 25 and 26 are to be applied somewhat differently. In *Cole* [7] the Court of Appeal held that, whereas under s. 25 the party seeking to exclude the statement must show affirmatively that it should be excluded on specific grounds, under s. 26 the court should not admit the statement unless it appears that it is in the interests of justice to do so. In other words, although many of the same factors are to be considered, the emphasis to be placed on them is different. In both cases, much will depend on how significant the statement is in relation to the issues the court has to decide, the language of the statement, the gravity of the charge, and the availability or otherwise of other prosecution witnesses who could give oral evidence to the same effect. It is also relevant to consider whether adequate notice has been given to the other side of an intention to rely on the statement, so as to allow time for investigation of the facts [8].

Documents produced by computers: Police and Criminal Evidence Act 1984, section 69

The fact that a document is produced by a computer does not necessarily mean that it is hearsay. Where the computer is used only to perform calculations, its output is not hearsay, and may be admitted as a piece of real evidence [9]. The same is true of less complicated machines, such as the Intoximeter [10] and the radar set [11], which produce automatic readouts. Nonetheless, where such readouts are produced by a computer, their admissibility is subject to the provisions of the Police and Criminal Evidence Act 1984, s. 69(1) (below), just as in the case of hearsay computer documents: *Shephard* [12].

To the extent that it is hearsay, because it is a record of information supplied to the computer, rather than a mere printout of automatic functions, a document produced by a computer may be admissible under the Criminal Justice Act 1988, s. 24, provided that it complies both with that section and with the Police and Criminal Evidence Act 1984, s. 69, which provides:

(1)   In any [criminal] proceedings, a statement in a document produced by a computer shall not be admissible as evidence of any fact stated therein unless it is shown—
    (a)   that there are no reasonable grounds for believing that the statement is inaccurate because of improper use of the computer;
    (b)   that at all material times the computer was operating properly, or if not, that any respect in which it was not operating properly or was out of operation was not such as to affect the production of the document or the accuracy of its contents; and
    (c)   [refers to rules of court, not yet promulgated].

The section does not create a new cateogory of admissible hearsay evidence. Any document produced by a computer must be admissible under other principles of law, and must in addition satisfy the requirements of s. 69(1) but, where the computer is used for the purposes of calculation only, the resulting evidence is not hearsay: *Minors* [13]. The conditions of admissibility under s. 69(1) may be met either by calling oral evidence about the proper working of the computer or by a certificate which complies with sch. 3, para. 8. Detailed provisions are in sch. 3, the full text of which can be found in the current edition of *Blackstone's Criminal Practice*. If oral evidence is called, it is unnecessary that the witness be a computer expert, unless the particular circumstances of the case require expert evidence. In general, the evidence of any person who is familiar with the operation of the computer, in the sense of knowing what the computer is required to do, and who can give evidence that it was operating properly, will suffice. But evidence is required; it is not enough to rely on the presumption of regularity (*Shephard* [14]).

In contrast to the former s. 5 of the Civil Evidence Act 1968, s. 69 gives no definition of a computer. In *Shephard* [14], the House of Lords considered that this omission was intentional, and was designed to allow the courts to apply the natural meaning of the word 'computer', rather than to be shackled by the consequences of an overly detailed description. Thus, a cash register would not be a computer in the ordinary sense of the word. And the mere fact that a document happens to be produced using a computer as a word processor (now a routine event) does not mean that the document is subject to the provisions of s. 69(1) [15]. This is an area in which the courts are expected to apply common sense, especially in view of the fact that computers are now used in every area of life with great and increasing regularity.

General considerations

As always in the magistrates' court, there is the problem of resolving the admissibility of evidence, discussed in Chapter 1. The considerations there discussed should be borne carefully in mind, in the light of the fact that the bench are enjoined by the Act to consider the contents of the statement in some instances. While this cannot be avoided, it is, of course, necessary to stress to the bench as strongly as possible the need to put out of their minds any documents they decide to exclude. In many cases, the bench can and should decide questions of admissibility on the basis of an agreed description of the nature, source and contents of the document, without actually seeing it, even though in some cases, this may be inappropriate.

There are no requirements of notice of intent to adduce hearsay evidence in criminal cases, corresponding to those with which we have to deal in the county court. Hence, the only rules that apply to hearsay statements in criminal cases are those applicable to the advance disclosure of evidence generally in criminal cases (as to which see Chapter 13).

The Criminal Justice Act 1988, sch. 2 (see appendix) contains provisions corresponding to those of s. 4 of the Civil Evidence Act 1995 (see Chapter 3). These deal with the weight to be accorded to admissible hearsay statements in criminal cases, and evidence which may be introduced to attack the credibility of the maker of the statement, including any previous inconsistent statements he may have made.

Further reading

Murphy on Evidence 6th ed., ch. 10, part B; *Blackstone's Criminal Practice 1998*, F. 16.

Notes

1. (1988) 88 Cr App R 354. As to the steps which may reasonably be required, see *Gonzales de Arango* (1991) 96 Cr App R 399; *Castillo* [1996] 1 Cr App R 438.

2. *Neill* v *North Antrim Magistrates' Court* [1992] 1 WLR 1220; *O'Loughlin* [1988] 3 All ER 431. As to the present state of mind exception, see *Murphy on Evidence*, 6th ed., p. 218 et seq.

3. *Acton Justices, ex parte McMullen* (1990) 92 Cr App R 98; see also *Ashford Magistrates' Court, ex parte Hilden* [1993] QB 555; *Ricketts* [1991] Crim LR 915.

4. *Cole* [1990] 1 WLR 866. See also *Price* [1991] Crim LR 707; *Scott* v *R* [1989] AC 1242.

5. See, e.g., *Martin* [1988] 1 WLR 655 (a case decided under the earlier provisions of the Police and Criminal Evidence Act 1984).

6. Glossaries will be admissible only pursuant to Crown Court Rules, and only in trials on indictment: see Criminal Justice Act 1988, s. 31.

7. [1990] 1 WLR 866.

8. *Iqbal* [1990] 1 WLR 756.

9. *Minors* [1989] 1 WLR 441; *Wood* (1982) 76 Cr App R 23.

10. *Castle* v *Cross* [1984] 1 WLR 1372.

11. *The Statue of Liberty* [1968] 1 WLR 739.

12. [1993] AC 380

13. [1989] 1 WLR 441.

14. [1993] AC 380.

15. *Blackburn* (1992) *The Times*, 1 December 1992.

Five

Confessions and the Codes of Practice

Introduction

It is the moment that every defence advocate dreads. It is the moment when the advocate hears the officer say, 'In reply to the caution, the defendant said . . .' or: 'I then interviewed the defendant on tape'. And you know what is coming next. The more matter-of-fact the officer's voice, the worse it is probably going to be. All advocates who practise in the criminal courts have experienced their own personal nightmare, and secretly fear the defence advocates' race-memory of some occasion on which some mythical defendant admitted everything and added his theft of the Crown Jewels to boot. It runs something like this: 'All right, guv, it's a fair cop. You got me bang to rights. I suppose with form like mine it will be straight inside this time.'

This is a therapeutic chapter, written for those haunted by the unspoken but deeply felt fear of the dénouement described above. We may as well start by facing facts. There is nothing that any advocate can do about a confession made in the absence of oppression and of circumstances likely to render any confession unreliable, and in full compliance with the Codes of Practice. A properly taken confession is admissible and powerful evidence of guilt, and rightly so. No prosecuting advocate should ever feel embarrassed about inviting a bench to convict on the evidence of a confession, even in the absence of other evidence, provided that the confession is shown to be admissible.

Let us start by considering what a confession is. A confession is the name given to an adverse admission made by the defendant in a criminal case which suggests or confirms his guilt of the offence charged. In common parlance, the word 'confession' implies a full admission of guilt, even a hint of melodrama. But the word carries no such implication in law. Any admission which, even partially, tends to incriminate the maker in the offence charged is termed a confession. The detailed rules of the common law dealing with the admissibility of confessions have been replaced by new statutory tests laid down by the Police and Criminal Evidence Act 1984, and s. 82(1) of the Act provides a statutory definition of the term 'confession' for the purposes of the Act, according to which that term 'includes any statement wholly or partly adverse to the person who made it, whether made to a person in authority or not and whether made in words or otherwise'.

Before the coming into effect of the Act, confessions were habitually made either orally in response to questioning by police officers, the only record of which was a note made subsequently in the officer's notebook, or in the form of a written statement under caution made on a standard form. In some cases, officers conducting an interview adopted the practice of recording the questions and answers as they were spoken, using one of their number as a scribe. This practice was clearly a sound one, was in general praised by the courts and came to be more frequently used, at least in serious cases.

However, the Police and Criminal Evidence Act 1984 and the Code of Practice for the Detention, Treatment and Questioning of Persons by Police Officers (Code of Practice C) introduced some important changes in this practice. It is now required that a record of an interview be made either contemporaneously or as soon as practicable after the conclusion of the interview. The record must contain at least the substance of the interview (and preferably be a verbatim account). The conduct of interviews at police stations is regulated in considerable detail by Code of Practice E, which requires interviews to be tape-recorded in most cases. Code E also sets out detailed requirements for the conduct of tape-recorded interviews. Where a contemporaneous record or a tape recording is made, it is envisaged that there should ordinarily be no need for the old-style written statement under caution. But Code of Practice C, Annex D, nonetheless lays down a detailed procedure for taking such statements when required.

For reasons which will become abundantly clear later in this chapter, it is essential for every advocate to familiarise himself or herself with the statutory provisions and with the Codes of Practice. In whatever form the confession is made, however, it will be subject to the same rules of admissibility which will shortly be discussed and which count among the most crucial rules of evidence in criminal cases.

Those who have made a careful study of Chapter 2 will ask why confessions should be admissible, since they appear to fall squarely within the definition of hearsay which we there considered. That is an intelligent and proper question. The answer to it is that at common law, admissions adverse to the interests of the maker are admissible, in both civil and criminal cases [1], as evidence of the facts admitted, as an exception to the rule against hearsay. The justification for this exception is that a voluntary admission by a party, contrary to that party's interest, is inherently reliable because of the unlikelihood of its being made except from a desire to tell the truth. Admissions against interest have always been regarded as evidence not only admissible, but also extremely cogent against the party making the admission.

The above observations are valid only where the admission (or confession, as we shall call it in this chapter, following the terminology in criminal cases) is made in the absence of oppression and of circumstances likely to render any confession unreliable, and in compliance with the Code of Practice. In a surprising number of instances, defence advocates are unaware of legitimate arguments which might be made to exclude or limit evidence of confessions, and prosecutors are unaware of potential weaknesses or potential strengths in their cases based on confessions. We hope that some of these problems will be resolved by what follows in this chapter.

Being there

Section 58 of the Police and Criminal Evidence Act 1984 gives a person in police custody the important right to consult privately with a solicitor at any time, if he so requests. Effectively, this means that the person detained may request that his solicitor be admitted to the police station to advise him during the progress of the police inquiry. This provision represents the first time English law has given statutory force to such a general right, and there can be no doubt that it is a most significant development, particularly when it is regarded in conjunction with Code of Practice C, which requires that the solicitor be permitted to be present at an interview if he is available when it commences or while it is in progress. Solicitors now have unprecedented opportunities to be present at interviews and to advise their clients before and during interviews. Refusing a solicitor permission to be present at an interview, removing him from an interview or refusing a solicitor admission to a police station are now extremely serious steps, which may be taken

only in closely defined circumstances (see Code of Practice C, para 6.1
et seq., annex B). An illustration of this is *Samuel* [2] in which the
Court of Appeal quashed the defendant's conviction, where it appeared
that he had been detained and questioned without access to legal
advice, and had made confessions. There was no question of the use of
oppression, or that any confession made was necessarily unreliable, but
there was no sufficient basis for denying the defendant access to legal
advice. The court's decision was based squarely on s. 78 of the Police
and Criminal Evidence Act 1984, in that the denial of advice had an
unacceptably adverse effect on the fairness of the proceedings. As we
shall see later in this chapter, exclusion is not automatic in such cases,
but it enjoys a high degree of likelihood.

It is the duty of a solicitor to attend the police station (personally or
by his articled clerk or legal executive) if so requested by a client in
custody, unless it is impracticable to do so or the duty solicitor is
available and agrees to attend. The point is that a solicitor will offer
some reassurance to a suspect in what may otherwise appear, especially
to the inexperienced, to be the overbearing atmosphere of a police
station.

Until the coming into force of the Criminal Justice and Public Order
Act 1994, one of the solicitor's most important functions was to remind
the client of his right to remain silent and advise him to exercise it.
This, of course, is now very often bad advice, since the client's silence,
including his failure to account for various matters, can be used as
evidence against him under the provisions of the 1994 Act. This is
explored more fully in Chapter 6. But this means only that the
solicitor's presence is more important than ever. Not only must a
decision be made as to whether or not the client should make a
statement, but, if it is decided that he should, the decision must also
address the form and content of the statement. This requires the
solicitor to make a mature judgment about the nature and strength of
the case against the client at an early stage, and a mistaken decision
may have drastic consequences.

The solicitor will, therefore, play a part in whatever statements his
client makes to the police, and will be a witness to the circumstances
under which those statements are made. Not only does this operate as
some guarantee that any confession will be made in circumstances
likely to render it admissible (a benefit to the prosecution of having a
solicitor present which the police tend to overlook) but it gives the
solicitor an insight into the conduct of the police inquiry which it

would be difficult to duplicate by simply taking instructions subsequently. It is important to note that the interview record must record the presence of and any removal of the solicitor and that the action taken on the suspect's request to see a solicitor must be documented in the custody record.

It is worth noting that, while a solicitor is generally entitled to send to the police station a suitably qualified clerk, a police officer of the rank of inspector or above may direct that the clerk be excluded on the ground that admitting the clerk would hinder the investigation of crime (see Code of Practice C, para. 6.12). While the police are not entitled to exclude a clerk as unqualified to give competent advice, they do not necessarily have to admit a purported clerk who is of bad character, particularly, of course, where the 'clerk' appears to have been sent for the purpose of hindering the investigation or relaying messages to accomplices. Although no reader of this book would act in this way, there are apparently some solicitors who do. The police cannot, of course, make a blanket exclusion of a class of clerks, but must consider each case individually: see *Chief Constable of Avon and Somerset Constabulary, ex parte Robinson* [3]. It is a step in every way equivalent to, and as serious as excluding a solicitor who attends in person.

If for any reason you, or someone on your behalf, should not be present while your client is interviewed, you must at a minimum take detailed instructions about what occurred.

Taking instructions about confessions

As a matter of practical preparation, there are few areas as crucial as confessions, so far as the taking of detailed instructions is concerned. Cross-examination of police officers is almost impossible without a vivid and detailed understanding of the circumstances in which an interview occurred, or a written statement under caution was made. In what place; at what time of day or night; in what frame of mind; whether it was the defendant's first experience of a police station; whether the defendant was allowed access to a solicitor. With each day that passes before instructions are taken, the defendant's memory will tend to fade, and perhaps even be subconsciously repressed, whereas the police officer's recollection is permanently recorded in his notes or in the recesses of his professional experience. If the period of detention and interrogation was long, the problem is intensified. Yet, in order to

have a serious chance of success in cross-examination about a confession, it is vital to have a full account of what happened: how many
interviews; in what order; who was present; and most importantly,
what did the officer say and what did your client say? Unless you can
challenge or otherwise deal with the detail of the confession line by
line, your cross-examination will lose something in terms of effectiveness. Similarly with a written statement under caution. How long did
it take to make? Who wrote what? Did they record word for word what
your client said? Were any questions interposed as he was dictating?
Did he sign the statement and initial any corrections? Was he told that
he could correct, alter or add anything he wished? What kind of
interview record was made? Was the interview tape-recorded? Does it
appear that Code of Practice C was complied with, both generally and
in specific instances called for by the fact that your client was sick,
unable to speak English or a juvenile?

Obviously, an early and lengthy conference with your client is called
for if you are to have any hope of getting instructions of this kind. In
many cases, for good reason or bad, the defendant will be unable to
give you instructions in sufficient detail. If this happens, you must do
what you can with the available material. But this should not be
accepted as an inevitable problem, and must not be permitted to occur
simply because of your failure to take the best possible instructions.

When dealing with an interview record or a written statement under
caution, you should always insist on seeing the original before trial.
Things leap out of the pages of an original which may be buried in a
typed or even a photographic copy. Nuances of signature (steady or
shaky?) of handwriting (hurried or leisurely?) or corrections (fluent or
hesitant?) become devastatingly apparent in many cases. The original
should also give away many secrets about the time a statement must
have taken to write, about the frame of mind of the maker and the
willingness or otherwise of the maker to make the statement. From
both the original and the copy, you may gain a useful insight from the
language used. Is this the style of language your client habitually
employs? Are there words or phrases which he could not spell or even
understand? In dealing with clients to whom English is a second
language, this can be a particularly fertile field of inquiry. For similar
reasons, if the interview was tape-recorded, you should make arrangements to listen to the tape, in addition to obtaining a copy of the
transcript, unless it is clear that this would serve no useful purpose.

Admissibility of confessions

At common law, confessions were admissible as an exception to the rule against hearsay, but because of the usually crucial role of confessions in deciding the outcome of criminal trials, and the potential for coerced confessions, the common law developed rules to ensure that a confession made to a 'person in authority' was not to be admissible unless the prosecution proved beyond reasonable doubt that it had been made 'voluntarily' and in the absence of 'oppression'. The terms in quotation marks acquired technical meanings through judicial interpretation, but they were part of the common law's concern with this aspect of criminal trials. Adverse admissions are admitted as an exception to the rule against hearsay, because the danger of unreliability traditionally associated with hearsay evidence is outweighed by the fact that a statement so clearly adverse to the interests of the maker is unlikely to have been made unless its contents are true. Of course, this proposition is destroyed where there is any real risk that the statement was made, not because of a desire to tell the truth, but because of threats, fear, unjustified hopes, weakness or any other circumstances which make it likely that, not only the confession actually made, but any confession which might have been made, may be unreliable.

The Police and Criminal Evidence Act 1984, which has now replaced the common law rules governing the admissibility of confessions with new statutory rules, has in no way changed this basic concern of the law. For reasons which need not be explored here, it has substituted differently worded tests of admissibility which have probably strengthened the position of defendants who have made confessions. Only the new statutory rules need be studied now, although, because certain concepts are preserved, we shall refer to the common law where necessary. The starting-point is now s. 76 of the Police and Criminal Evidence Act 1984, which provides as follows:

(1) In any proceedings a confession made by an accused person may be given in evidence against him insofar as it is relevant to any matter in issue in the proceedings and is not excluded by the court in pursuance of this section.

(2) If, in any proceedings where the prosecution proposes to give in evidence a confession made by an accused person, it is represented to the court that the confession was or may have been obtained—

(a)   by oppression of the person who made it; or

(b)   in consequence of anything said or done which was likely, in the circumstances existing at the time, to render unreliable any confession which might be made by him in consequence thereof, the court shall not allow the confession to be given in evidence against him except insofar as the prosecution proves to the court beyond reasonable doubt that the confession (notwithstanding that it may be true) was not obtained as aforesaid.

(3)   In any proceedings where the prosecution proposes to give in evidence a confession made by an accused person, the court may of its own motion require the prosecution, as a condition of allowing it to do so, to prove that the confession was not obtained as mentioned in subsection (2) above.

The power of the court to require proof of its own motion is a valuable protection to the unrepresented defendant, but it need hardly be said that such a situation should never be necessary where the defendant is represented — his solicitor or counsel must be vigilant in seeing that the rules are observed. The procedure to be followed where the admissibility of a confession is disputed was dealt with in Chapter 1. Another important point is that the test of admissibility is not whether the confession is true (which is a question of fact arising only if it is admitted in evidence) but how it was obtained (which will determine, as a matter of law, whether it may be admitted).

At common law, the rules of admissibility applied technically only where the confession was made to a 'person in authority' — usually a police officer or other professional investigator — and there was much learning on the question of who was or was not such a person. Happily, this arcane distinction has now been abolished, and the new rules apply to all confessions. Having said this, three questions arise for examination:

(a)   Who has the burden of proof and what is the standard of proof?

(b)   What amounts to oppression?

(c)   What makes a confession unreliable?

Burden and standard of proof   Here, the Act follows the common-law rule and requires proof by the prosecution to the same standard as on the issue of guilt itself, whether the dispute is raised by the defence or by the court of its own motion. The standard is, of course, that beyond reasonable doubt. It follows that you should address the bench on the issue of admissibility by pointing out to them that they must exclude the confession not only if they find that it was obtained in one of the ways proscribed by s. 76(2) but if it *may* have been so obtained.

Confessions obtained by oppression The concept of oppression is a test recognised by the common law which the Act has preserved, and to which it has added a partial statutory definition. By s. 76(8):

> In this section 'oppression' includes torture, inhuman or degrading treatment, and the use or threat of violence (whether or not amounting to torture).

At common law, there was no comprehensive definition of the term 'oppression', and, indeed, it appears to have been considered judicially only once before the enactment of the 1984 Act [4]. Nor was its meaning completely clarified by s. 76(8), which, because of the use of the word 'includes' is obviously not intended to be exhaustive. But the question was considered by the Court of Appeal in *Fulling* [5], in which it was held that 'oppression' should be given its ordinary dictionary meaning. The court referred in particular to one meaning assigned to the word by the *Oxford English Dictionary:* 'Exercise of authority or power in a burdensome, harsh, or wrongful manner; unjust or cruel treatment of subjects, inferiors, etc.; the imposition of unreasonable or unjust burdens'.

In *Fulling,* it was alleged that the police had, during interrogation of a female defendant, deliberately told her that her boyfriend had been having an affair with another woman, who had also been arrested and was in the next cell. The defendant alleged that as a result of this, she became bitterly distressed, and made a statement just to get out of custody (though she did not allege that the police offered her bail in return for the statement). The Court of Appeal held that, even if true, these allegations were not sufficient to amount to oppression. It is clear from this decision that oppression involves both extreme conduct and impropriety on the part of the interrogating officers, and that its availability as a ground of exclusion will be comparatively rare. Where these elements are not present, any application to exclude must be based on the unreliability ground, dealt with below.

It has also been held that the mere fact that a police officer becomes impatient or angry, or gives way to bad language, during an interview is not sufficient to amount to oppression: *Emmerson* [6]. But in *Paris* [7], the Court of Appeal held that a confession should have been excluded on the ground of oppression, where the defendant had been 'bullied and hectored' in a way which, in the opinion of the Court, could not have been more hostile and intimidating short of actual violence. The court may take into account the personal attributes of the defendant in assessing the effect of interrogation on him. In *Seelig* [8] the Court of Appeal held that the trial judge had been correct in taking account of the fact that the defendant, a merchant banker, was 'experienced', 'intelligent', and 'sophisticated'. Conversely, if the defendant is of low intelligence, poorly educated, or lacking in self-assertiveness, the court should take these factors into account in his favour. What is oppressive in the case of one defendant may be no more than a wholly justifiable attempt to obtain information in the case of another. Each case must be considered on its own facts.

Unreliable confessions   The second ground for exclusion of confessions is wide and represents a welcome extension of the common law requirement of voluntariness. The use of the word 'unreliable'and the emphasis on 'circumstances' rather than conduct suggest that the court is to consider the whole picture and not just whether or not any deliberate 'oppressive' acts or omissions on the part of the interrogators may have induced the confession. This is important in the light of the fact that the common-law concept of voluntariness no longer applies. The common-law concept of voluntariness was defined as requiring the exclusion of any confession obtained by means of exciting in the suspect a 'hope of advantage' or 'fear of prejudice'. Thus, where it was alleged that the police offered bail or threatened to withhold it, threatened to have a member of the family charged, promised to 'put in a good word with the bench' or to allow other offences to be taken into consideration, the concept of voluntariness was invoked. It is true that such conduct could also be described colloquially as oppressive, but it does not accord with the decision in *Fulling* [5] and is much more aptly described as rendering any confession that might be made unreliable.

This is particularly significant in cases where the police do not indulge in any deliberate conduct, but unintentionally permit circumstances to exist which put pressure on a suspect to confess. In such a case it would be difficult to argue oppression.

It has been held that s. 76(2) obliges the judge to consider everything said and done by the police, which means that the judge must evaluate the totality of the circumstances surrounding the making of the confession: *Barry* [9]. These circumstances may include the personal characteristics of the defendant. In a number of cases, the Court of Appeal has made it clear that the trial court should scrutinise carefully the circumstances surrounding any confession made by a person of low intelligence or suffering from any psychiatric or psychological disorder, even though such a defendant is also entitled to additional protection at trial conferred by the Police and Criminal Evidence Act 1984, s. 77. Thus in *Harvey* [10], a confession made by a woman who was found to be psychopathic and of low intelligence was excluded, where it appeared that the confession might have been made because of a child-like desire to protect her lover from suspicion.

However, following the decision in *Rennie* [11], which was based on the common law, the Court of Appeal held in *Goldenberg* [12] that it will not be sufficient to exclude a confession under s. 76(2) if the circumstances relied on consist entirely of things said or done by the defendant or the defendant's state of mind at the time of the interview. The defendant in *Goldenberg* was a heroin addict who alleged that, because of his addiction, he had no choice but to make a confession in order to be released from custody. The Court held that there must be a causal link between what was said or done by the police officers and the making of the confession. With respect, it is hard to see a sensible distinction between the facts of this case and the facts of those cases in which the Court of Appeal has held it to be proper to consider the low intelligence or abnormality of the defendant, but it seems the distinction must somehow be made. [13]

The Act does not define what it means by 'unreliable', but you can probably address the bench safely on the basis that the word simply imports that the confession is such that no court could conscientiously permit it to be adduced because in view of the possibly decisive nature of such evidence, and having regard to the high standard of proof required of the prosecution, it would be dangerous and unjust to do so.

It should be noted that the test is whether *any* confession which might have been made by the defendant in consequence of the circumstances might be unreliable. The court need not, and should not, limit itself to the question of the reliability of the confession actually made. Indeed, in a sense, the actual contents of the confession are irrelevant to the question of admissibility, since the test is not whether the confession is true. It is the effect of the circumstances on the state of mind of the suspect (which would affect *any* confession he might have made) that is relevant.

Whether or not a confession was obtained by oppression or under circumstances likely to render any confession unreliable is a question of fact in each case. There is no such thing as conduct or circumstances which are enough to exclude as a matter of law, because the ultimate question is one of causation: what led, or may have led, the defendant to confess? Of course, where there has been oppression of the kind referred to in s. 76(8) it would hopefully be unthinkable that a court would entertain any resulting confession. But this is still a question of fact. In the days of the common law voluntariness rule, it was held that the categories of threats and inducements were never closed. No doubt the same is true of oppression and circumstances under the Act. Nonetheless, even if not closed, the categories become familiar to every practising advocate through sheer repetition. The same allegations are made and refuted daily in courts throughout the land, and seem to change little over the course of time. A statement in return for bail, in return for abstaining from violence, in return for forbearing to bring other charges, in return for allowing other offences to be taken into consideration, in return for a 'good word' to the bench, in return for not arresting or charging a member of the family. Even though the rules of admissibility are now different, there is no reason to suppose that these facts and more are not amply covered by s. 76.

The case for exclusion is always a difficult one to argue. The bench will, quite naturally and rightly, want to hear all available evidence and will tend to resent attempts to keep evidence out. The best prospects for success are afforded by the two techniques of (a) emphasising the burden and standard of proof, and (b) avoiding, wherever legitimately possible, any suggestion of deliberate misconduct on the part of the police. The latter technique is, of course, available only where consistent with the facts. It is pointless and self-defeating to sacrifice all sense of reality by holding back in a case where, if the defendant is to be believed, the officers were plainly guilty of gross misconduct or a serious breach of the Code of Practice. Moreover, any bad faith on the part of the officers will be an important factor in the possible exercise of the court's discretion to exclude (below). In such a case, you must argue the facts openly and fearlessly. Only professional judgment will supply the correct approach in any given case.

Nonetheless, the two techniques suggested enjoy, for self-evident reasons, a proven record of success. The bench will naturally feel more inclined to sympathise with the defence where they can do so without having to hold, expressly or impliedly, that the police officers who appear as witnesses in their court on a regular basis have been guilty of misconduct. The bench may quite properly find that a confession is unreliable because of some circumstances created by the police with no improper intent and even possibly with the best of motives. In the case of an inexperienced defendant, who finds himself in a police station for the first time in his life, this is by no means an uncommon occurrence. The defendant may well have believed that he was in some way threatened without any real basis for his fear. His confession may nonetheless be unreliable, and you can argue the point without any attack on the police. Similar arguments may be available where the defendant's capacity to look after himself was reduced or eliminated by some illness or personal problems of which the police may have been unaware.

Confessions and the Codes of Practice

Between 1912 and 1985, the rules for the guidance of police officers in connection with the detention and interrogation of suspects, first laid down by the judges of the King's Bench Division and known generally as the Judges' Rules, provided the guidance required by the police and by the criminal courts in this area, subject to statutory provisions and the common law. The Judges' Rules were not rules of law, but rules of practice, and the effect of a breach of the Rules on the admissibility of any resulting confession was never satisfactorily stated by the courts. The preamble to the Rules made it clear that they did not affect the overriding principles of law concerning the admissibility of confessions, but added that a breach of the Rules might render answers and statements inadmissible in subsequent criminal proceedings.

In practice, the main significance of the Judges' Rules came to be that a serious breach of the Rules was relevant to the issue of whether or not a confession obtained following or by means of such a breach must be excluded because the prosecution could not prove that it had been voluntary and obtained without oppression, which was the test of admissibility at common law. In addition, the courts appear to have assumed that a judge might exercise his discretion to exclude a confession where a relevant breach of the Rules had occurred [14]. The courts exhibited no enthusiasm for excluding confessions merely because a breach had occurred, and in practice it was necessary for the defendant to show not only that a substantial breach had occurred, but also that the breach had had a significant effect on the making of the confession sufficient to call into question its admissibility as a matter of law.

The Police and Criminal Evidence Act 1984 introduced radical new provisions dealing with the arrest, detention and interrogation of suspects and, by s. 66, required the Secretary of State to issue Codes of Practice dealing with:

    (a)   the exercise by police officers of statutory powers—
        (i)   to search a person without first arresting him; or
        (ii)   to search a vehicle without making an arrest;
    (b)   the detention, treatment, questioning and identification of persons by police officers;
    (c)   searches of premises by police officers; and
    (d)   the seizure of property found by police officers on persons or premises.

Section 60 of the Act required the Secretary of State to issue a Code of Practice in connection with the tape recording of interviews.

Four codes were promulgated pursuant to s. 66, and came into effect on 1 January 1986. These are: Code A relating to the exercise by police officers of statutory powers to stop and search; Code B relating to the searching of premises by police officers and the seizure of property found by police officers on persons or premises; Code C relating to the detention, treatment and questioning of persons by police officers; and Code D relating to the identification of persons by police officers. This chapter will be concerned principally with Code C, which deals with much the same subject-matter as did the Judges' Rules. Code C was amended, with effect from 10 April 1995, to take account of the Criminal Justice and Public Order Act 1994.

Code of Practice E relating to tape-recording of interviews was promulgated later, pursuant to s. 60, and came into effect on 29 July 1988.

Unfortunately, Parliament did not specifically provide for the effect of a breach of the Codes of Practice on the admissibility of confessions, but hinted at the solution by making the Codes admissible in evidence. By s. 67(11) of the Act:

In all criminal and civil proceedings any such code shall be admissible in evidence; and if any provision of such a code appears to the court or tribunal conducting the proceedings to be relevant to any question arising in the proceedings it shall be taken into account in determining that question.

From this, it is clear that the Codes of Practice may be used as relevant evidence in determining whether a confession must be excluded because it was obtained by oppression or in circumstances likely to render unreliable any confession which might have been made by a defendant. There is no doubt that a substantial breach of the Code may be relevant in persuading the bench that this is the case, and you can argue that the Act intends the Codes of Practice to be enforced by being adduced in evidence and applied to the issue of admissibility. Of course, as with the Judges' Rules, a minor, technical or inconsequential breach, which appears to the court not to have influenced the making of the confession, will not be enough to exclude. On the other hand, the court should undoubtedly exclude a confession which has been obtained by means of or following a serious and substantial breach of the Code.

This exclusion may be based either on legal grounds, relying on the Police and Criminal Evidence Act 1984, s. 76, or on the court's general discretion to exclude evidence under s. 78 of the Act, which was discussed in Chapter 1. The courts have shown themselves willing to exclude under s. 78 on grounds of unfairness which may be based on something other than a breach of the Codes of Practice. An example is the case of *Mason* [15] in which police officers obtained a confession by misrepresenting to the defendant the strength of the case against him (see Chapter 1). But here we are concerned with unfairness arising from a breach of a provision of the 1984 Act, or of Codes C and E.

A clear example is the case in which the defendant has been denied access to legal advice, in breach of the Police and Criminal Evidence Act 1984, s. 58. One case in which it was held that this should have been sufficient to exclude a confession has already been discussed in this chapter (*Samuel* [16]). And in *Walsh* [17], the Court of Appeal held that if any 'significant and substantial' breach of s. 58 or Code C occurred, then '*prima facie* at least, the standards of fairness set by Parliament have not been met'. Even in these circumstances, however, exclusion is not automatic, though it may normally be expected. In *Alladice* [18], the Court of Appeal held that a confession had been properly admitted where, despite denial of access to legal advice, the defendant admitted in evidence that he had been able to cope adequately with the interviews, that he had received and understood the caution, and that he knew his legal rights. And conversely, the fact that the defendant's solicitor is present during an interview may be considered a factor in deciding to admit the confession, despite some breach of the Code: see, e.g., *Dunn* [19]. But the Court of Appeal also made it clear, in *Keenan* [20], that the provisions of Code C dealing with interviews must be strictly complied with, and that any substantial breach should ordinarily result in exclusion.

In this connection, some doubt has arisen about the meaning of the word 'interview' as used in the Code. Paragraph 11.1A of Code C defines an interview as the questioning of a person regarding his involvement or suspected involvement in an offence. In *Cox* [21], it was held that an interview occurs at the time of arrest, when questions are put with a view to obtaining an admission on a vital part of the case from the person arrested. On the other hand, questioning to obtain information in the normal course of an officer's activities does not constitute an interview: *Marsh* [22]. It is obviously important for the court to know whether or not an interview was occurring when a statement was made. Code C, para. 11, provides that, with certain narrow exceptions, interviews should take place at a police station, and Code E, also subject to exceptions, requires interviews to be tape-recorded. It would seem that the crucial test is whether the person being questioned is a suspect in the case and is being questioned with a view to obtaining a confession. It also seems clear that the court will sometimes have to use its discretion in determining whether some less formal exchange, for example, at the scene of the offence, amounts to an interview, and should therefore be subject to the provisions of Code C. There is clearly room for concern about informal conversations, which under the previous law, gave rise to so many complaints about alleged 'verballing'. In *Cox* [23] the Court of Appeal held that the word 'interview' should not be construed strictly, as if it were a statutory provision, but rather the courts should judge each situation on its merits having regard to what might be fair. An example of the kind of problem which can arise is *Matthews* [24] where the defendant asked that a conversation with an officer be kept 'off the record' but the confession was held to have been rightly admitted, even though the officer had failed to make a note of it. In *Christou* [25] it was held to be improper for police officers to adopt a disguise to enable them to ask questions of a suspect without having to observe the provisions of Code C.

At common law, the courts held that exclusion of a confession should be based on the effect produced on the defendant by the conduct of the officers, rather than the state of mind or intent of the officers [26]. However, it has also been held that, where the officers act 'in bad faith', i.e., in deliberate contravention of the Police and Criminal Evidence Act 1984 or of the Codes, this will be an important factor in deciding to exclude a confession: see, e.g., *Alladice* [27]. On the other hand, a substantial breach which is committed 'in good faith', i.e., unintentionally or inadvertently, will not be excused solely for that reason.

The fact that a confession is excluded because of a breach does not necessarily mean that a subsequent confession, properly obtained, must also be excluded. But if the effect of the breach continued to affect the defendant at the time of the later interview, then it, too, should be excluded: *Gillard* [28].

Recognising breaches of the Codes

Some of the most important provisions of Code C relating to detention, arrest and questioning are set out in the Appendix to this book. But it cannot be emphasised too strongly that you must obtain and study a complete text of all the Codes. They are set out in full in the current edition of *Blackstone's Criminal Practice*. Even given a thorough working knowledge of the Codes, it is obvious that the range of possible breaches is not inconsiderable and that a breach may not always be easy to recognise. In a summary trial, in which the defence advocate works without sight of the prosecution statements, this can present problems in identifying areas of complaint while there is still time to act on them. One useful technique in overcoming this problem is to carry a checklist of areas in which a breach is most likely to occur. The following, while not exhaustive, may serve as the basis of such a checklist in relation to Code C. You will be able to modify and supplement it in the way you find most helpful.

Question	Code C, paragraph
1. Is my client a juvenile?	1.5
Was the appropriate adult present?	1.7
Was my client treated as required by the Code in relation to:	
detention?	8.8, 8.12
searches?	Annex A
interviews?	Section 12 and Annex C
being charged?	16.1–3, 16.6, 16.9

Question	Code C, paragraph
2. Is my client mentally handicapped? (Same questions as above)	See summary Annex E
3. Is my client a foreign national or handicapped by blindness or deafness?	1.6
Was an interpreter called or steps taken to ensure his understanding at all times especially during interviews?	3.6, 3.14, section 13
Was he enabled to speak to the consul?	Section 7
4. Was my client detained for an unnecessary length of time?	1.1
5. Was he given access to Code C?	1.2
Was he notified of his rights to see the Code? to have someone informed? to consult a solicitor?	3.1, 3.2
6. If held incommunicado, was my client permitted: to have someone informed? to receive visits? to have writing materials, letters, messages?	5.1, 5.2 5.4 5.7
7. Did my client request legal advice?	
Was action taken reasonably promptly?	6.1, 6.2
Was he interviewed without access to advice?	6.6–11
Was the solicitor refused access to the police station altogether?	6.14
Was all action recorded?	6.16, 6.17
8. Was my client treated as required throughout his period of detention? general conditions meals etc. medical treatment	8.1–5 8.6–7 Section 9(b)
Was a record made?	8.11, 9.7–9

Question	Code C, paragraph

9.   Was my client cautioned as required?

On suspicion?	10.1
Prior to arrest?	10.2
On arrest?	10.3
After breaks in questioning?	10.5
On being charged?	16.2
Was a record made of the cautions?	10.7

10.   Was each interview properly conducted?

What was my client told about refusal to answer or make a statement?	11.3
Did he have access to legal advice?	See Question 7
Was the interview conducted in proper physical surroundings and with required physical reliefs for the client?	Section 12(a)
Was the client fit to be interviewed?	Annex C
Was an interview record made and:	
made promptly?	11.5, 11.7
signed and timed by the maker?	11.8, 11.9
Was the client allowed to see and sign the record?	11.10–12
Is the content of the record satisfactory?	11.5, section 12(b)

11.   Was a written statement under caution taken?

Did the taking comply with Annex D?	12.13, Annex D

12.   When my client was charged:

Was there improper delay?	16.1
Was he cautioned and given written notice?	16.2, 16.3
Did questioning then cease?	16.5
Was improper use made of a statement made by a co-defendant?	16.4
Was a record made of everything said at and after the charging?	Section 16(b)

The following is a suggested checklist for use in connection with tape-recorded interviews.

Question	Code E, paragraph
1. Was this an interview that should have been recorded?	3.1–3.4
2. Was the whole of the interview recorded?	3.5
3. Was the taping carried out openly?	2.1, 4.1
4. Was my client sufficiently informed about the tape-recording?	4.2
5. Was my client cautioned?	4.3
6. Was a master tape made? sealed?	2.2
7. Were any objections made by my client? If so, were those objections recorded?	4.5
8. Were any changes of tape made or breaks taken?	4.8, 4.9
9. Was there any equipment failure?	4.12, 3.3
10. Were the tapes properly identified and preserved at the conclusion of taping?	4.13–4.15
11. Has security of the master tape been preserved?	6.1–6.3
12. Was my client given a notice explaining the use to be made of the tapes and arrangements for access to them?	4.16
13. Was an interview record prepared?	5.1–5.4
14. Is my client wholly or partially deaf? Was a contemporaneous note also taken?	4.4

As to the making of objections to tape-recorded interviews, arrangements for editing of such statements and for the playing of tapes to the court, see *Practice Direction (Crime: Tape Recording Police Interviews)* [1989] 1 WLR 631.

You should work on organising and supplementing these checklists as you may find most advantageous for your own use. In time, the major items will become so familiar that you will become sensitive to facts which suggest a potential breach. Incidentally, there is no objection to cross-examining (or re-examining) a police officer about his knowledge of the Codes of Practice. This was commonly done with the Judges' Rules, and though it should be used with some discretion it is sometimes a worthwhile weapon.

Challenging the weight of confessions

If the bench find that a confession is admissible in law and further find that there is no ground to exclude the confession in the exercise of their discretion, the confession will be admitted in evidence. Some defence advocates seem to give up at this point, and assume that there is nothing more that they can do. This is far from the truth. The whole question of weight remains open to challenge. This may be done during cross-examination of the officers, and by calling your client and other witnesses, and of course during your closing speech. It is important, of course, to bear in mind that the issue is no longer just the absence of oppression or the circumstances in which the confession was made, but whether the bench should give the confession enough weight to justify their acting on it to convict.

Confessions implicating co-defendants

It is a cardinal rule of evidence that any confession is evidence against the maker of the admission only, and not against any other person implicated by it. Because the maker may have had motives of his own for implicating others, and because the person or persons implicated had no opportunity to be present and refute what was said about them by the maker, the implication against those others is inherently unreliable, and would not justify the departure from the rule against hearsay that would be necessary to render the confession admissible against them.

It is, of course, commonplace for one defendant to try to put the blame on another, or at least to try to share the blame with another, and a confession, particularly when enshrined in an interview record or a written statement under caution, is an ideal tool for the job. This poses an intractable procedural and evidential problem if the defendants are tried jointly. Suppose that you represent defendant A. Defendant B, jointly charged and tried with A, has made a written statement under caution implicating A. The prosecution wish to place B's confession before the bench, because, even if it is not evidence against A, it is certainly evidence against B as the maker. The very fact that B has tried to implicate A in a certain way may even be cogent evidence against B himself. On the other hand, if the confession goes before the court, there will be prejudice to A, consisting of evidence which is not admissible against A.

In almost every case, the confession will be admitted in full, and the prejudice to A must be accepted as one of the risks of a joint trial. Nor will the situation be an adequate ground for separate trials, unless the prejudice is very great. Although this seems unfair on the face of it, the rule does correspond to certain of the realities of practice. Firstly, the prosecution are entitled to use the confession against B. Secondly, the confession should be admitted as a whole unless there are very good reasons for not doing so, because the court should ordinarily be told exactly what a defendant states in his confession. Thirdly, the evidential value of the confession as against B would be weakened by omitting the reference to A. Fourthly, the confession may effectively be made evidence against A in the course of your cross-examination of B. Although B's out-of-court statement is not evidence against A, what B says from the witness-box on oath at the trial is evidence in the case generally. In many cases, you will be unable to cross-examine effectively without referring to the statement, and there is accordingly no real ground for excluding the passages referring to A, to which B's advocate will be entitled to refer during re-examination, in order to re-establish B's credibility.

In most cases, you will wish to cross-examine B as strenuously as possible, since the best way to nullify the effect of his confession is to demonstrate his dishonesty or unreliability. Remember always that the order of cross-examination dictates that you must cross-examine B before the prosecutor does so. Even if you ask no questions about that part of B's confession which concerns A, the prosecutor will, and you may have no chance to rebut whatever B says in answer to that cross-examination. In short, it is almost always a serious mistake not to cross-examine B fully. You may as well face the full impact of the statement and try to demolish it.

Certainly, there are cases where the reference to A is relatively insignificant to the case against B, and where the risk of prejudice to A is very great, where the court should either grant separate trials or agree to the editing of B's statement [29]. Any application for such relief should, of course, be made by explaining the position to the bench in general terms, without referring to the details of the evidence, so as to avoid exposing the bench to prejudicial material.

It is the duty of A's advocate, in the situation where B's confession is admitted without editing on a joint trial, to remind the bench very forcefully that nothing in the statement is evidence against A. This must be done deliberately and pointedly in the course of your closing speech. Make a point of emphasising that B's statement is not evidence against A for any purpose, and that the prosecution cannot rely on the statement to prove the case against A.

Confessions made in response to confessions of co-defendants

In certain cases, defendant A may make a confession after being shown the record of an interview with defendant B or a written statement made by defendant B, whether or not the record or written statement actually implicates A. Although B's statement is not evidence against A, for the reasons discussed above, what A says to the police in response to B's statement may be evidence against A if it amounts to a confession. This is sometimes described as A adopting B's statement, though it is actually A's own statement that is evidence against him. The prosecution may, of course, refer to B's statement in such a case, in order to explain or provide the background for A's statement. If, having been shown B's statement, A denies what B says, then he has in no way adopted B's statement, and in this case neither A's denial nor B's statement have any evidential value against A.

Where both A and B have been charged with an offence, or informed that they may be prosecuted for the offence, and a police officer wishes at that stage to show B's interview record or statement to A, Code of Practice C provides restrictions on what may be done, because the cut-off point for interrogation for the offence has passed, and there are obvious dangers in inviting A to comment on B's statement at that stage. Paragraph 16.4 provides that in such circumstances, the officer shall:

hand to that person [A] a true copy of any such written statement or bring to his attention the content of the interview record, but shall say or do nothing to invite any reply or comment save to warn him that he does not have to say anything but that anything he does say may be given in evidence and to remind him of his right to legal advice in accordance with paragraph 6.5.

Moreover, the proceedings should be tape-recorded: see Code of Practice E, para. 3.1(c).

Whether or not paragraph 16.4 applies, you should take very careful instructions about the circumstances in which B's statement was shown to A, particularly where the police officers have recorded that A has agreed with the statement, with some such phrase as 'Well, if B has told you all about it, there's nothing I can say'. Such a situation is very likely to arise, particularly where there has been a breach of paragraph 16.4. Your client may not know or understand why B said what he did, but may have assumed that B would be believed, rather than he himself. It is essential to identify the dangers in each individual situation, and deal with them in cross-examination and by adducing evidence, and, if possible, excluding any adoption by A of B's statement.

Confessions which reveal previous bad character

It is desirable that a confession should be recorded as made in the defendant's own words. This occasionally has disadvantages for the defence, in that the defendant himself may refer in his statement to some matter which is inadmissible against him, but which has the potential for prejudice. A reference to previous bad character is the most usual example. Although the prosecution would not be permitted to use the defendant's bad character as evidence of his guilt, the defendant may not object, as a matter of strict law, to the admission of his statement containing the unfortunate revelation [30].

In practice, however, a more lenient rule generally prevails, since references to character are incidental and accidental, and add nothing to the evidential value of the confession. The practice is to edit out of the statement the offending references. This is achieved, in the case of a written confession, interview record or transcript by physically striking the passages concerned (providing edited copies for the use of the court) and in the case of an oral statement, by instructing the witnesses to omit the passages from their evidence (to avoid accidental allusions, it is advisable to have the officers mark their notebooks in pencil, and have the prosecutor use leading questions to avoid the offending passages and maintain a smooth narrative). The practice of editing in these circumstances enjoys the express sanction of the courts [31], and responsible prosecutors will unhesitatingly agree to defence requests for such editing, unless the case is an unusual one. Unusual cases, in which editing may not be appropriate, are those where the confession would be so emasculated by the editing as to be wholly or virtually unintelligible to the bench (in which case the confession should either be omitted altogether, or presented to the bench intact with copious warnings to ignore the reference to character), or cases where the reference to character actually has some relevance to guilt, for example where the defendant's admission of his presence in prison at a given time proves his association with a co-defendant (in which case the prosecution can and should insist upon the statement going into evidence as it stands).

In any case where the statement is presented to the bench without editing, it is the duty of the defence advocate to emphasise to the bench that the reference to bad character has no evidential value in proving the defendant's guilt. But it should be stressed that such a situation ought to be exceptional.

Further reading

Murphy on Evidence, 6th ed., ch. 8; *Blackstone's Criminal Practice 1998*, F17.

Notes

1. In civil cases, the admissibility of adverse admissions is now also governed by statute, Civil Evidence Act 1995, s. 7(1).
2. [1988] QB 615.
3. [1989] 1 WLR 793.
4. By Sachs J, in *Priestly* (1965) 51 Cr App R 1.
5. [1987] 1 WLR 1196.
6. (1990) 92 Cr App R 284.
7. (1992) 97 Cr App R 99.
8. [1992] 1 WLR 148.
9. (1991) 95 Cr App R 355.

10. [1988] Crim LR 241. See also *Everett* [1988] Crim LR 826; *McGovern* (1990) 92 Cr App R 228.
11. [1982] 1 WLR 64.
12. (1988) 88 Cr App R 285. See also *Crampton* (1990) 92 Cr App R 369.
13. See also *Effik* (1992) 95 Cr App R 427.
14. *May* (1952) 36 Cr App R 91; *Prager* [1972] 1 WLR 260.
15. [1988] 1 WLR 139
16. [1988] QB 615.
17. (1989) 91 Cr App R 161.
18. (1988) 87 Cr App R 380; *Seelig* [1992] 1 WLR 148.
19. (1990) 91 Cr App R 237.
20. [1990] 2 QB 54. See also *Absolam* (1988) 88 Cr App R 332; *Canale* [1990] 2 All ER 187.
21. (1992) 96 Cr App R 464.
22. [1991] Crim LR 455.
23. (1992) 96 Cr App R 464.
24. (1989) 91 Cr App R 43.
25. [1992] QB 979; see also *Bryce* [1992] 4 All ER 567; *Okafor* [1994] 3 All ER 741; *Weedersteyn* [1995] 1 Cr App R 405.
26. See, e.g., *DPP* v *Ping Lin* [1976] AC 574.
27. (1988) 87 Cr App R 380.
28. (1990) 92 Cr App R 61; *Y* v *DPP* [1991] Crim LR 917.
29. *Rogers* [1971] Crim LR 413; *Lake* (1976) 64 Cr App R 172.
30. *Turner* v *Underwood* [1948] 2 KB 284.
31. *Knight* (1946) 31 Cr App R 52.

Six

The Defendant's Denials, Mixed Statements, and Silence

Not every defendant confesses. Some remain stoically silent, while others vigorously assert their innocence. Very many at least try to persuade the police that their involvement in an offence is not as culpable as it may appear. The rules which apply in these situations are quite different from those relating to confessions. Because of the Criminal Justice and Public Order Act 1994 the position when the defendant remains silent at any stage of the proceedings is now very different from what it once was, and this change affects every aspect of a solicitor's representation of the defendant, from interrogation and arrest to the trial itself. In this chapter, we will examine the principles of law which apply to these situations.

Denials

Where the defendant is questioned about an offence and denies it, his denials have no evidential value against him and, in principle, should be excluded. You often see attempts to adduce evidence which consists of no more than a police officer putting allegations to the defendant and the defendant denying those allegations. Of course, it does no harm to the prosecution case to have the allegations repeated to the court through this evidence, but such allegations are inadmissible hearsay, unless the defendant turns them into a confession by admitting them. This was stated succinctly by Pickford J in *Norton* [1], when he said:

> If the answer given amount to an admission of the statements or some part of them, they or that part become relevant as showing what facts are admitted; if the answer be not such an admission, the

statements are irrelevant to the matter under consideration and should be disregarded.

The same approach was taken by the House of Lords in *Christie* [2] in which Lord Reading said that such evidence was inadmissible unless the defendant somehow acknowledged the truth of the allegations. This should be more than enough authority to persuade the court to exclude such an interview, if you wish the court to do so. Some advocates prefer to allow the interview to be given in evidence, hoping to derive some advantage from the fact that the defendant denied the allegations against him at the first opportunity presented to him. This is a perfectly legitimate approach if your judgment commends it to you, as is a decision by the prosecutor not to attempt to adduce the evidence of the defendant's denials at all. But if either side demurs, the correct ruling by the court is that the evidence is inadmissible.

It should be emphasised, however, that a false explanation is not the same as a denial. If the defendant, when originally questioned, gives the police a false story, for example, an alibi which is later disproved, he cannot claim that what he said amounted to a denial. The giving of a false explanation is relevant and admissible evidence of guilt, and the prosecution will be fully entitled to adduce evidence of it at trial.

Mixed statements

In a great many cases, of course, it is not quite so simple. Life is not always so obliging as to offer us such easily identifiable cases, and the psychology of interrogation does not lend itself readily either to complete confession or to complete denial. More probably, the defendant's response to the questioning will be partly incriminating and partly exculpatory. It is usual to refer to such statements as mixed statements.

Where the defendant makes a mixed statement, the bench must consider the entire statement in order to ascertain where the truth lies. Before the more recent cases, the courts had developed the logical, though very inconvenient rule that only the incriminating parts of the statement were admissible (as a confession) as evidence of the truth of any facts stated by the defendant. The exculpatory parts were held to be self-serving and hearsay, and accordingly were not admissible as evidence of any facts stated. Thus, the exculpatory parts could be accepted only for the purpose of 'looking at the whole picture', or assessing the defendant's reaction when taxed with the offence, or as evidence tending to contradict or modify the incriminating passages [3]. This rule was obviously extremely difficult for any bench or jury to follow scrupulously, and produced a high degree of artificiality.

The Court of Appeal in *Duncan* [4] and the House of Lords in *Sharp* [5] altered the rule in a way which makes it much easier for the bench to deal with mixed statements. Rather than try to distinguish between parts of a statement which are and are not evidence of the facts stated, the bench should now read the statement as a whole, and have regard to its total effect in deciding whether or not it is sufficiently incriminating to amount to a confession, and, if so, what weight should be given to it. Such issues, of course, are a fertile source of points for a closing speech.

However, please note one extremely important point. The rule developed in *Duncan* and *Sharp* applies only in cases where the statement is adduced by the prosecution as an alleged confession, and must be evaluated by the bench as prosecution evidence. The defendant may not himself adduce statements he may have made out of court, however exculpatory they may be, as evidence of the truth of the facts stated or as an alternative to giving evidence. For this purpose, they remain hearsay and self-serving. If the defendant wishes to establish such facts, he must adduce admissible evidence of them, as in any other case, in accordance with the cases cited in note [3].

The defendant's silence

The defendant's silence is a rather complicated subject, which must now be considered under three separate headings:

(a) the effect of the defendant's failure to mention facts favourable to his defence when questioned by the police, arrested, or charged with or informed that he may be prosecuted for an offence;

(b) the defendant's failure to give evidence at trial; and

(c) the defendant's failure to comply with requirements to disclose aspects of his defence before trial.

At common law, the defendant was under no obligation to do any of these things, and any failure to do so could not be made the subject of comment by the prosecution, although in a trial on indictment, the judge might venture some moderate and balanced comment [6], and, therefore, it may be assumed that the bench in a summary trial might at least take them into consideration in assessing the weight to be accorded to the defence case. Some very limited inroad on these principles was made. For example, it was suggested that, where the defendant was 'on even terms' with the police officers questioning him, it might be reasonable to expect him to make some reply to the allegations against him [7]. And s. 11 of the Criminal Justice Act 1967 imposed on the defendant a procedural requirement to disclose before a trial details of any alibi on which he proposed to rely, failure to comply leading to a possible exclusion of alibi evidence in the court's discretion. But these were very limited incursions, and had little general effect on the defendant's common law position.

However, there was considerable judicial dissatisfaction with this position, based on a feeling that in many cases, the defence, if true, could be put forward before trial easily and without any danger of prejudice to the defendant. This is no doubt correct in cases where the defence is straightforward, for example, an alibi, but is questionable where the charges are technical in nature, or where the defence should legitimately be considered in detail. In the latter cases, it may not be reasonable to expect the defendant to divulge the defence immediately, though it may be that he might be expected to do so at some time before trial. In any event, the judicial dissatisfaction has led to radical statutory incursions into the defendant's common law rights to remain silent.

The defendant's silence when questioned

Sections 34, 36 and 37 of the Criminal Justice and Public Order Act 1994 provide that the court may draw an inference adverse to the defendant if he fails to mention certain matters on being questioned about, arrested for, or charged with or informed that he may be prosecuted for an offence. These sections provide as follows:

34.—(1) Where, in any proceedings against a person for an offence, evidence is given that the accused—
(a)   at any time before he was charged with the offence, on being questioned under caution by a constable trying to discover whether or by whom the offence had been committed, failed to mention any fact relied on in his defence in those proceedings; or
(b)   on being charged with the offence or officially informed that he might be prosecuted for it, failed to mention any such fact, being a fact which in the circumstances existing at the time the accused could reasonably have been expected to mention when so

questioned, charged or informed, as the case may be, subsection (2) below applies.

(2) Where this subsection applies—

(a) a magistrates' court inquiring into the offence as examining justices;

(b) a judge, in deciding whether to grant an application made by the accused under—

(i) section 6 of the Criminal Justice Act 1987 (application for dismissal of charge of serious fraud in respect of which notice of transfer has been given under section 4 of that Act); or

(ii) paragraph 5 of Schedule 6 to the Criminal Justice Act 1991 (application for dismissal of charge of violent or sexual offence involving child in respect of which notice of transfer has been given under section 53 of that Act);

(c) the court, in determining whether there is a case to answer; and

(d) the court or jury, in determining whether the accused is guilty of the offence charged,
may draw such inferences from the failure as appear proper.

(3) Subject to any directions by the court, evidence tending to establish the failure may be given before or after evidence tending to establish the fact which the accused is alleged to have failed to mention.

(4) This section applies in relation to questioning by persons (other than constables) charged with the duty of investigating offences or charging offenders as it applies in relation to questioning by constables; and in subsection (1) above 'officially informed' means informed by a constable or any such person.

(5) This section does not—

(a) prejudice the admissibility in evidence of the silence or other reaction of the accused in the face of anything said in his presence relating to the conduct in respect of which he is charged, in so far as evidence thereof would be admissible apart from this section; or

(b) preclude the drawing of any inference from any such silence or other reaction of the accused which could properly be drawn apart from this section.

(6) This section does not apply in relation to a failure to mention a fact if the failure occurred before the commencement of this section.

(7) [Repealed.]

36.—(1) Where—

    (a) a person is arrested by a constable, and there is—

        (i) on his person; or

        (ii) in or on his clothing or footwear; or

        (iii) otherwise in his possession; or

        (iv) in any place in which he is at the time of his arrest,

any object, substance or mark, or there is any mark on any such object; and

    (b) that or another constable investigating the case reasonably believes that the presence of the object, substance or mark may be attributable to the participation of the person arrested in the commission of an offence specified by the constable; and

    (c) the constable informs the person arrested that he so believes, and requests him to account for the presence of the object, substance or mark; and

    (d) the person fails or refuses to do so,

then if, in any proceedings against the person for the offence so specified, evidence of those matters is given, subsection (2) below applies.

    (2) Where this subsection applies—

    (a) a magistrates' court inquiring into the offence as examining justices;

    (b) a judge, in deciding whether to grant an application made by the accused under—

        (i) section 6 of the Criminal Justice Act 1987 (application for dismissal of charge of serious fraud in respect of which notice of transfer has been given under section 4 of that Act); or

        (ii) paragraph 5 of Schedule 6 to the Criminal Justice Act 1991 (application for dismissal of charge of violent or sexual offence involving child in respect of which notice of transfer has been given under section 53 of that Act);

    (c) the court, in determining whether there is a case to answer; and

    (d) the court or jury, in determining whether the accused is guilty of the offence charged,

may draw such inferences from the failure or refusal as appear proper.

    (3) Subsections (1) and (2) above apply to the condition of clothing or footwear as they apply to a substance or mark thereon.

    (4) Subsections (1) and (2) above do not apply unless the accused was told in ordinary language by the constable when making

the request mentioned in subsection (1)(c) above what the effect of this section would be if he failed or refused to comply with the request.

(5)   This section applies in relation to officers of customs and excise as it applies in relation to constables.

(6)   This section does not preclude the drawing of any inference from a failure or refusal of the accused to account for the presence of an object, substance or mark or from the condition of clothing or footwear which could properly be drawn apart from this section.

(7)   This section does not apply in relation to a failure or refusal which occurred before the commencement of this section.

(8)   [Repealed.]

37.—(1)   Where—

(a)   a person arrested by a constable was found by him at a place at or about the time the offence for which he was arrested is alleged to have been committed; and

(b)   that or another constable investigating the offence reasonably believes that the presence of the person at that place and at that time may be attributable to his participation in the commission of the offence; and

(c)   the constable informs the person that he so believes, and requests him to account for that presence; and

(d)   the person fails or refuses to do so,

then if, in any proceedings against the person for the offence, evidence of those matters is given, subsection (2) below applies.

(2)   Where this subsection applies—

(a)   a magistrates' court in inquiring into the offence as examining justices;

(b)   a judge, in deciding whether to grant an application made by the accused under—

(i)   section 6 of the Criminal Justice Act 1987 (application for dismissal of charge of serious fraud in respect of which notice of transfer has been given under section 4 of that Act); or

(ii)   paragraph 5 of Schedule 6 to the Criminal Justice Act 1991 (application for dismissal of charge of violent or sexual offence involving child in respect of which notice of transfer has been given under section 53 of that Act);

(c)   the court, in determining whether there is a case to answer; and

(d)   the court or jury, in determining whether the accused is guilty of the offence charged,
may draw such inferences from the failure or refusal as appear proper.

(3)   Subsections (1) and (2) do not apply unless the accused was told in ordinary language by the constable when making the request mentioned in subsection (1)(c) above what the effect of this section would be if he failed or refused to comply with the request.

(4)   This section applies in relation to officers of customs and excise as it applies in relation to constables.

(5)   This section does not preclude the drawing of any inference from a failure or refusal of the accused to account for his presence at a place which could properly be drawn apart from this section.

(6)   This section does not apply in relation to a failure or refusal which occurred before the commencement of this section.

(7)   [Repealed].

Section 34 applies when the defendant is questioned under caution, is charged, or is informed that he may be prosecuted for an offence, whereas ss. 36 and 37 apply only where the defendant is arrested for the offence. As we saw in Chapter 5, Code of Practice C requires a police officer to caution the defendant before interviewing him about an offence, and the form of caution was revised to reflect the possibility of an adverse inference being drawn against him if he fails to mention facts on which he may rely at trial.

What facts the defendant could reasonably have been expected to mention must, of course, be a question of fact in each case. As we noted earlier, where the defence is straightforward and available to the defendant immediately, for example, an alibi, it may well be reasonable for the defendant to mention it at once, and his failure to do so provides an obvious logical basis for thinking that it may have been concocted after the event. But in many cases, the nature of the defence can be determined only after consideration of the details of the offence (which may not be fully apparent at the time of an interview). Much may depend on the amount of information given to the defendant by the police. If he or his solicitor are not given enough information to enable them to understand the nature of the charge, it hardly seems reasonable to expect a response to the allegations [8]. Moreover, there may be cases in which the defendant has been injured or shocked, or has requested legal advice, in which it is not unreasonable for him to withhold comment at that stage. It was also held in *Argent* [9] that the defendant's mental state, intelligence, articulateness, command of the English language, and general level of sophistication may be relevant in assessing the reasonableness or otherwise of his failure to mention facts.

All of this, of course, has made the role of a solicitor in advising the defendant at this stage extremely difficult. In *Condron* [10] it was held that the fact that the defendant fails to mention facts based on his solicitor's advice will not generally prevent an adverse inference from being drawn against him if the court thinks that it was reasonable to expect certain facts to be mentioned. Obviously much depends upon the professional judgment of the solicitor in each individual case. In some instances, the solicitor may advise handing to the police a written statement of the client's position. If this is not clear at the time of the interview, the statement may be handed in at the time when the defendant is charged, although there is obviously still some possibility that the failure to comment at the time of the interview may lead to adverse inferences [11]. It certainly seems necessary for the solicitor to make the fullest possible inquiry of the police officers about the state of the evidence against the defendant. If anything is withheld, it may certainly cast a failure to comment in a different light. In *Pointer* [12] it was observed that the extent of the evidence may even make it appear that continued interview of the defendant is a violation of Code of Practice C, though the court seems to have accepted that, even if he believes that he has enough evidence to charge, the officer is entitled to ascertain whether or not the defendant has anything to say.

From the decisions in *Condron* and *Argent* it seems clear that a solicitor may have to give evidence on the issue of reasonableness. Although there is no basis for thinking that the court will consider the apparent correctness or otherwise of the solicitor's advice to be in any way conclusive, it seems important for the solicitor to make some statement at the interview to indicate the basis of it. The court may conclude that the defendant could not, in the circumstances, reasonably be expected to do anything but follow the advice. The solicitor should certainly make clear, in a proper case, that he is advising the defendant to make no comment because of a lack of information about the case. There is some reason to think that the courts will prefer substantive legal reasons to 'tactical' reasons, even though this distinction appears meaningless in the light of the solicitor's duty to represent his client's interests as fully a possible.

It has been suggested that the solicitor distinguish between cases in which giving reasons might lead to a waiver of privilege (because the advice is based on instructions given by the client) and those in which it will not (because it is based on external factors). This may be good advice, but does not always solve the problem, because it may require the solicitor to make an uncomfortable choice between putting on the record matters which may make a failure to mention facts reasonable, and the possibility of being compelled later to give evidence about what was said by the client. Whether a waiver of privilege is involved in this situation has not been decided definitively, but the court in *Condron* acknowledged that it is a possibility.

The defendant's failure to give evidence at trial

Section 35 of the Criminal Justice and Public Order Act 1994 provides:

> **35.**—(1) At the trial of any person who has attained the age of fourteen years for an offence, subsections (2) and (3) below apply unless—
>
>   (a)   the accused's guilt is not in issue; or
>
>   (b)   it appears to the court that the physical or mental condition of the accused makes it undesirable for him to give evidence; but subsection (2) below does not apply if, at the conclusion of the evidence for the prosecution, his legal representative informs the court that the accused will give evidence or, where he is unrepresented, the court ascertains from him that he will give evidence.
>
>   (2)   Where this subsection applies, the court shall, at the conclusion of the evidence for the prosecution, satisfy itself (in the case of proceedings on indictment, in the presence of the jury) that the accused is aware that the stage has been reached at which evidence can be given for the defence and that he can, if he wishes, give evidence and that, if he chooses not to give evidence, or having been sworn, without good cause refuses to answer any question, it will be permissible for the court or jury to draw such inferences as appear proper from his failure to give evidence or his refusal, without good cause, to answer any question.
>
>   (3)   Where this subsection applies, the court or jury, in determining whether the accused is guilty of the offence charged, may draw such inferences as appear proper from the failure of the accused to give evidence or his refusal, without good cause, to answer any question.

(4)   This section does not render the accused compellable to give evidence on his own behalf, and he shall accordingly not be guilty of contempt of court by reason of a failure to do so.

(5)   For the purposes of this section a person who, having been sworn, refuses to answer any question shall be taken to do so without good cause unless—

(a)   he is entitled to refuse to answer the question by virtue of any enactment, whenever passed or made, or on the ground of privilege; or

(b)   the court in the exercise of its general discretion excuses him from answering it.

(6)   Where the age of any person is material for the purposes of subsection (1) above, his age shall for those purposes be taken to be that which appears to the court to be his age.

(7)   This section applies—

(a)   in relation to proceedings on indictment for an offence, only if the person charged with the offence is arraigned on or after the commencement of this section;

(b)   in relation to proceedings in a magistrates' court, only if the time when the court begins to receive evidence in the proceedings falls after the commencement of this section.

The inquiry to be made by the court under s. 35(2) arises only where the defendant's representative does not inform the court that the defendant intends to give evidence. It extends only to the question of whether or not the defendant has been made aware of the statutory position, and not to the reasons underlying the defendant's decision whether or not to give evidence. Thus, it does not violate the lawyer–client privilege (*Cowan* [13]).

Whether it is proper to draw any inference, and if so, what inference is proper from the defendant's failure to give evidence must depend on the facts of each particular case. In *Cowan*, the Court of Appeal laid down important principles applicable to this situation. Although couched in terms of directions to the jury in cases tried on indictment, no doubt the same principles should apply to the way in which the bench directs itself in a summary trial. The principles correspond with the Judicial Studies Board's specimen jury direction for s. 35 cases, which the Court of Appeal approved. They may be summarised as follows:

(a)   The jury must receive a proper direction on the burden and standard of proof, i.e., the prosecution must prove the guilt of the accused so that the jury feel sure of guilt.

(b)   The judge must make it clear that the accused continues to be entitled not to give evidence.

(c)   The judge must explain that, pursuant to s. 38(3) of the Act, the accused's failure to give evidence cannot be sufficient in itself to prove his guilt. (We will consider this point below.)

(d)   The judge must make it clear that the jury must be satisfied that the prosecution have established a case to answer, based on the prosecution's evidence, before any inference against the accused may be drawn from the accused's failure to give evidence.

(e)   If the jury conclude, having regard to any explanation advanced to explain the accused's silence or the absence of explanation, that the accused's silence can only sensibly be attributed to the accused's having no answer to the case against him, or no answer likely to stand up to cross-examination, they may draw an adverse inference against him.

In the magistrates' court, a decision to advise the defendant not to give evidence has always been suspect, both because of experience that magistrates are significantly more likely to acquit after hearing a defendant's side of the case, and because the argument of pure points of law is more difficult in a court in which the tribunals of law and fact are combined. The enactment of s. 35 has strengthened this principle enormously. Although each case must be dealt with individually, and there is no substitute for the professional judgment of advocates, it may now be stated with some confidence that the defendant should be called to give evidence unless there is some very compelling reason to the contrary. Such a reason, it is submitted, could only be that the case against him is virtually non-existent, or has a fatal legal flaw.

General provisions affecting sections 34 to 37

Section 38 of the Criminal Justice and Public Order Act 1994 makes the following general provisions applicable to ss. 34 to 37:

38.—(1)   In sections 34, 35, 36 and 37 of this Act—
'legal representative' means an authorised advocate or authorised litigator, as defined by section 119(1) of the Courts and Legal Services Act 1990; and
'place' includes any building or part of a building, any vehicle, vessel, aircraft or hovercraft and any other place whatsoever.

(2) In sections 34(2), 35(3), 36(2) and 37(2), references to an offence charged include references to any other offence of which the accused could lawfully be convicted on that charge.

(3) A person shall not have the proceedings against him transferred to the Crown Court for trial, have a case to answer or be convicted of an offence solely on an inference drawn from such a failure or refusal as is mentioned in section 34(2), 35(3), 36(2) or 37(2).

(4) A judge shall not refuse to grant such an application as is mentioned in section 34(2)(b), 36(2)(b) and 37(2)(b) solely on an inference drawn from such a failure as is mentioned in section 34(2), 36(2) or 37(2).

(5) Nothing in sections 34, 35, 36 or 37 prejudices the operation of a provision of any enactment which provides (in whatever words) that any answer or evidence given by a person in specified circumstances shall not be admissible in evidence against him or some other person in any proceedings or class of proceedings (however described, and whether civil or criminal).

In this subsection, the reference to giving evidence is a reference to giving evidence in any manner, whether by furnishing information, making discovery, producing documents or otherwise.

(6) Nothing in sections 34, 35, 36 or 37 prejudices any power of a court, in any proceedings, to exclude evidence (whether by preventing questions being put or otherwise) at its discretion.

Subsections (3) and (4) provide that inferences drawn under ss. 34 to 37 may not be the sole basis for a conviction or committal of a defendant for trial. Thus, a case cannot be based solely upon a defendant's failure to respond to allegations made against him. Some substantive evidence, at least sufficient for a *prima facie* case, is required. Where the defendant applies to dismiss a charge, however, a refusal may be based on an inference from the defendant's failure to give evidence — yet a further indication that the defendant should almost always be called as a witness in the magistrates' court.

Subsections (5) and (6) ensure that nothing in ss. 34 to 37 shall be construed to render admissible evidence which is not otherwise admissible under the rules of evidence generally, or to restrict the power of the bench to exclude any prosecution evidence as a matter of discretion.

The defendant's failure to comply with disclosure provisions

Section 5 of the Criminal Procedure and Investigations Act 1996 imposes duties of pre-trial disclosure of evidence on both the prosecution and the defence in cases tried on indictment. Those imposed on the defence represent a radical change in the law. Before the 1996 Act, the duty to disclose was limited to one or two specific kinds of evidence, such as evidence supporting an alibi (Criminal Justice Act 1967, s. 11, which is superseded by the 1996 Act) and proposed expert evidence (Police and Criminal Evidence Act 1984, s. 81; Crown Court (Advance Notice of Expert Evidence) Rules 1987). However, s. 5 of the 1996 Act provides that after primary disclosure has been, or purports to have been made by the prosecution, and the accused has been served with the required papers, including copies of the indictment and the prosecution's evidence, the accused must provide disclosure of the defence to be presented at trial. Primary disclosure is defined by s. 3 of the Act as a disclosure of any prosecution material which has not previously been disclosed and which in the prosecutor's opinion might undermine the case for the prosecution, or a statement that no such material exists.

The mandatory procedure under s. 5 does not apply to summary trials in the magistrates' court, but, by virtue of s. 6, the defence may engage voluntarily in disclosure in the interests of obtaining the secondary disclosure required of the prosecution by s. 7 of the Act. Secondary disclosure is defined as disclosure of any prosecution material which has not previously been disclosed and which might be reasonably expected to assist the accused's defence as disclosed by the defence statement, or a statement that no such material exists.

The pertinent provisions of s. 5 are as follows:

(5)   Where this section applies, the accused must give a defence statement to the court and the prosecutor.

(6)   For the purposes of this section a defence statement is a written statement—

(a)   setting out in general terms the nature of the accused's defence,

(b)   indicating the matters on which he takes issue with the prosecution, and

(c)   setting out, in the case of each such matter, the reason why he takes issue with the prosecution.

(7) If the defence statement discloses an alibi the accused must give particulars of the alibi in the statement, including—

(a) the name and address of any witness the accused believes is able to give evidence in support of the alibi, if the name and address are known to the accused when the statement is given;

(b) any information in the accused's possession which might be of material assistance in finding any such witness, if his name or address is not known to the accused when the statement is given.

(8) For the purposes of this section evidence in support of an alibi is evidence tending to show that by reason of the presence of the accused at a particular place or in a particular area at a particular time he was not, or was unlikely to have been, at the place where the offence is alleged to have been committed at the time of its alleged commission.

(9) The accused must give a defence statement under this section during the period which, by virtue of section 12, is the relevant period for this section.

Section 6 provides that, in any case to which s. 5 applies, the defendant may give a defence statement to the prosecutor (and must then give it also to the court). Where this is done, subsections (6) to (8) of s. 5 apply, and the defendant must further comply with the rules as to time made under s. 12.

Section 6 is supplemented by the following enforcement provisions of s. 11:

(2) This section also applies where section 6 applies, the accused gives a defence statement under that section, and the accused—

(a) gives the statement after the end of the period which, by virtue of section 12, is the relevant period for section 6,

(b) sets out inconsistent defences in the statement,

(c) at his trial puts forward a defence which is different from any defence set out in the statement,

(d) at his trial adduces evidence in support of an alibi without having given particulars of the alibi in the statement, or

(e) at his trial calls a witness to give evidence in support of an alibi without having complied with subsection 7(a) or (b) of section 5 (as applied by section 6) as regards the witness in giving the statement.

(3)   Where this section applies—

(a)   the court or, with the leave of the court, any other party may make such comment as appears appropriate;

(b)   the court or jury may draw such inferences as appear proper in deciding whether the accused is guilty of the offence concerned.

(4)   Where the accused puts forward a defence which is different from any defence set out in a defence statement given under section 5 or 6, in doing anything under subsection (3) or in deciding whether to do anything under it the court shall have regard—

(a)   to the extent of the difference in the defences, and

(b)   to whether there is any justification for it.

(5)   A person shall not be convicted of an offence solely on an inference drawn under subsection (3).

The provisions that adverse inferences may be drawn, and the rule that a conviction may not be based solely on such inferences, are similar to the provisions of the Criminal Justice and Public Order Act 1994, which we have already considered. It is clear that there are abundant opportunities for factual disputes as to whether a defence raised at trial differs from that set out in the defence statement, whether there is a justification for any such difference, and the circumstances in which defences set out in the defence statement should be regarded as inconsistent. In the case of an alibi, the Act adopts a different approach from that of the Criminal Justice Act 1967, under which the accused's failure to supply the required details barred him from adducing evidence of the alibi, unless the judge exercised his discretion to permit it despite the failure. In practice, judges and magistrates habitually gave permission because of the drastic consequences of ruling otherwise, so that the disclosure rule was not particularly effective.

An interesting distinction between the provisions of the Criminal Procedure and Investigations Act 1996 and those of the Criminal Justice and Public Order Act 1994 is that s. 11(3)(a) of the 1996 Act requires a party to obtain the leave of the court before making a comment on the defence position. This seems puzzling, inasmuch as the 1994 Act abolished the rule laid down by s. 1(b) of the Criminal Justice Act 1898 that the prosecution could not comment on the accused's failure to give evidence, and imposes no requirement to obtain leave. It is reasonable to assume that there is no bar to comment in cases arising under ss. 34

to 37 of the 1994 Act, and the position under the 1996 Act appears anomalous. It may be that it is justified by the potential for disputes about whether any comment is appropriate. But any such requirement is obviously difficult to apply to summary proceedings.

Clearly, it will not be in every case that the defence will make a voluntary disclosure of the nature of the defence before trial. However, there will be cases in which this should be done, for example, where the defence is an alibi, or in any other case in which it is straightforward. In such cases, the provisions of ss. 34, 36 or 37 of the Criminal Justice and Public order Act 1994 may have dictated earlier disclosure in any case, so that there is nothing to lose. In such cases, it may be worth finding out whether the prosecution have any secondary material to disclose. There may be other cases also in which this is worthwhile, if there is some specific ground for believing that such material exists. This must, of course, remain a matter of judgment in each individual case.

Civil cases

In civil cases in the county court, the position is much simpler. It has always been accepted that a failure to respond to allegations, in circumstances in which an innocent person might reasonably have been expected to respond, may provide the basis for an inference adverse to the party who fails to respond. This may occur where the party remains silent in the face of allegations made personally, by failing to answer correspondence in which the allegations are made, or failing to take steps which an innocent party might reasonably have been expected to take [14].

Further reading

Murphy on Evidence, 6th ed., ch. 9; *Blackstone's Criminal Practice* 1998, F19.

Notes

1. [1910] 2 KB 496.
2. [1914] AC 545.
3. *Storey* (1968) 52 Cr App R 334; *Donaldson* (1976) 64 Cr App R 59.

4. (1981) 73 Cr App R 359.
5. [1988] 1 WLR 7.
6. Criminal Evidence Act 1898, s. 1(b), repealed by the Criminal Justice and Public Order Act 1994.
7. *Mitchell* (1892) 17 Cox CC 503; *Chandler* [1976] 1 WLR 585; but see also *Hall* v *R* [1971] 1 WLR 298; *Gilbert* (1977) 66 Cr App R 237.
8. *Roble* [1997] Crim LR 449.
9. *Argent* [1997] 2 Cr App R 247.
10. [1997] 1 Cr App. R 185.
11. See E. Cape and J. Luqmani, *Defending Suspects at Police Stations* (London: Legal Action Group, 1998) Legal Action Group, and E. Cape, *Sidelining defence lawyers: police station advice after Condron* (1997) 1 E & P 386.
12. 17 April 1997, unreported.
13. [1996] QB 373. See also *Practice Direction (Crown Court: Defendant's Evidence)* [1995] 1 WLR 657.
14. *Wiedemann* v *Walpole* [1891] 2 QB 534, 537–8; *Bessela* v *Stern* (1877) 2 CPD 265.

Seven

Evidence of Character

Introduction

This chapter is of primary, though not exclusive concern in criminal cases. There is probably no criminal case in which the defendant's character, be it good or bad, does not pose some problem for the advocate. Usually, the problems are more on the defence side than the prosecution side, though this is by no means an invariable rule. Nor are the problems confined to cases in which the defendant's character is bad, though in such cases the problems differ from those in which his character is good. It is, therefore, a safe assumption that whether the defendant models his life-style on St Francis of Assisi or on Fagin, or on some representative of humanity somewhere between the two, his character will have to be considered in some detail.

Such consideration can be hampered by the client who will not tell even his own advocate the truth about his character, or who cannot remember all the painful details. It is always worthwhile spending time taking really detailed instructions about the defendant's previous convictions, since there are few things worse than having the true picture exposed for the first time in court. This process usually refreshes the defendant's memory, or brings home to him the futility of further disingenuity, as the case may be. But if he insists upon his version of events, do not be sceptical. In this age of computerised records, mistakes are alarmingly common, and the defendant may well be telling the truth. In such a case, you will need time to check the original court records. These instructions are essential at every stage of criminal proceedings — for bail applications, at trial and during mitigation, and the importance of taking them with great attention to detail cannot be overstated.

It is often assumed that the term 'character' refers only to previous convictions. But the existence of previous convictions is not the sum total of bad character, any more than their absence is the sum total of good character. Character, whether good or bad, comprises three distinct areas, all of which are the concern of the law of evidence. These are:

(a)   A person's general reputation in his community.

(b)   A person's propensity or disposition to behave in a certain way.

(c)   Previous specific acts, including but not limited to previous convictions.

In practice, the term 'character' is used to denote the existence or absence of previous convictions. Since the possession of previous convictions makes all the difference between good and bad character, the usage is harmless, as long as it is not allowed to obscure the wider meaning of the term.

This chapter is concerned with the extent to which evidence of each of these three matters may be introduced into evidence, or, if unfavourable, excluded. The simplest way to examine this subject is to analyse separately good and bad character in relation to the rules of evidence.

Good character

In representing a client of previous good character, it is fundamental to remember that evidence of his good character is not only admissible, but actually constitutes some evidence tending to show his innocence of the charge. This is a remarkable rule, since in the exceptional cases when evidence of bad character is admissible, such evidence usually affects only the credit of the defendant as a witness, and is not evidence of his guilt. The rule as to good character is one of fairness to the defendant, and was restated by the Court of Appeal in *Bryant* [1]. The defendant, whose good character had been put before the jury, elected not to give evidence. The trial judge directed the jury that, since the defendant had not given evidence, his credit was not an issue and that accordingly the evidence of good character was irrelevant and should be disregarded. The Court of Appeal held this direction to be too restrictive. The evidence did not affect credit only, but operated to influence the jury to say 'whether they think it likely that a person with such a character would have committed the offence'. The jury were therefore entitled to consider it in the defendant's favour in any event.

Since the decision in *Bryant*, the courts have considered the question of the defendant's good character further in the context of giving appropriate directions to juries in trials on indictment. Difficult situations arise in cases where two or more defendants are charged together, and not all of them are of good character. In such a case, it is inevitable that the jury may be tempted to compare the defendants of bad character unfavourably with those of good character. The same situation may arise in the magistrates' court, and the principles developed in relation to trial on indictment must be applied to summary trials. In *Vye* [2] the Court of Appeal held that the jury must be directed that the defendant's good character is some evidence that he may not be guilty of the offence charged, whether or not he has given evidence. If the defendant has given evidence, they must be directed further that his good character is some evidence supporting his credibility as a witness. In a joint trial in which some only of the defendants are of good character, the same directions must be given as to those defendants, but the judge must take all possible steps to see that no undue prejudice is caused to the defendants of bad character. The guidelines laid down in *Vye* were confirmed by the House of Lords in *Aziz* [3]. It follows that, in the magistrates' court, the bench should advise themselves accordingly, with the assistance of submissions from the defence advocates. The task of representing a defendant of bad character in such a case is obviously a difficult one. It is essential to remind the bench that the question of character is not decisive, but is only one factor bearing on the question of guilt or innocence.

Another problematic situation is that in which the previous good character of a defendant has been compromised by his conduct in relation to the instant case, or by his plea of guilty to some of the charges against him. The first situation arose in *Aziz*, in which the defendants, though otherwise of good character, admitted to some acts of dishonesty not covered by the indictment in the case against them. The House of Lords held that the standard direction to the jury should be given in such a case, but that the judge should qualify the direction by reminding the jury of the acts admitted by the defendants. Clearly, any other approach would result in the jury being misled, and it is submitted that the same practice should be followed in the magistrates' court. Where the defendant has pleaded guilty to one or more charges in relation to the instant case, it is submitted that the defendant should be given the choice of having nothing said about his character, or being presented as a person of good character subject to the pleas of guilty. However, it cannot be said that any such rule has yet been adopted. In *Teasdale* [4] it was held that a good character direction should be given, but in *Challenger* [5] (which sought to distinguish *Teasdale* on a somewhat technical ground) it was held that the judge had a discretion to withhold the direction in such a case. The position here is, therefore, rather unclear and there is room for argument in any particular case. Such an argument in the magistrates' court should be made to the clerk in the first instance, in the hope of preventing the bench from being exposed to unnecessary information about the defendant's character. In the light of the clerk's view, the wisest course may be to say nothing about the defendant's character.

Remember always that, although you can certainly argue to the bench that your client's good character makes it less likely that he committed the offence charged, good advocacy dictates that this argument should not be pressed too far; taken to absurd lengths, it could suggest that no one should ever be convicted of a first offence, and this the bench are unlikely to swallow.

Evidence of good character can be presented to the court in three ways, which are acceptable individually or in combination, and all of which should be used wherever possible. These are:

(a)   Cross-examination of the prosecution witnesses. The usual form of this cross-examination is to elicit from the officer in charge of the case that the defendant has no previous convictions. The question should be phrased specifically in terms of the absence of previous convictions, and should not be a general enquiry about the defendant's 'good character'. The officer will have to concede a demonstrable absence of previous convictions, but he may be less helpful if he happens to think that good fortune in escaping convictions in the past is the main foundation of your client's good character. Sometimes, other prosecution witnesses can give evidence about your client's reputation in the community, though for obvious reasons you should be very sure of the likely answers before embarking on such cross-examination; if such circumstances exist, you can probably call your own character witness, which is much safer.

(b)   Calling the defendant to give evidence and putting the appropriate questions in chief. This is an auspicious introduction to any evidence in chief, and should be dealt with at the outset, because it puts everything else in perspective.

(c)   Calling character witnesses. The value of this is sadly underestimated in modern trial practice. It is always worth asking the defendant whether there is someone who can speak for him. Preferably, this should be a person of standing in the community; ministers of religion, professional persons and community leaders are ideal, though employers and family are often more effective than is popularly supposed. The fact that someone is prepared to attend court and go into the witness-box to attest to your client's character is a fact which compels the attention of almost every court.

The facts which may be proved in support of your client's good character are that he has no previous convictions, and that he is of good reputation in his community. Strictly speaking, the defendant may not introduce evidence of the personal opinion of a character witness about his character: *Rowton* [6]; or of previous specific creditable acts, such as handing in lost property at a police station; or of the defendant's general disposition to behave in certain ways: *Redgrave* [7]. For largely historical reasons, these latter facts are inadmissible, although, except in the case of previous creditable acts, which are never admitted, this rule seems generally to be ignored in practice, either because it is not widely known or because of considerations of fairness to the defence.

When seeking to prove the defendant's good reputation within his community, you have the advantage that the concept of community is now given a broad meaning, rightly so in these days of widespread social mobility. Most courts will now accept that the proper term of reference is the defendant's own circle, which need not be a strictly geographic circle in the old neighbourhood sense, but may be a social, professional, ethnic or other appropriate circle; good reputation is a positive fact in any of these contexts. The proper method of questioning a character witness is therefore: 'Are you aware of what people generally in [describe the circle] think of [the defendant] with respect to honesty or dishonesty?', and 'What is the general opinion of [the defendant] within this circle?' The first of these questions is an essential foundation for the second.

From a prosecution standpoint, apart from any objection to the inadmissible facts referred to above, the main area of concern is the case in which the defendant falsely states that he is of good character, whereas in fact he has previous convictions. The existence of previous convictions is the only area in which good character can be refuted effectively. Trying to refute an assertion of good reputation is like trying to punch a sponge, unless you happen to have a character witness who is unaware of some discreditable episode in the defendant's past. Where the defendant misrepresents his character to the court, the prosecution are in an enviable position, even where the misrepresentation is unintentional, as can be the case. If this happens, the prosecution have two weapons available:

(a) Cross-examination of the defendant. Unlike any other witness, the defendant giving evidence for the defence in a criminal trial enjoys a general immunity against being cross-examined about his bad character or previous convictions. This immunity was conferred by s. 1 of the Criminal Evidence Act 1898, the statute which first made the defendant a competent witness for the defence. The immunity is usually described as the defendant's 'shield'. The shield is created by s. 1(f) of the Act in the following terms:

A person charged and called as a witness in pursuance of this Act shall not be asked, and if asked shall not be required to answer, any question tending to show that he has committed or been convicted of or been charged with any offence other than that wherewith he is then charged, or is of bad character.

The shield is not, however, absolute. In certain circumstances, the shield may be lost, with the result that the defendant becomes, like any other witness, liable to cross-examination about the generally prohibited matters. Each of the three sets of circumstances in which the shield may be lost will be considered in this chapter. This is the moment to deal with one of them. Section 1(f) continues:

unless — . . .
(ii) he has personally or by his advocate asked questions of the witnesses for the prosecution with a view to establish his own good character, or has given evidence of his good character.

Determination of whether the effect of the defendant's cross-examination or evidence is such as to forfeit the shield is a matter of law for the bench, and it is improper to begin to cross-examine about character without asking the bench to rule, however obvious the matter may appear. There are cases in which it is genuinely doubtful whether the shield has been lost. It may be clear enough if the defendant gives evidence that he is a builder, and is hard-working, when such evidence can have no relevance to the case other than in terms of an assertion of good character. But what if the defendant asserts his trade in order to establish his innocent possession of apparent burglary tools? In such a case, any assertion of good character would seem to be no more than a necessary ancillary to proof of a relevant fact. A good illustration is *Thomson* [8], in which the defendant explained his act of running away from a police officer, which might otherwise have appeared incriminating, by giving evidence that he had been fined on an earlier occasion, and thought he was going to be arrested for non-payment of the fine. On appeal, it was held that the trial judge had erred in compelling him to say for what offence he had been fined, and in permitting cross-examination about his previous convictions. Clearly, the defendant had neither misled the court about his character, nor sought to assert his good character. Many courts and prosecutors would feel it to be unfair to cross-examine a defendant about his character in a case where he must deal with some aspect of his personal circumstances in order to give evidence in support of his defence, though regrettably, there are those who would seek to do so. A defence advocate may have to argue strongly that the shield has not been lost, if faced with such an unreasonable approach. It is good and professional for a prosecutor to recognise and act on the distinction between presentation of the defence and assertion of good character.

In conducting the cross-examination, it should be borne in mind that, although you can put the previous convictions to the defendant directly, and ask him about the sentences imposed and the general nature of the offences, it is not permissible to explore the detail of the previous offences so as to suggest guilt of the offence charged, even where the previous offences are similar in nature to the offence charged. The previous convictions are admissible only for the purpose of refuting the defendant's assertion of good character, and are not evidence of his guilt as charged: *France* [9]. This is not too much of a handicap, since the previous convictions are quite potent enough in their proper role. If you feel that the similarity between the offence charged and the previous offences is sufficiently compelling to be directly relevant to the issue of guilt as charged, you should be asking the court to rule that the previous convictions are admissible as similar-fact evidence, which is in no way dependent upon the question of whether or not the defendant asserts his good character. Similar-fact evidence is considered later in this chapter.

(b) Cross-examination of a defendant is naturally possible only when the defendant has given evidence on which he may be cross-examined. It is not unknown for a defendant to suggest his asserted good character by cross-examination of the prosecution witnesses, or by calling a character witness, while exercising his right not to give evidence. In such a case, it seems that the prosecution would be entitled to call evidence in rebuttal, to demonstrate the defendant's true character. Although the authorities to this effect are cases in which the defendant avoided giving evidence by exercising the now abolished right to make an unsworn statement from the dock, the principle is unaffected. The leave of the court must be obtained by an application to adduce such evidence, but it should not be refused in any case where the defendant has misled the court with regard to his character.

Bad character

It is one of the fundamental principles of the English law of evidence that the prosecution may not adduce evidence of the defendant's previous bad character in order to prove merely that he acted in conformity with it in relation to the offence charged. In English law, you cannot give a dog a bad name and hang it. The rule has never been better stated than in the following words of Lord Herschell LC in *Makin* v *Attorney-General for New South Wales* [10]:

> It is undoubtedly not competent for the prosecution to adduce evidence tending to show that the accused has been guilty of criminal acts other than those covered by the indictment, for the purpose of leading to the conclusion that the accused is a person likely from his criminal conduct or character to have committed the offence for which he is being tried.

This does not, of course, mean that there will be no occasion when the previous bad character of the defendant may be referred to in the course of the evidence. It means that the defendant's bad character may not, as such, be made part of the prosecution case against him. If the defendant is alleged to have assaulted a fellow prisoner while serving a sentence of imprisonment, the case cannot be presented without reference to the fact of the defendant's condition in life at the time of the offence. But evidence that the defendant was then a serving prisoner is not a use of his bad character to prove his guilt; it is simply necessary, relevant evidence of the circumstances of the offence charged. The bench will not be told why he was in prison, because such evidence would be both irrelevant and inadmissible as evidence of bad character. The fact that he was in prison at the time of the offence is all that is relevant. The reason why an aspect of the defendant's character may be adduced in evidence in such a case is that it is relevant to the issue of guilt of the offence charged. Lord Herschell's dictum does not mean that evidence of character must be excluded if it is relevant to guilt, but that it must be excluded if its *only* relevance is to show that the defendant acted in conformity with his known character, in relation to the offence charged — in other words, if its only relevance is to suggest to the bench in effect: 'He's done it before; isn't it more likely that he has done it again?' In fact, Lord Herschell continued his speech by saying:

> On the other hand, the mere fact that the evidence adduced tends to show the commission of other crimes does not render it inadmissible if it be relevant to an issue before the jury.

In *Jones* v *DPP* [11], the defendant was convicted of the murder of a girl guide in October 1960. He had previously been convicted of raping another guide during September 1960. In statements to the police about the murder charge, the defendant gave an alibi which was false. He then replaced this with a second alibi, which was almost identical to an alibi he had advanced at his earlier trial on the rape charge. The similarity extended to details such as conversations which the defendant claimed to have had with his wife, which were almost word for word the same. At trial, the defendant sought to explain away the first, false alibi by stating in evidence that he had been 'in trouble' with the police before. He was cross-examined about the suspicious similarity of his second alibi on the murder charge to his alibi on what was referred to as 'another occasion' — no details of the previous conviction being revealed to the jury. The defendant appealed unsuccessfully to the House of Lords on the ground that the cross-examination should not have been permitted. The House found no error. The similarity of the alibis was clearly relevant to the guilt of the defendant, since it tended to show that he was prepared to concoct false alibis. This being so, there was no objection to the cross-examination or to the proof of the fact that the defendant had previously set up the same alibi, even though the jury must have realised that he had on some previous occasion been charged with some other offence. Note that, correctly, the jury were given no details of the other offence, with which they were not concerned.

Another and more specific example is to be found in what is termed similar-fact evidence. Similar-fact evidence is evidence of other acts, including but not limited to previous convictions, which are so strikingly similar in their nature to the facts of the offence charged that the court is justified in concluding that the similar features represent a hallmark of a particular offender, and that the same offender must have been responsible for each offence. In the rare cases where such a conclusion is justified, the evidence of similar acts is relevant to the issue of the defendant's guilt as charged. The degree of similarity required to make evidence of similar acts admissible is extremely high, simply because anything less would amount simply to evidence of bad character. Consequently, similar-fact evidence is rarely used, especially in the magistrates' court. It might have been omitted from this book altogether, were it not for a recent trend on the part of prosecutors to abuse the rule by seeking to introduce evidence of other acts which bear only a superficial similarity to the facts of the offence charged, for example evidence that the defendant stole goods of a similar nature during a previous shoplifting expedition.

The degree of similarity required before evidence of similar acts becomes admissible was vividly illustrated by Lord Hailsham of St Marylebone in *DPP* v *Boardman* [12] using the following illustrations:

Whilst it would certainly not be enough to identify the culprit in a series of burglaries that he climbed in through a ground-floor window, the fact that he left the same humorous limerick on the walls of the sitting-room, or an esoteric symbol written in lipstick on the mirror, might well be enough. In a sex case, to adopt an example given in argument in the Court of Appeal, whilst a repeated homosexual act by itself might be quite insufficient to admit the evidence as confirmatory of identity or design, the fact that it was alleged to have been performed wearing the ceremonial head-dress of a Red Indian chief or other eccentric garb might well in appropriate circumstances suffice.

No better example of the proper use of similar-fact evidence could be imagined than that provided by the facts of one of the earliest of modern cases, *George Joseph Smith* [13], otherwise known to posterity as the 'brides-in-the-bath' case. The defendant was charged with the murder of a woman with whom he had gone through a ceremony of marriage. Evidence of the deaths of two other women, with whom the defendant had also gone through ceremonies of marriage, was held to have been rightly admitted. In each case, the deceased woman was found dead in her bath; in each case the door of the bathroom would not lock; in each case, the defendant had informed a doctor that the woman suffered from epileptic fits; and in each case, the woman's life was insured for the benefit of the defendant. The devastating degree of similarity in the different cases was not mere evidence of bad character, but was the clearest possible evidence of systematic crime, stamped with the hallmark of the individual defendant, from which the jury were justified in drawing the inference that each killing was murder, and murder by the same individual. But nothing short of this degree of similarity will do, for if the hallmark of the individual cannot be clearly shown, the evidence would be merely evidence of bad character, and not only inadmissible but so prejudicial as to make a fair trial almost impossible. Prosecutors should consider this with great care, before making any application to admit similar-fact evidence, and defence advocates should be vigilant to object to any apparent abuse of the rule.

It should be noted that striking similarity is not a ground of admissibility in itself, but rather a case in which evidence of bad character is admissible because it is relevant to the issue of guilt. In *DPP v P* [14] Lord Mackay of Clashfern LC said that to regard striking similarity as the only such case would be too restrictive. Other cases include evidence of crimes of preparation, or crimes which are effectively part of the same transaction as the offence charged; for example, where the defendant steals a car to use in a subsequent robbery, forges a cheque for use in a subsequent fraud, kills someone by dangerous driving while fleeing the scene of some other crime, or attempts to bribe a police officer to give him bail when arrested for some other offence.

Note that such cases are fundamentally different from those in which character is purely incidental (for example, the defendant who commits an offence while a serving prisoner). In the 'incidental' cases, the defendant's character is not directly relevant to guilt, but is only a part of the background circumstances. It may not be explored in detail during the evidence, or in cross-examination. But if the evidence is relevant, not only may the prosecution adduce such evidence as part of their case, they may also cross-examine the defendant about it, if he elects to give evidence. Section 1(e) of the Criminal Evidence Act 1898 provides:

A person charged and being a witness in pursuance of this Act may be asked any question in cross-examination notwithstanding that it would tend to criminate him as to the offence charged.

And s. 1(f) of the same Act, which created the shield of the defendant against cross-examination about his bad character, provides as its first exception that the defendant may be so cross-examined if:

> (i) the proof that he has committed or been convicted of such other offence is <u>admissible evidence</u> to show that he is guilty of the offence wherewith he is then charged.

Cross-examination about bad character

Section 1 of the Criminal Evidence Act 1898, which, for the first time, rendered the defendant a competent witness for the defence, invested the defendant witness with a shield against cross-examination about his bad character. The shield is not absolute, but may be lost in certain circumstances. We have considered the loss of the shield where the defendant asserts his own good character, and where cross-examination about character is relevant to the defendant's guilt of the offence charged. Two further situations in which the shield may be lost remain to be considered. These situations arise from the provisions of s. 1(f) (as amended) that the defendant may be cross-examined about his character in either of the following two sets of circumstances, that is to say if:

> (ii) . . . the nature or conduct of the defence is such as to involve imputations on the character of the prosecutor or the witnesses for the prosecution; or the deceased victim of the alleged crime; or
> (iii) he [the defendant] has given evidence against any other person charged in the same proceedings.

These different cases must be considered separately.

Defences involving imputations on character

The defendant may make imputations on the character of the prosecutor or the witnesses for the prosecution either in the course of cross-examination (whether in person or by his advocate) or during the course of his evidence, or both. And unfortunately, unlike the case in the first part of s. 1(f)(ii) in which the defendant asserts his own good character, there may be little or nothing that you, as an advocate, can do to prevent loss of the shield. Some defences, by their very nature, involve making imputations on the character of the prosecutor or the witnesses for the prosecution. If the defendant is to be believed, the imputations may well be justified, but in any event you have a duty to make them if essential to the defence.

As originally enacted, s.1(f)(ii) mentioned only the character of the prosecutor and the witnesses for the prosecution. The reference to the deceased victim of the alleged crime was added by s. 31 of the Criminal Justice and Public Order Act 1994. This will not arise in summary trials but may do so in prosecutions for homicide in the Crown Court.

An imputation on character is any allegation which, if believed, a court would consider to be seriously discreditable to the witness. The most obvious examples are allegations that a prosecution witness has committed perjury, or fabricated evidence, for example where it is alleged that a police officer obtained a confession by force or fraud, or invented the contents of an interview. But any allegation of perjury, fabrication of evidence, serious misconduct or dishonest or immoral behaviour, including an imputation of criminal convictions, may suffice. Conversely a mere allegation of mistake or unreliability is insufficient to lose the shield. And where the defendant does no more than assert his innocence, even in strong terms, he does not lose his shield, even though the implication may be that the evidence against him is untrue. The shield is lost only by an express and affirmative allegation of some seriously discreditable conduct.

The mere fact that the making of imputations is inevitable, and is an essential part of the defence, is no answer to the loss of the shield. In *Bishop* [15], a defendant charged with burglary sought to show that he was not a trespasser in the building concerned by alleging that he had had a homosexual relationship with the occupier. Clearly, this was no more than a necessary part of the defence, and was designed not to attack the character of the occupier, but to refute an essential element of the offence charged, by suggesting that the defendant had permission to enter the building and so was not a trespasser. The shield was nonetheless lost.

The advocate does, however, retain a certain degree of control, in that it may be possible to conduct the defence without recourse to the making of imputations on character. This will occur where the 'nature' of the defence does not necessarily involve imputations, but the 'conduct' of the defence may or may not involve them, depending upon the manner in which it is undertaken. As an advocate, you should not make an imputation on the character of any witness, unless you are credibly instructed that the imputation can be made, and unless it is essential to the conduct of the defence. The first 'unless' represents a rule of professional conduct; the second represents a rule of professional judgment, in the sense that it is a cardinal error to throw away your client's shield without good reason. In certain cases, you will have absolutely no choice but to suffer the loss of the shield, since the very essence of your defence may be that the prosecution witnesses are lying, or have fabricated evidence against your client. The tactical implications of this, and one method of minimising the damage, are considered in Chapter 13.

The purpose of permitting cross-examination about character in such circumstances is that the court is entitled to evaluate the attack made on the prosecution witnesses in the light of the character of the person who makes it. An imputation on character will carry more weight if it emanates from a defendant of good character than if it emanates from a defendant with numerous previous convictions. For this reason, even where the shield is lost, the evidence of the defendant's bad character is admissible only as evidence of the defendant's credit as the author of the imputations, and may not be used as evidence of his guilt.

Discretionary exclusion of character

In earlier chapters it has been stated that, by virtue of s. 78 of the Police and Criminal Evidence Act 1984, the bench have a discretion to exclude technically admissible prosecution evidence on the ground that its admission would result in unfairness. This discretion may be exercised to prevent cross-examination of the defendant about his previous bad character, or to limit such cross-examination to relevant aspects of that bad character, even where the cross-examination is technically permissible. For example, in *Watts* [16], where a defendant charged with a minor indecent assault on an adult woman became liable to be cross-examined about his previous convictions because he had made imputations on the character of prosecution witnesses, the Court of Appeal held that it had been wrong to permit him to be cross-examined about previous convictions for indecent assault on young girls. The danger that the jury might be misled into thinking that the evidence could be admissible to prove guilt, instead of going to credit only, was too grave, and the trial judge should have exercised his discretion to exclude.

Conversely, in *Powell* [17], where the defendant was charged with living off immoral earnings, and where he not only alleged that the prosecution case was fabricated, but also made a false assertion of good character, the Court of Appeal held that it was proper for both reasons to permit cross-examination about his similar conviction for allowing premises to be used for the purposes of prostitution.

In *Britzman* [18], the Court of Appeal laid down guidelines for the exercise of discretion in such cases. The court said that cross-examination should not be permitted on the basis that there has been an imputation on character merely because the defendant denies allegations against him, even if he does so firmly and even offensively. Cross-examination should be permitted only where the court is sure that there can be no possibility of mistake, misunderstanding or confusion and that the jury (or, interpolating, the bench) will inevitably have to decide who is telling the truth with regard to the imputations. Allowances should be made for the strain of giving evidence, and particularly where the imputations are made during cross-examination by the prosecution. Moreover, the prosecution should not seek to cross-examine about character where the evidence against the defendant is otherwise overwhelming. Similar guidelines are to be found in the judgment of Ackner LJ in *Burke* [19].

Two further observations should be added. The first is that in the magistrates' court, even to ask for the exercise of discretion inevitably reveals that there may be some bad character to exclude — another consequence of having no jury as a separate tribunal of fact. However, since you can ask for discretion without divulging the full details of the defendant's past, it is worth making the application. Remember that the prosecution must ask for leave before proceeding to cross-examine (object if they do not) and your asking for discretion should give nothing away that is not apparent to the bench already.

The second is that the bench can decide to allow cross-examination only as to a part of the defendant's character that appears relevant to the issue. For example, if the defendant is charged with indecent assault and makes imputations on the character of the prosecution witnesses, as in *Watts,* it may well be terribly prejudicial (and actually irrelevant to the proper purpose of the evidence) to permit cross-examination about other sexual assaults. But it may be perfectly proper to permit cross-examination about offences involving dishonesty or false statement. These help the bench to assess the veracity of the imputation, but do not prejudice the defendant in any other respect.

This limited application of the discretion may often commend itself to the bench more than a blanket exclusion. When making an application for the exercise of discretion, ensure that you say no more than that the bench should limit itself to offences involving dishonesty; otherwise you may indeed give the game away.

Giving evidence against co-defendants

Section 1(f)(iii) removes the shield in cross-examination not by the prosecution, but by co-defendants. It is comparatively simple to determine when the shield has been lost in these circumstances, although this too is a question of law for the bench, and leave to cross-examine is required. The difference is that the judge has no power to restrain cross-examination by a co-defendant if the shield is lost as a matter of law.

A defendant 'gives evidence against' another, if he gives evidence which assists the prosecution case against the other, or undermines the other's defence, in either case making it more likely that the other will be convicted: *Bruce* [20]. This does not mean that the defendant must testify as a prosecution witness against the co-defendant; indeed, he is an incompetent witness for this purpose. What is envisaged is the by no means uncommon situation in which a defendant will seek, during his evidence in chief on his own behalf, to inculpate a co-defendant, in order to exculpate himself. However, he need not give evidence with that intention; if his evidence in fact has the required detrimental effect on the co-defendant's case, the shield is lost: *Murdoch* v *Taylor* [21].

In *Varley* [22] the Court of Appeal laid down guidelines for judges who are called upon to decide whether a defendant is entitled to cross-examine a co-defendant under s. 1(f)(iii). The most important of these are that the judge must first be satisfied that '. . . the evidence either supports the prosecution case in a material respect or undermines the defence of the co-accused. A hostile intent is irrelevant'. It must be clear that the defence of the co-accused is undermined; mere inconvenience or inconsistency with the defence is not enough. Mere denial of participation in a joint venture is also insufficient, unless the denial necessarily leads to the conclusion that, if the witness did not participate, then the co-accused must have done so (e.g., in a case where one of two defendants must have committed the offence charged).

'Any other person charged in the same proceedings' means any other person also charged and before the court in the same trial, even though the charges against that co-defendant may not be identical to those against the defendant witness.

As in the case of imputations against prosecution witnesses, there are many cases in which loss of the shield is inevitable. However, good advocacy demands that the shield should not be lost unnecessarily, where the defendant's case does not call for an assault on the defence of co-defendants. Also similar to the rule in the case of imputations on character is the principle that, since the object of the permitted cross-examination is to allow the court to assess the weight to be attached to the evidence against the co-defendant by reference to the character of the defendant witness, the evidence of bad character is evidence only of the credit of the defendant witness as the author of the evidence adverse to the co-defendant, and is not evidence of the guilt of the defendant witness.

Improper references to character

A reference during a criminal trial to the previous bad character of a defendant, other than when permitted by the rules of evidence, is a serious irregularity. The proper course for a defence advocate, unless he intends for the tactical reasons outlined in Chapter 13 to introduce his client's character anyway, or it is inevitable that the shield will be lost at a later stage, is to apply immediately for a retrial before a differently constituted bench. The prejudice that may otherwise operate against the defendant, even though the bench may be fair-minded and may try to exclude the reference from their minds, may preclude a fair trial, and will almost certainly preclude the appearance of a fair trial.

Improper references to character can occur in various ways, by inadvertence or malevolence from the mouth of a prosecution witness or co-defendant, or through a mistake on the part of the defendant himself. Of these, the last is the most embarrassing possibility. However, even in this case, a properly advised bench should grant the retrial, particularly where the answer which reveals character has been induced by cross-examination. The only exception is where the defendant, seeing his defence coming apart at the seams, deliberately sabotages the trial by an unprovoked revelation of his past record. This is a mercifully rare occurrence.

Oddly enough, there are situations even more embarrassing than the voluntary disclosure of bad character by the defendant. These are situations where the defendant's advocate invites an improper reference to character in the course of cross-examination of the prosecution witnesses. If this seems unlikely, consider the effect of questions such as the following:

(a) 'Why were you following my client?'

(b) 'What exactly was being discussed at the police station, while you were not interviewing my client about this offence?'

(c) 'How did you know my client's name when you first saw him on the street?'

(d) 'What did my client tell you that you have not given in evidence today?'

If these questions have one thing in common, it is that they are questions which defendants often urge you to put. If they have a second thing in common, it is that they are all potentially disastrous, for even though the answers may be inadmissible, it is no use objecting after they have been given, when you yourself have induced them. The bench will assume that you have some good reason for doing so. A good advocate will sense that he is straying into dangerous territory, merely by the fact that the police officer has (following his training better than some advocates follow theirs) stayed carefully away from the subject in chief, and exhibits an embarrassed reluctance to answer in cross-examination. The latter is often misinterpreted by the inexperienced advocate as a sign of evasion, with terrible results. Pressed far enough, the officer will tell the court what he knows.

Finally, it should be noted that the Rehabilitation of Offenders Act 1974 and the Children and Young Persons Act 1963, s. 16(2), provide some restriction on the disclosure of certain previous convictions that occurred long ago, or while a person was a child or young person. In the case of the former statute, the restriction is only one of first obtaining leave before referring to a spent conviction in open court, for the Act does not apply to references during criminal proceedings [23]. The latter prohibits the disclosure of the covered offences in any event. Quite apart from these restrictions, a wise prosecutor will often refrain from dredging up ancient convictions even though he may technically be entitled to do so, especially where the defendant's recent record is good. Quite often, such an error of judgment forfeits the sympathy of the court and transfers it to the defendant, and accomplishes nothing in terms of attacking the defendant's credit.

A person who has only spent convictions may, with the leave of the court, be presented as a person of good character: *Nye* [24]. Once again, this is less effective than in the Crown Court, where the judge will decide this, and the jury will never hear about convictions. But, even in the magistrates' court, it is well worth pursuing, because not only will the bench not hear the details of the convictions, but also they will probably be reluctant to hold spent convictions against the defendant; indeed, in some cases, the defendant may even get some credit for having reformed. Note, however, that the issue must be addressed with care. The Court of Appeal in *Nye* emphasised that the trial court must not be misled about the defendant's character in any way.

It has never been decided whether a person is of good character if his record consists solely of road traffic offences. It was suggested, *obiter*, in *Callum* [25] that this might be so, but clearly this must be approached with caution. It is submitted that it might be a proper approach if the offences were essentially regulatory, for example, driving without lights, or even speeding, but that it would not be proper if they involved more deliberate disregard for the law, for example, driving while disqualified or failing to stop or report an accident. In such a case, caution dictates not representing the defendant to be of good character, and this would certainly be true if he were charged with another road traffic offence.

Further reading

Murphy on Evidence, 6th ed., ch. 5 and 6; *Blackstone's Criminal Practice 1998*, F12–F14.

Notes

1. [1979] QB 108. See also *Vye* [1993] 1 WLR 471.
2. [1993] 1 WLR 471.
3. [1996] AC 41: see also *Fulcher* [1995] 2 Cr App R 251.
4. [1993] 4 All ER 290.
5. [1994] Crim LR 202.
6. (1865) Le & Ca 520.
7. (1981) 74 Cr App R 10.
8. [1966] 1 WLR 405.
9. [1979] Crim LR 48; *McLeod* [1994] 1 WLR 1500.
10. [1894] AC 57, 65.
11. [1962] AC 635. See also *Anderson* [1988] QB 678.

12. [1975] AC 421, 454.
13. (1915) 11 Cr App R 229.
14. [1991] 2 AC 447.
15. [1975] QB 274.
16. [1983] 3 All ER 101.
17. [1985] 1 WLR 1364.
18. [1983] 1 WLR 350, 355.
19. (1985) 82 Cr App R 156; *McLeod* [1994] 1 WLR 1500.
20. [1975] 1 WLR 1252.
21. [1965] AC 574. See also *Mir* [1989] Crim LR 894.
22. [1982] 2 All ER 519.
23. *Practice Direction (Crime: Spent Convictions)* [1975] 1 WLR 1065.
24. (1982) 75 Cr App R 247
25. [1975] RTR 415.

EIGHT

Witnesses

Introduction

In Chapter 1, it was said that there are different varieties of evidence which may be presented to a court. Oral evidence is one of these varieties, and it is presented to the court by witnesses. Chapter 11 will say much more about the actual evidence which witnesses may give, and about the preparation and presentation of evidence given in chief, in cross-examination and in re-examination. This chapter examines some very basic questions about witnesses which are often overlooked in the course of concentrating on the substance of the witnesses' evidence. These are questions affecting the witnesses themselves, as distinguished from the evidence which they may give. Because witnesses are the foundation of almost every contested case, an understanding of the rules that affect them is a basic tool of advocacy.

In order to study these rules concerning witnesses, we shall try to answer four questions which you should ask, namely:

    (a)   What witnesses can I call to give evidence?
    (b)   What witnesses can I compel to attend to give evidence?
    (c)   What kinds of witnesses should I call to give evidence?
    (d)   How many witnesses should I call to give evidence?

What witnesses can I call to give evidence?

This question focuses, not upon the actual evidence that a witness may be able to give, but upon the personal qualification or disqualification of a witness to be called to give evidence at all. A person who is personally qualified to give evidence is said to be 'competent' and one who is disqualified on personal grounds, to be 'incompetent'. To the modern mind, the idea that any witness should be incompetent to give evidence seems rather strange, given that the court should have access to as much relevant evidence as possible, and certainly, the court will favour competence wherever incompetence can properly be avoided. But, as in so many instances, the rules of evidence regarding competence remain shackled to some extent by their historical development.

At common law, there were a number of general incompetences, based on the premise that there were certain persons whose evidence must always be too suspect or unreliable to be accepted by a court, for example, persons convicted of infamous crimes and non-Christians. But the common law also recognised specific incompetences, which arose from the relationship of a person to the case in question. The parties to a case and their spouses were incompetent because of their personal interest in the outcome. The general incompetences based on character or inability to take the prescribed oath have long since been abolished by statute, and general incompetence is now significant only with respect to the evidence of children of tender years, and persons of defective intellect. The specific incompetences affecting the parties and their spouses likewise survive only in a much emasculated form, and only in relation to criminal cases. In civil cases, the parties and their spouses have long been competent by statute.

We shall look first at the specific incompetences of the defendant and the spouse of the defendant in criminal cases, and then turn to the general incompetence affecting children of tender years and persons of defective intellect.

Defendants in criminal cases   At common law, the defendant in a criminal case was, like any other party, incompetent to give evidence. In an age of harsh punishments and frequent denial of counsel, this incompetence gradually came to be regarded as unjust and it was eventually removed by s. 1 of the Criminal Evidence Act 1898. The Act provided that:

> Every person charged with an offence . . . shall be a competent witness for the defence at every stage of the proceedings, whether the person so charged is charged solely or jointly with any other person.

This section still forms the basis of the right of the defendant to go into the witness-box in his defence, in any criminal trial, whether summary or on indictment. Note that the phrase 'at every stage of the proceedings' is broad enough to encompass the right to give evidence not only at trial, but also in ancillary proceedings such as applications for bail and committal proceedings and in mitigation of sentence: *Wheeler* [1].

Whenever a defendant does give evidence in his defence as permitted by the Act, the bench must weigh his evidence as they would that of any other witness. It is always proper, and often desirable to remind the bench in tactful terms that they should not view his evidence with suspicion merely because he moves from the dock to the witness-box to give it. The Act, incidentally, gives the defendant the right to give evidence from the witness-box, unless the court otherwise orders: s. 1(g). The court may so order only in a case of necessity, for example where the defendant is of violent disposition and may be difficult to control: *Symonds* [2]. Failure to observe this principle may lead to a conviction being quashed (*Farnham Justices, ex parte Gibson* [3]).

Because s. 1 makes the defendant a competent witness 'for the defence' and not just on his own personal behalf, he may (with his consent) be called as a witness by a co-defendant. However, since he would thereby subject himself to cross-examination about the case as a whole, including his own involvement, it is difficult to imagine a case in which he would consent to be called for a co-defendant, having declined to be called by his own advocate.

The Act renders the defendant a competent witness only for the defence. It is important to note that the defendant remains incompetent as a witness for the prosecution: *Grant* [4]. For various reasons, it is usually the hope of the prosecution that the defendant will give evidence. The prosecution cannot require a reluctant defendant A to go into the witness-box to give evidence in his own defence, for the Act precludes any such compulsion. But can the prosecution call a willing defendant A to give evidence for them against co-defendant B? Defendant A's motive for such treachery might be the hope of attracting a more lenient sentence, or the expectation that the prosecution might play down his involvement in the case, at the expense of defendant B. Whatever the motive on either side, it cannot be done while A is a defendant in the case; he is incompetent for the prosecution.

Of course, if defendant A ceases to be a defendant, because he is no longer a person charged and before the court, his incompetence is removed. This will be the case if he has pleaded guilty to all the charges against him, or the prosecution decide not to proceed with any charges to which he has not pleaded guilty, or not to proceed against him at all. Where the prosecution propose to call such a witness, the situation requires delicate handling by all the advocates in the case. Even though he may thus become a competent prosecution witness, A's credit as a witness is open to powerful challenge.

A's credit as a witness can be protected to some extent if the bench are prepared to sentence A before the trial proceeds against B. This can take some of the steam out of the inevitable cross-examination about his motive for giving evidence for the prosecution. Having received a reasonably lenient sentence, A may prove less enthusiastic in his evidence on behalf of the prosecution. Nonetheless if you are defending B, your position is generally rendered somewhat easier if sentence is deferred until the end of the trial. In this case, it may be easier to ensure by cross-examination that the bench understand that A has something to gain by giving evidence against B, or at least believes that he has something to gain. As to the correct moment at which to sentence a former defendant whom the prosecution require as a witness, fashion varies. Often, however, the bench will accept that they do not have enough facts to sentence A fairly before the respective roles of A and B have been fully explored. There are no limitations on the magistrates' freedom to choose which course to follow.

The defendant's spouse   Until recently, the question of the competence of the spouse of the defendant was a somewhat complicated one. At common law, the spouse was incompetent as a prosecution witness, except in cases of high treason and in cases which may be described broadly as involving acts of violence or neglect against the witness spouse or a child of the family of the spouses. There was uncertainty about the position of a spouse as a defence witness, particularly on behalf of a person jointly charged with the defendant spouse. The common law position as to competence was refined by a series of statutory provisions spanning the period between the Criminal Evidence Act 1898 and the Theft Act 1968, which made the witness spouse competent in an ever-increasing number of cases. The provisions of s. 30 of the Theft Act 1968 were so broad as effectively to make the spouse competent, with some exceptions, rather than the other way around. This position was recognised and rationalised by the Police and Criminal Evidence Act 1984. Section 80 of the Act provides:

(1)   In any proceedings the wife or husband of the accused shall be competent to give evidence—

    (a)   subject to subsection (4) below, for the prosecution; and

    (b)   on behalf of the accused or any person jointly charged with the accused. . . .

(4)   Where a husband and wife are jointly charged with an offence neither spouse shall at the trial be competent . . . by virtue of subsection (1)(a) . . . above to give evidence in respect of that offence unless that spouse is not, or is no longer, liable to be convicted of that offence at the trial as a result of pleading guilty or for any other reason.

The result of this is that the witness spouse is always a competent witness, either for the prosecution or the defence, unless the husband and wife are jointly charged with an offence of which the witness spouse remains liable to be convicted. Section 80(8) of the Act preserves the position that the prosecution may not comment on the failure of the husband or wife of the accused to give evidence.

The term 'spouse' denotes a person who is lawfully married, i.e., whose marriage is recognised as valid by English law [5] and, therefore, excludes those whose marriage is void, 'common law spouses', mistresses and others, regardless of the apparent seriousness or permanence of the relationship.

Two other provisions should also be noted. First, by s. 80(5) of the Act:

In any [criminal] proceedings a person who has been but is no longer married to the accused shall be competent and compellable to give evidence as if that person and the accused had never been married.

At common law, there was originally a rule that former spouses retained their incompetence as witnesses with respect to any matters that occurred during the marriage. However, although never formally abrogated, the rule is plainly obsolete, since existing spouses, so to speak, have by statute long been declared to be competent in civil cases, and it would be absurd that former spouses should have remained incompetent while existing spouses are not. It has for some long time been certain that the old common law rule would no longer be applied in civil cases. It enjoyed a somewhat longer life in criminal cases, but the 1984 Act has now recognised that it should be laid to rest in those cases also.

Secondly, it should be noted that s. 80(9) of the Act abolishes in criminal cases two privileges that had previously been abolished in civil cases, namely the privilege against compelled disclosure of communications between husband and wife and compelled evidence about the occurrence or non-occurrence of marital intercourse.

Children of tender years At common law, the original test of competence in the case of children was whether or not the child was capable of understanding the significance of the oath [6]. But this test gave way to a more pragmatic approach, based on the child's maturity, and his understanding of the importance of telling the truth in the context of giving evidence. In *Hayes* [7], the Court of Appeal said:

> The important consideration, we think, when a judge has to decide whether a child should properly be sworn, is whether the child has a sufficient appreciation of the solemnity of the occasion and the added responsibility to tell the truth which is involved in taking an oath, over and above the duty to tell the truth which is an ordinary duty of normal social conduct.

There was, at common law, no absolute age at which a child ceased to be 'of tender years'. The court in *Hayes* observed that: '. . . the watershed dividing children who are normally considered old enough to take the oath and children normally considered too young to take the oath, probably falls between the ages of eight and ten'. But all the authorities agreed that the ability of the actual child in question, as perceived by the court, was the determining factor.

Before the change in the test laid down in *Hayes*, however, frustration with the older rule had led Parliament to provide, by the Children and Young Persons Act 1933, s. 38(1), that, in criminal cases, children could be permitted to give evidence unsworn, provided the judge was satisfied that the child possessed sufficient intelligence. Section 38(2) of the Act created an offence akin to perjury to cover such evidence. The fact that children might give evidence either sworn or unsworn gave rise to numerous problems, especially in the area of corroboration. The corroboration problem lost much of its force when the Criminal Justice Act 1988, s. 34, abolished the requirement for a corroboration warning to the extent that it had been required solely because the witness was a child. But there remained much concern about the anomaly. The evidence of children in criminal cases is now governed by the Criminal Justice Act 1991, s. 52(1), which inserted the following new s. 33A into the 1988 Act:

(1) A child's evidence in criminal proceedings shall be given unsworn.

(2) A deposition of a child's unsworn evidence may be taken for the purposes of criminal proceedings as if that evidence had been given on oath.

(3) In this section 'child' means a person under 14 years of age.

The offence akin to perjury with respect to such unsworn evidence is recreated by the Criminal Justice Act 1991, s. 100 and sch. 11, para. 1.

The provision governing competence is now s. 33A(2A) of the Criminal Justice Act 1988, which was inserted by the Criminal Justice and Public Order Act 1994, sch. 9, para. 33:

A child's evidence shall be received unless it appears to the court that the child is incapable of giving intelligible testimony.

It would seem that it is no longer necessary for the judge to inquire into the competence of a child in every case. But, as in the case of an adult witness, the judge may do so if it seems appropriate, having regard to the child's apparent ability to express himself or herself intelligibly. This was the holding in *Hampshire* [8], decided under an earlier statutory provision governing competence, s. 52(2) of the Criminal Justice Act 1991, but apparently applicable equally to the present law.

In *Hampshire*, the accused was charged with offences of indecency with two girls, aged eight and nine. The evidence in chief of the children was admitted in the form of videotaped interviews, but, in breach of the guidelines for the conduct of such interviews [9], no one had impressed on the children the importance of speaking the truth. The trial judge admitted the evidence without any consideration of the issue of competence, but later formed the view that he ought to have investigated the matter, and then purported to find that the children were competent. The Court of Appeal held that there was no longer any duty on the judge to inquire about the competence of a child in every case, though he retained the power to do so, if it appeared necessary in a particular case. A review of the videotaped evidence of a child would normally be enough to enable the judge to make a decision. The court also held, consistently with earlier common law authority, such as *Hayes*, that while competence, in relation to a child, had traditionally included understanding the duty of telling the truth in a court of law, in addition to the ability to testify intelligibly, the intention of Parliament in enacting s. 52(2) of the Criminal Justice Act 1991 had been to alter that position. The court interpreted the subsection to mean that the 'ordinary' test of competence, i.e., that applicable to an adult, should be applied in the case of children, 'regardless of any real or notional additional test previously imposed on them if they gave evidence on oath', i.e., not including the test of understanding the special importance of telling the truth in court. It seems that the present provision under s. 33A(2A) must be construed in the same way.

In *Hampshire*, the Court of Appeal approved the practice of the trial judge reminding a child of the duty of speaking the truth, though there now appears to be no basis in law for the practice, and it remains to be seen whether it will continue in the light of the present law.

In civil cases, the competence of children is governed by s. 96(1) and (2) of the Children Act 1989, in which it is provided that where a child called as a witness in any civil proceedings does not, in the opinion of the court, understand the nature of an oath, his evidence may be received unsworn if the court finds that the child understands the duty of speaking the truth and has sufficient understanding to justify his evidence being heard. This provision effectively combines the provisions of s. 38(1) of the 1933 Act with the provisions laid down in *Hayes*, and, ironically, affords greater scrutiny of the competence and reliability of a child's evidence in civil cases than is now available in criminal cases.

Quite apart from questions of competence, the treatment of child witnesses is one of the most delicate and demanding tasks that can face an advocate, particularly in sexual cases. The potential for alienating the bench is never greater than in the context of a decision of whether or not to call a child, or of how to cross-examine a child. The task of the defence advocate is especially demanding, because regardless of the important considerations of the physical and mental welfare of the child, the advocate must not forget that hysterical invention and exaggeration are a real possibility in the evidence of a young child. There can be no objection to a thorough and testing cross-examination, provided that it is conducted with restraint and tact.

As a prosecutor, you should ensure that a responsible adult attends court with the child, and that the child is physically and mentally fit to give evidence. Your examination-in-chief should be as short as is consistent with your duty to elicit the facts. As a defender, you must put your client's case fully, but you should vary your style of cross-examination from that which you might employ in the case of an adult witness. Bear in mind that you can emphasise to the court in your closing speech the dangers of the evidence of children. You need not make all your points in cross-examination, and it is usually unnecessary to drive home points of inconsistency or weakness at this stage. The bench will be receptive to them during your closing speech, and will appreciate your restraint and consideration in reserving them until that time.

In youth courts, the evidence in chief of child witnesses may, under certain circumstances, be presented in the form of a videotaped interview of the child by an adult, or by means of testimony by live television link. These possibilities are dealt with in Chapter 11.

Both sides should bear in mind the important statutory provisions dealing with the evidence of child witnesses in committal proceedings, contained in ss. 42 and 43 of the Children and Young Persons Act 1933 and s. 103 of the Magistrates' Courts Act 1980 (as substituted by the Criminal Justice Act 1988, s. 33), and designed to reduce as far as possible the ordeal involved in giving evidence which will be repeated at the trial on indictment.

Persons of defective intellect   Witnesses whose intellectual powers are diminished for any reason are competent to the extent that the court is satisfied that they understand the nature of the proceedings and the duty to tell the truth, and are capable of giving comprehensible evidence. In *Bellamy* [10], the test was explained as being the same as that laid down at common law in the case of children in the case of *Hayes* (above). Many witnesses can assist the court with relevant facts, despite some degree of mental handicap. If necessary, the court may adjourn the case in order for the witness to recover his or her capacity. This is sometimes done in the case of witnesses who are suffering from temporary mental incapacity caused by alcohol or drugs. The court will permit any witness to give evidence whenever possible (unless outraged by any self-induced incapacity) although the weight of the evidence given may not be great.

What witnesses can I compel to attend to give evidence?

The general rule in both civil and criminal cases is that any witness who is competent to give evidence is also compellable to do so. By compellable is meant that the witness may be lawfully required by the court, under penalty of sanction for refusal to obey, to attend and give evidence. The purpose of the rule is to prevent the court from being deprived of relevant evidence, merely because of the refusal of a witness to cooperate. However, for reasons which have already been explored in this chapter, when discussing competence, there are exceptions in the cases of a defendant and the spouse of a defendant in a criminal case.

The defendant   Section 1 of the Criminal Evidence Act 1898, which for the first time made a defendant and his or her spouse competent witnesses for the defence, provided that the defendant should not be called as a witness 'except on his own application', and that the spouse should not be called as a witness for the defence 'except on the application of the person . . . charged'. It is clear from the wording of the section that the defendant is not a compellable witness. It follows that the defendant need never give evidence unless he wishes to do so, and the question of whether it may ever be advisable not to call the defendant is dealt with in Chapters 6 and 13. Of course, in this regard, the position under the provisions of the Criminal Justice and Public Order Act 1994 is radically different from what it was at common law. It should be noted, however, that if the defendant does elect to give evidence, he becomes a witness and his evidence becomes evidence for all purposes in the case, and he cannot object to being cross-examined on behalf of the prosecution and any co-defendants, once he has been sworn.

The defendant's spouse   As with competence, the question of the compellability of the spouse of the defendant gave rise to much uncertainty at common law. In fact, it was not until the end of the 1970s that the House of Lords in *Hoskyn v Commissioner of Police for the Metropolis* [11] decided that the spouse should never be a compellable prosecution witness, even when competent. Although this case is now history, it is worth noting one important point. The basis of the majority decision was that it was undesirable that one spouse should be compelled to testify against the other. However, Lord Edmund Davies, in a powerful dissent, noted that some offences are too grave to be compromised merely because a spouse changes his or her mind about testifying, and that being compellable is a useful protection for a spouse who is subject to violence or intimidation and does not wish to be seen to give evidence voluntarily.

In enacting the Police and Criminal Evidence Act 1984, Parliament adopted in part the reasoning of Lord Edmund Davies and in part reversed the majority in *Hoskyn.* The portion of s. 80 dealing with competence has already been dealt with in this chapter. The remainder of the section, dealing with compellability, provides as follows:

(2)   In any proceedings the wife or husband of the accused shall, subject to subsection (4) below, be compellable to give evidence on behalf of the accused.

(3)   In any proceedings the wife or husband of the accused shall, subject to subsection (4) below, be compellable to give evidence for the prosecution or on behalf of any person jointly charged with the accused if and only if—

(a)   the offence charged involves an assault on, or injury or a threat of injury to, the wife or husband of the accused or a person who was at the material time under the age of 16; or

(b)   the offence charged is a sexual offence alleged to have been committed in respect of a person who was at the material time under that age; or

(c)   the offence charged consists of attempting or conspiring to commit, or of aiding, abetting, counselling, procuring or inciting the commission of, an offence falling within paragraph (a) or (b) above.

The full text of subsection (4) should now be added:

(4)   Where a husband and wife are jointly charged with an offence neither spouse shall at the trial be competent or compellable by virtue of subsection (1)(a), (2) or (3) above to give evidence in respect of that offence unless that spouse is not, or is no longer, liable to be convicted of that offence at the trial as a result of pleading guilty or for any other reason.

Parliament has recognised that certain offences (broadly similar to those in which the spouse was originally competent for the prosecution at common law) are too serious to permit the spouse to be in a category separate from other witnesses. These are also just the cases in which the witness spouse is most likely to come under pressure from the defendant spouse not to testify, and Lord Edmund Davies's protection argument has surely been heeded here. It applies also to cases where the witness spouse is to testify for a co-accused, as well as those in which he or she is to testify for the prosecution.

If you are a prosecutor, you will have to make some delicate and important decisions in the area of compelling spouse witnesses, especially in cases that are essentially 'domestic' in nature. You should appreciate that you will often find it pointless to compel a reluctant spouse, who may genuinely wish to be reconciled to the defendant and who does not want to jeopardise that reconciliation by testifying. You may also be guilty of unnecessary insensitivity. But the Act does give you the power to compel in cases where the charge is a serious one, or is against a young child, or where it seems apparent that the reluctance of a spouse to testify is the product of violence or intimidation. It is important to exercise sound professional judgment in such cases.

In *Pitt* [12] it was held that a spouse who was a competent, but not compellable, witness against the defendant retains the choice of whether or not to give evidence right up to the moment of taking the oath, even if the spouse has previously made a witness statement, or even given evidence in earlier proceedings. This case was decided under the common law rules which preceded those under s. 80 of the Police and Criminal Evidence Act 1984, but there seems to be no good reason to depart from it.

Merely to know whether a witness is compellable is not enough. Prosecuting and defending advocates alike should be familiar with the procedure in the magistrates' court for compelling the attendance of witnesses, by applying before trial to the court for the issuance of a witness summons: Magistrates' Courts Act 1980, s. 97(1). The summons, which may be issued by the clerk to the justices as well as the justices themselves, is available in any case where the bench or clerk is satisfied that any person in England or Wales is likely to be able to give material evidence, or produce any document or thing likely to be material evidence, and that the person will not voluntarily attend as a witness or produce the document or thing. The summons directs the witness to attend before the court at the time and date stated, to give evidence or to produce the document or thing. The witness summons must be served personally on the witness, and the compelling party must tender with the summons a sum of money reasonably sufficient to defray the witness's expenses involved in attending.

By s. 97(2) of the Magistrates' Courts Act 1980, if a justice of the peace (not the clerk in this instance) is satisfied by evidence on oath that it is probable that a witness summons would be insufficient to procure the attendance of the witness, the justice may issue a warrant to arrest the witness and bring him before the court. This is a drastic step, and justices are likely to grant this relief only where it appears strictly necessary, for example where the witness has already failed to obey a witness summons. Furthermore, if the witness attends, but refuses without just cause to be sworn or to give evidence, or to produce the document or object, the court has power to commit him to custody for up to seven days or until he sooner complies with the order of the court.

In the county court, a witness summons may also be issued on the request of a party under CCR Ord. 20, r. 12, for the attendance of a witness or the production of any document or object. Failure to obey the summons may be visited by a fine as provided for by the County Courts Act 1984, s. 55.

When one looks at the available procedure, it is surprising that one so often hears advocates complaining that their cases are being hindered by reluctant witnesses. Having said that, there will be occasions when, as a matter of professional judgment, you will decide not to call a reluctant witness. The mere fact that the power to compel exists does not mean that it is tactically correct to make use of it in every case. There will be cases in which the witness's evidence will be so affected by his reluctance or hostility that it would be too dangerous to call him. On the other hand, there will also be cases in which the witness's evidence is of great importance to your case, and where it would be irresponsible not to make use of the power to compel. Even though a witness may have expressed reluctance to attend court, this may amount to no more than a natural disinclination to take time off work and spend a good part of a day waiting around a magistrates' or county court. Service of a witness summons often reminds a witness of his civic duties, and you will often find that, when presented with a document to show to his employer, the witness may suddenly find that he is not quite as reluctant to take a day off work as he initially appeared. If in doubt, always have the witness attend. You do not have to call the witness merely because he is at court (though bear in mind that the other side may do so) but his presence gives you an opportunity to assess his mood.

How many witnesses should I call to give evidence?

The number of witnesses to be called is almost always governed by an advocate's tactical and professional judgment. In some instances, it is governed by his or her duty as a prosecutor. In a very few situations, it is governed by the rules of law concerning corroboration. The last-named cases were always few in number, because the rule of English law is that any case may be proved by the evidence of one witness, in the absence of some specific rule to the contrary. The rules requiring corroboration have, for the most part, been abolished in recent years.

In most cases, you are entitled to decide the order in which you will call your witnesses, though in civil cases it is usual and desirable to call first the party you represent. There may be cases in which, for good reason, you will want to call first another witness, for example an expert. In one instance, however, the order of witnesses is dictated by statute, subject to the discretion of the court. By s. 79 of the Police and Criminal Evidence Act 1984:

If at the trial of any person for an offence—
   (a)   the defence intends to call two or more witnesses to the facts of the case; and
   (b) those witnesses include the accused,
the accused shall be called before the other witness or witnesses unless the court in its discretion otherwise directs.

The expression 'witnesses to the facts of the case' would seem to exclude expert and character witnesses who are not called for the purpose of giving testimony directly about the actual facts of the case.

Considerations of judgment   The days of compurgators are long gone. Modern advocacy does not depend on the number of witnesses called on one side or the other. Of course, if two or more credible witnesses corroborate each other, that is to say support each other's evidence, then the weight of their combined evidence is likely to be greater than the uncorroborated evidence of either. It is, therefore, safe to state that you should call all the credible, available evidence that supports your case. But this should not be taken as an absolute rule. There is no substitute for professional judgment in this matter, any more than in any other aspect of successful advocacy. If one witness has accurately and forcibly given evidence of the relevant facts, and has emerged unshaken from cross-examination, you will not necessarily wish to risk losing some of the impact of that evidence by calling a less impressive witness to repeat the same evidence. Sometimes, a client will present you with a number of witnesses whose very availability in quantity should arouse your suspicion. You are not obliged to call them all. Any court will find its suspicions aroused on seeing a veritable procession of friends and relatives of the defendant, or any party, follow each other into the witness-box in quick succession to say exactly the same thing.

For prosecutors, the above principles are modified to some extent by the duty of the prosecution to see that a fair trial is had, so far as possible. This does not mean that the prosecution should not also seek to make their case as persuasive as possible, and it is certainly within the discretion of a prosecutor not to call a witness who appears not to be credible. However, it is a general rule that the prosecution should either call or make available at court all witnesses from whom the prosecution have taken a statement, even though their evidence may not support the prosecution case, and may even be inconsistent with the prosecution case: *Bryant* [13]. Calling a witness does not necessarily mean eliciting his evidence in chief: in the prosecutor's discretion, the witness may be sworn and then tendered for cross-examination. There is no duty on the prosecution to supply the defence with the witness's statement.

Corroboration and suspect witnesses   The expression 'corroboration' in the law of evidence means support or confirmation by evidence independent of the evidence to be corroborated. The general rule of the common law is that a conviction or judgment may be based on the evidence of a single witness or piece of evidence. There were, however, some instances in which the common law provided that a conviction for a criminal offence could not be sustained unless the jury were directed to look for corroboration of the evidence of certain witnesses, because of the perceived danger of evidence given by such witnesses. The same principle, strictly, was applied in the magistrates' court, in that the magistrates were to warn themselves of the danger of convicting based on the uncorroborated evidence of such witnesses. These 'dangerous' witnesses were identified judicially [14] as being the evidence of accomplices in the offence charged, the evidence of children and the evidence of complainants in sexual cases. These cases were referred to as cases in which corroboration was to be looked for as a matter of practice, because, as long as the jury were properly directed, it was open to them to convict even in the absence of corroboration. The warning was all that was required. Corroboration warnings became, through judicial interpretation, extremely technical, and often operated to impose unnecessary restrictions on evidence tendered in criminal cases. These requirements have now been abolished by statute [15] and it has been held that no further requirements for corroboration as a matter of practice exist or should be created [16].

It remains proper, however, for the magistrates to warn themselves to approach any evidence with caution if it seems to them to come from a suspect source, for example, a witness with an obvious motive to serve in giving his evidence, or a witness whose evidence appears to be affected by mental instability [17]. While the Court of Appeal held firmly in *Makanjuola* that no corroboration warning is required in such cases, the court may, of course, take note of and act on any apparent characteristics of evidence which suggest that it may carry some danger, and it is the duty of the defence advocate to direct the court's attention to such matters.

In a small group of cases created by statute, there is a requirement of corroboration as a matter of law. These cases differ from the practice cases, in that a conviction cannot be sustained in the absence of corroboration of certain evidence. A warning is not enough. The number of these cases has also been eroded steadily by statute, but several remain. The only one likely to be of importance in the magistrates' court is that of speeding. By s. 89 of the Road Traffic Regulation Act 1984 a person charged with speeding 'shall not be liable to be convicted solely on the evidence of one witness to the effect that in the opinion of the witness the person prosecuted was driving the vehicle at a speed exceeding a specified limit'. The effect of the corroboration must be to support the evidence of the witness [18]. But no other kind of evidence of speeding requires corroboration, so that evidence of the reading of a device which measures speed does not require corroboration, and may itself provide corroboration of the evidence of a witness [19].

Perhaps the most important point to make about the whole issue of corroboration and suspect witnesses is that, even though the requirements of law for corroboration have been reduced to virtually none, the presence or absence of corroboration may be very important as a factual matter when it comes to the weight of evidence. Any bench or judge will concede that evidence often enjoys far more weight when supported by other evidence than would otherwise be the case. Accordingly, the presence or absence of support makes an excellent subject for your closing speech, and should always be mentioned.

What kinds of witnesses should I call to give evidence?

At first, this may appear to be a somewhat strange question. It is intended, not to refer to the personal characteristics of a witness, or even to draw attention to the fact that there are good and bad witnesses, but to point out that some species of witness are often overlooked and excluded from consideration. It is deceptively easy to get into the habit of thinking that witnesses must necessarily be percipient witnesses, that is to say witnesses who perceived relevant facts and who are called to give direct evidence of what they perceived. This way of thinking omits reference to two valuable and underused species of witness, namely the expert witness and the character witness.

Expert witnesses   As long ago as 1782, Lord Mansfield said in *Folkes v Chadd* [20] that the opinion of scientific men, upon proven facts, might be given by men of science within their own science. It was a recognition of the plain truth that courts may be equipped to decide questions within the common experience of judges, jurors and magistrates, but are not equipped to deal with technical matters calling for specialised expertise. Experts are therefore permitted to state their opinion on such matters, on the basis of proven, admitted or even hypothetical facts, in order to assist the court in reaching a conclusion which it would be incapable of reaching properly unaided.

An expert is somebody who, in the context of the specialised area facing the court, knows what he or she is talking about and is therefore capable of rendering to the court the necessary advice. There are provisions for courts to obtain expert assistance, independently of the parties, but in most cases, expert witnesses are called by the parties. It is often, though erroneously, assumed that experts are an expensive luxury inappropriate to the magistrates' or the county court. Such is not the case. Since the only qualification to be an expert is to know what you are talking about, experts may be recruited in back-street garages as well as engineering departments of universities. Qualification by long experience is almost always just as persuasive as qualification on paper, and frequently more so. Experts qualified by experience are often inexpensive, often enthusiastic and often decisive. The court is concerned with actual expertise, and not with the means by which that expertise has been obtained. In *Silverlock* [21], a solicitor who had made a study of handwriting was permitted to give evidence as an expert in that field, notwithstanding his lack of formal qualification. Stories abound of cases won by witnesses with a lifetime's experience of nuts and bolts, over 'highly qualified' theoretical engineers.

It is certainly true that qualification in the relevant field is necessary. It is, in fact, a question of competence to give evidence, since with very limited exceptions, only experts are permitted to state their opinion rather than to give evidence of facts. You must, therefore, present evidence of the qualifications of the witness to the court and specifically invite the court to accept the witness as an expert, before leading the witness on to deal with substantive matters. This, however, is easily accomplished by asking the witness about paper qualifications or experience in the field, or preferably both. The modern practice is to permit a witness to testify as an expert, if he or she has any serious claim to do so. The weight of an expert's evidence is quite another matter, and depends on how far the expert can persuade the court that his or her opinion can be treated as reliable.

For these very reasons, you are entitled to cross-examine a witness tendered as an expert, before he or she testifies about any substantive matter, concerning the question of qualification, with a view to suggesting that the witness is not qualified to be an expert, and that the proposed evidence is therefore inadmissible from the witness tendered. This cross-examination should take place after the credentials of the witness have been presented in chief, and before substantive opinion evidence is given. It is proper and sometimes necessary to interrupt the evidence in chief at the right moment, and ask the court for leave to cross-examine, which should not be refused, since the cross-examination is relevant to competence as a witness and must be conducted at that stage. While the court will usually decide to hear the witness, such cross-examination is never wasted. It plants in the mind of the court some doubt as to the weight of the evidence to come, and enables you to begin your attack on the other side's expert evidence even before it is given.

In the next chapter, we shall consider expert evidence in more detail, dealing with the handling of expert witnesses and with the important rules of court calling for disclosure of expert reports.

Character witnesses   The evidence which may be given by character witnesses has been dealt with in Chapter 7. However, it is well worth noting again that such witnesses are a proper and sadly underused weapon available to an advocate representing a defendant of good or reformed character. The witness must, of course, know the defendant well enough to speak with some authority, and must himself be demonstrably credible and respectable. Always ask your client if such a person is available to speak for him. Ensure, of course, that your witness is familiar with the defendant's character including any previous convictions, especially if the defendant is a reformed character. Few things are worse than having your character witness learn for the first time in cross-examination that the defendant's record is not quite as unblemished as he believed and came to court to say.

Further reading

Murphy on Evidence, 6th ed., ch. 15 and 18; *Blackstone's Criminal Practice 1998*, F4–F5.

Notes

1. [1917] 1 KB 283.
2. (1924) 18 Cr App R 100.
3. [1991] RTR 309.
4. [1944] 2 All ER 311.
5. *Khan* (1986) 84 Cr App R 44; and see the Private International Law (Miscellaneous Provisions) Act 1995, ss. 5–8.
6. *Brasier* (1779) 1 Leach 199, 1 East PC 443.
7. [1977] 1 WLR 234.
8. [1996] QB 1.
9. *Memorandum of Good Practice on Video Recorded Interviews with Child Witnesses for Criminal Proceedings* (1992), para. 3.10.
10. *Bellamy* (1985) 82 Cr App R 223.
11. [1979] AC 474.
12. [1983] QB 25.
13. (1946) 31 Cr App R 146.
14. *Baskerville* [1916] 2 QB 658; *Davies* v *DPP* [1954] AC 378.
15. Criminal Justice Act 1988 s. 34(2) Criminal Justice and Public Order Act 1994, s. 32(1).
16. *Makanjuola* [1995] 1 WLR 1348.
17. *Spencer* [1987] AC 128; *Makanjuola* [1995] 1 WLR 1348.
18. *Brighty* v *Pearson* [1938] 4 All ER 127.
19. *Nicholas* v *Penny* [1950] 2 KB 466; *Swain* v *Gillett* [1974] RTR 446.
20. (1782) 3 Doug KB 157.
21. [1894] 2 QB 766.

Nine

Expert Evidence*

Introduction

Witnesses are called in a court of law to state the facts which they have observed and they are not allowed to give their opinion to the court on those facts. So, for example, a witness can say that a car was being driven on the wrong side of the road or at a speed of 60 miles per hour, but strictly speaking he is not allowed to say that in his opinion the driving that he saw was dangerous. Although often nobody bothers to take the point when a witness oversteps the mark and ventures his opinion it is still a basic rule of law that witnesses are not in court to give their views about the matters in issue. There is, however, a very important exception to this rule and that relates to the evidence of expert witnesses. A person who has acquired expertise in a specialised field either by learning and studying or by experience (or both) is entitled to state his opinion to the court because he has a knowledge and understanding of the specialised matters in question which the judge or magistrates cannot possibly hope to have. Therefore the court will allow him to give to them an 'informed opinion'.

The fact that expert witnesses may be qualified by experience, as well as formal education, should not be overlooked, especially when considering the selection of an expert for an action in the county court, in which the client's financial resources may be limited. Witnesses with a lifetime of experience are not infrequently more persuasive than those with extensive paper qualifications. In *Silverlock* [1], a solicitor who had made an extensive study of the science of comparing samples of handwriting was permitted to give expert evidence on that subject, notwithstanding his lack of formal training. And in *Oakley* [2], a police

---

* This chapter was originally written by David Barnard.

officer who had received training in accident investigation was allowed to give evidence in a prosecution for causing death by dangerous driving about the likely cause of an accident.

Expert evidence should be confined to subjects outside the normal experience of magistrates, judges and juries. Thus, questions of a person's intent or belief, or the reasonableness or otherwise of a person's actions, are usually matters which the bench or the judge can decide by using their experience of life to weigh the evidence. However, there will be cases where that experience is insufficient, for example, where the defendant's state of mind has been affected by mental illness, or where the reasonableness of a professional judgment is called into question in a medical or legal negligence case. In such cases, expert evidence is appropriate and necessary. In *Ward* [3], it was held that expert evidence may be given on the issue of the reliability of a confession, if the defendant, at the time of making the confession, suffered from a mental state so severe as to amount to a mental disorder.

Expert witnesses are not often called to give evidence orally in cases in magistrates' courts; instead their evidence is given usually in the form of witness statements which are not challenged (for example, fingerprint evidence or the evidence of blood/alcohol analysis). In county court actions, on the other hand, expert evidence is very frequently presented orally and is often challenged; indeed, in many cases, the principal area of dispute will lie in the conflicting opinions of expert witnesses. For example, the court may have to resolve differences between the opinions given by architects called to give evidence about what went wrong with a building or the court may have to decide between two expert engineers who have each attempted to explain why a motor-car engine has broken down. Because expert opinion is so important in county court actions the lawyer needs a very good understanding of the rules relating to such evidence and the techniques whereby it can be tested.

Preparation of expert evidence

When you have to consider your own expert's opinion you will be faced immediately with a problem which will never arise when you are dealing with the proofs of the other witnesses you are going to call. Those witnesses will speak about the facts — what was said before the contract was made, what manoeuvres were executed by the vehicles prior to the collision taking place — and you can apply your own common sense and knowledge in determining the value which is to be placed upon the accounts given by the different witnesses. In the same way, you will be able to rely upon your own experience of people and events to decide on the line of cross-examination you should take in dealing with the witnesses of fact called on the other side.

The position is altogether different when you are considering expert testimony. You are called upon to understand and decide the value of evidence on a subject of which you will have, at best, only a rudimentary knowledge; and you will be required to undertake the very difficult task of challenging evidence given on the other side by a person with years of experience in the field in question. This is obviously a formidable task.

The key to dealing successfully with expert evidence is *preparation*. The preparation starts when you first have the report of your own expert to hand. Whatever the subject-matter, whether it is a medical report, a surveyor's report, an engineer's report, whatever it may be, you must begin by making a very serious effort to understand your own expert's evidence. You should build up a library of useful reference books — a medical dictionary, a simple guide to house building and repairs, a book with good diagrams showing the workings of a motor car — such reference books (the simpler the better) can be indispensable.

Once you as the advocate have had a chance to form some idea of the points your expert is making in his report you may well feel that you need to see him in conference. If he is going to be called as a witness at the trial, you will not get very far unless you have had a chance to go over in detail with him the report which he has made.

When you see your expert in conference do not worry about knowing less of the subject than the expert does. No lawyer likes to confess ignorance (particularly in front of a client) but the advocate cannot afford to pretend to an expert witness an understanding that he or she does not possess. The only sensible technique is to start off by telling the expert quite frankly that you have no knowledge of this particular field — and neither will the judge who at the end of the day will have to decide the case. Your expert must therefore be prepared to teach you just so much of the subject as is necessary for you to understand the points that will be made in evidence. If you do not understand the explanation, make the expert go back over it again. Ask the expert to draw simple diagrams to explain to you the points that will be covered. This can be time consuming but in doing it you will not only be teaching yourself the essential matters you have to understand before you can conduct your case, you will also be working out how the expert's evidence can be presented in the most attractive and readily understood way when you arrive at court.

At some stage, assuming the case is going to be contested, you should receive copies of the expert evidence which your opponent proposes to adduce. The rules of court relating to this will be dealt with later, but it may be assumed as a basic principle that you are never going to allow the other side to put you in the position where you have to go into court in a contested case without seeing in advance the expert evidence against you. What do you do when you have obtained the report from the other side?

You are going to need the assistance of your own expert again. You could not possibly cross-examine the expert on the other side until you have had the advice of your own expert on this new report. So you must persuade your expert first to explain to you what is being said in the other side's report; then, ask for an explanation of why (if it be the case) your expert says the other expert is wrong. He may be wrong for a number of reasons: he may be acting on a version of the facts which you can prove is untrue; he may have omitted to notice some important point picked up by your expert; his opinion may be based on knowledge which is outdated. But, before you can even attempt to cross-examine, you will need to understand why it is that your expert has come to a different conclusion from the expert on the other side.

Be careful not to be overwhelmed by your own expert. It can be very easy to give up when an expert has lost you midway through an explanation of some technical matter. You must not do this because the chances are that if the expert has lost you, in due course, he will lose the judge too. Lastly, be prepared for the possibility that your expert is wrong; if he is wrong, it is best to discover this before costs are expended on a full-scale trial of the action; bear in mind that you are under a duty to your client to make sure that the expert evidence you have obtained will stand up in court.

In practice, expert evidence is usually exchanged well before the trial. Our court system is only able to cope with the volume of work which it has because most cases are settled before trial; often an important consideration in determining whether or not to advise your client to settle an action is the view which you as an advocate have formed upon the strength of the expert evidence. Sometimes, of course, it will be clear from the moment you read your own report that your case simply cannot proceed; more often it will not be until after an overall picture can be built up, by looking at the documentation revealed on discovery and the views of the experts on both sides, that you will be able to form a good idea of whether or not you are going to win at the end of the day, and whether or not you should settle and if so on what terms.

Therefore, both from the point of view of preparing your own case and as a means of deciding whether or not you should settle, you will need to see the other side's expert evidence. The next part of this chapter considers the law and the rules of court on this topic.

Disclosure of expert evidence before trial

The basic rule at common law is that you are *not* entitled to know your opponent's expert evidence before the trial takes place unless he is willing to disclose it to you. The reason for this is that expert evidence is covered by legal professional privilege [4]. Letters, conversations, any communications between a lay person and his solicitor for the purpose of obtaining legal advice are privileged: they cannot be revealed without the client's consent. In the same way, a proof of evidence or a letter from a witness to a solicitor is covered by professional privilege and for the purpose of such privilege it makes no difference whether that proof of evidence or letter comes from a lay witness or an expert witness. The rule of the law of evidence which underlies the whole practice concerning the exchange of experts' reports is this: you are entitled to refuse disclosure of expert evidence because it is privileged. This means that if you obtain an expert report which does not say what you were hoping to hear, then you are completely free to discard that opinion and try another expert to see if you can do better. There is no duty on you to disclose evidence which you do not propose to use in court. There is now, however, an important exception to this in cases involving the welfare of children. This is dealt with in Chapter 10.

On the other hand, when you have obtained a report which you decide to use at trial, then a different set of rules applies. The Civil Evidence Act 1972 expressly provides that the rule concerning privilege is not to be used as a way of concealing expert evidence until the trial; the Act provides for rules of court to be made to require each side to give notice to the other of the expert evidence they intend to call at the trial. CCR, Ord. 20, r. 27, requires that (unless all the parties agree or the judge gives special permission) no expert evidence can be given at the trial unless the party wishing to call that evidence has applied in advance to the district judge to determine whether there should be disclosure of the evidence and has complied with any order that the district judge has made.

This means that by the time of the pretrial review you should have made up your mind whether you are going to need expert evidence, and should have obtained that evidence and be in a position to decide whether or not you want to argue that there should not be disclosure.

The district judge is directed by CCR, Ord. 20, r. 28, to apply the High Court rules which may be found in full in the appendix to this book. RSC, Ord. 38, r. 37, provides that:

> Where in any cause or matter an application is made . . . in respect of oral expert evidence, then, unless the court considers that there are special reasons for not doing so, it shall direct that the substance of the evidence be disclosed in the form of a written report or reports to such other parties and within such period as the court may specify.

The rule does not specify what the court might properly regard as 'special reasons'. Under an older version of r. 37, there were defined special cases, in particular, those involving an allegation of medical negligence, in which disclosure was the exception, rather than the rule. But there are no longer any such defined special cases, and the courts now take the view that disclosure should be ordered in all cases, unless it would result in obvious unfairness.

It is likely that at the pre-trial review the district judge will order *mutual* disclosure of expert evidence. By that, he means you are bound to disclose your expert evidence to the other side when they tell you that they are ready to disclose their reports. This does not mean that you have to produce the reports of experts you have decided not to call; nor does it mean that you have to show the other side every letter from your own expert or every attendance note that you may have made; what you are required to do is to give the other side a written report fairly setting out the evidence which your expert will give at trial.

Usually, the court will order mutual disclosure at a given time [5], though in the interests of fairness, of preventing a party from being taken by surprise, or of the saving of costs at trial, there may be cases in which one party may be directed to disclose before the other. One such case might be where the defendant's expert cannot be expected to form any sensible opinion except by being asked to consider and comment on the plaintiff's expert reports [6].

Of course, it is one thing to have an order in your favour and it is another thing to see that your opponent complies with that order. What should you do if you have your report ready and are willing to exchange it but your opponent says he has not yet obtained a report? Sometimes the best advice is not to disclose; if you do disclose your report you may find that your opponent will then take it to an expert who will proceed to tear your expert's opinion into shreds. If you feel that this could happen, do not disclose your report but go back to the district judge and ask him to make an 'unless order', i.e., an order that unless the other side produce a report and disclose it within so many days they shall be debarred from calling expert evidence. This technique is a sensible one to employ in High Court litigation and in a substantial claim in the county court. However, there will be other cases where you may decide that it would be sensible to reveal your report even though the other side have not yet obtained a report themselves; it may be that on seeing your report the other side will give up and put forward sensible terms of compromise. This matter obviously requires careful judgment. What you should never allow is a situation in which you are going into court to face expert evidence which has not been disclosed to you.

There are rules governing the pre-trial disclosure of expert evidence in trials on indictment in the Crown Court, made pursuant to s. 81 of the Police and Criminal Evidence Act 1984 [7]. Provision for similar rules for the magistrates' court is made by s. 20(3) and (4) of the Criminal Procedure and Investigations Act 1996. At the time of writing no such rules have been promulgated. However, where the defence make a voluntary disclosure of the nature of the defence in a summary trial, pursuant to s. 6 of the Act, and that defence involves expert evidence, it would seem inevitable that the nature of that evidence should be disclosed to the prosecution. The subject of voluntary disclosure is dealt with in more detail in Chapters 6 and 13.

Admissibility of expert reports

Having disclosed your expert evidence, you will now be in a position at trial both to call oral expert evidence and put your expert reports in evidence. Expert reports are admissible in civil cases in the county court by virtue of the Civil Evidence Act 1995. As we saw in Chapter 3, s. 1(2)(a) of the Act defines hearsay as follows:

'hearsay' means a statement made otherwise than by a person while giving oral evidence in the proceedings which is tendered as evidence of the matters stated.

Section 13 of the Act defines 'statement' as meaning 'any representation of fact or opinion, however made'. Thus, expert reports are now admissible by virtue of s. 1 of the Act subject to any other applicable provisions.

It will, of course, be preferable, wherever possible, to have your expert give oral evidence, in addition to presenting his report, but it should be noted that if, for any reason, the expert is not available to give oral evidence at trial, his report may still be admitted, even if it may carry somewhat less weight because he is not available for cross-examination.

In criminal cases, expert reports were not admissible until the coming into effect of s. 30 of the Criminal Justice Act 1988. The report is admissible as of right if the expert also attends to give oral evidence. But if it is not proposed to call the expert to give oral evidence then the report may not be admitted without leave of the court. Section 30(3) sets out the matters which the court is to take into account in deciding whether or not to give leave. These include the contents of the report, the reasons why the expert is not being called and the risk of unfairness to the defendant. The section defines an expert report in the same way as the Civil Evidence Act 1972. In addressing the court on this point for the defence, it is proper to point out the dangers of admitting evidence that cannot be tested by cross-examination, the fact that the evidence is challenged, and any unsatisfactory reason for not bringing the expert to court. In many cases, of course, for example, those involving blood tests in excess-alcohol cases, the expert's evidence may well not be in dispute, so that there will be no objection to the admission of his expert report.

Presentation of expert evidence at trial

How do you deal with your own expert when you arrive at court? First, of course, have the original of his report ready for the judge and ask the judge to read this immediately before your expert is called to give evidence. Then, remembering the things you did not understand when you first read the report, ask your expert to go over those points.

You must work out an acceptable formula to conceal from the judge the fact that you are concerned he may not have understood some of the points in the report. Every advocate has to determine such a formula for himself; but what is important is that you should make sure that all the points which are in any way obscure are cleared up before your expert is tendered for cross-examination. Bear in mind that, unlike other witnesses, an expert may not only state his opinion, but may explain and justify that opinion by reference to the exhibits, results of tests, analyses or experiments, or authoritative published works.

There are many other useful devices for presenting the evidence of an expert, which cannot be employed with a lay witness. For example, the expert may refer to charts, diagrams or models, or may be asked hypothetical questions in order to illustrate his opinion. A hypothetical question is one which invites the expert to assume certain facts to be true (facts, of course, which you hope to prove by other evidence) and to express an opinion based on that assumption. In cross-examination, of course, other assumed facts may be presented to the witness, causing him to concede that his opinion would be different, if the underlying facts were to differ from those he was asked to assume in chief. Since all tribunals find expert evidence much easier to follow when there is some visual aid to look at or even to hold, it is well worth planning the preparation and use of such aids with your expert. Examples might include an enlarged diagram of the working of the internal combustion engine, or of a part of the human anatomy, or a photograph of the *locus in quo*. The only limit is the imagination of the advocate or the expert. The old adage that a picture is worth a thousand words is as true in the court room as anywhere else.

When you come to cross-examine you should have in front of you a list of questions prepared by your expert and you should understand the point of each of those questions. Expert witnesses usually charge considerable fees and you are entitled to insist that they remain in court for all the relevant evidence including the evidence of the expert on the other side. It may well be that in hearing the evidence of the lay witnesses your expert will decide that he has to qualify or change his opinion. It may also be that in hearing the testimony given by the expert on the other side he will want to alter or re-emphasise certain points in his own evidence. You are entitled to expect your expert to be on hand throughout all those parts of the trial where his presence would be helpful. It is normally a false economy to call the expert for half an hour and then let him depart.

Summary

To sum up the points in this chapter, there are three essential points which you need to remember if you are to succeed in putting forward expert evidence. First, preparation — you must be willing to spend three or even four times as long in preparing expert evidence as you would in proofing witnesses who are merely speaking about the facts. Secondly, candour — you must be frank with your expert so that he understands your own ignorance of the subject and explains it to you with such clarity that before you go into court you fully understand the points that he is making; if you do not understand the evidence he is going to give, there is little chance that you will be able to present your case properly. Lastly, a knowledge of the rules — the advocate must know what the rules say and be able to use them to his client's advantage; in the field of expert evidence this means that the advocate must be able to use the rules so as to prevent himself from being taken in any way by surprise.

Further reading

Murphy on Evidence, 6th ed., ch. 11; *Blackstone's Criminal Practice 1998*, F10.

Notes

1. [1894] 2 QB 766.
2. (1979) 70 Cr App R 7.
3. [1993] 1 WLR 619.
4. *Causton* v *Mann Egerton (Johnsons) Ltd* [1974] 1 WLR 162.
5. *Practice Direction (Evidence: Expert)* [1974] 1 WLR 904.
6. *Kirkup* v *British Rail Engineering Ltd* [1983] 1 WLR 190, affirmed [1983] 1 WLR 1165.
7. See the Crown Court (Advance Notice of Expert Evidence) Rules 1987; *Blackstone's Criminal Practice 1998*, D12.22.

Ten

Privileges

Introduction

A privilege is a rule of law which permits a person to refuse to disclose certain kinds of confidential information, even though that information, if disclosed, might be relevant to some proceedings and might be admissible and of significant weight in those proceedings. Because the general policy of the law favours disclosure, so as to enable courts and tribunals to receive and act on the fullest possible information, rules of privilege are quite narrow and restrictively interpreted. English law recognises few privileges by comparison to some other jurisdictions, and those which are recognised are, from time to time, narrowed even more by the courts.

Nonetheless the law relating to privileges and to the related subject of evidence excluded by considerations of public policy is complex and, for the most part, outside the scope of this work. Fortunately, the more complicated issues, especially those concerned with public policy, arise very rarely in the magistrates' and county courts, and, when they do arise, there will be ample time to refer to more detailed works (such as the further reading suggested at the end of this chapter). This chapter will deal very briefly with the most important aspects of legal professional privilege, the privilege against self-incrimination, and the privilege in without-prejudice communications. These are the rules most likely to be encountered in everyday practice.

General principles

There are several principles applicable to privileges generally which should be mentioned before embarking on the individual privileges.

Waiver The most important of these is that privileges must be jealously guarded, and claimed on behalf of the person entitled to them. Privilege is only a protection against the compelled disclosure of information. A person entitled to claim a privilege is also entitled to disclose the information voluntarily. When he does so, the person is said to waive the privilege. Not infrequently, it is in the holder's best interests to waive a privilege, for example, because he himself wishes to rely on evidence contained in the privileged information, or because his cause of action necessarily involves a waiver [1], for example, where he sues a former solicitor for negligence arising from the solicitor's handling of a transaction during which privileged communications were made.

The decision whether or not to waive a privilege is one which may be made only by the holder of the privilege, having regard to the interests of the holder [2]. But the question of waiver is of vital interest to every legal adviser, because, as a matter of practical reality, the holder must rely on his lawyer's advice in making this crucial decision. It is an essential part of every lawyer's duty to consider this issue, to advise the holder of the privilege on it, and to take all necessary steps to claim and defend the privilege, if the decision to claim is made. It is vital to understand that, once a voluntary decision is made to waive a privilege, it is waived forever, regardless of any subsequent regret. If a deliberate disclosure of privileged information is made, it is irrelevant whether or not the decision to do so was advisable, or even whether or not it was intended [3]. Once privileged information is disclosed, it may be used as evidence by any party. Moreover, the waiver extends not only to the information actually disclosed, but to any other information which is factually linked to it. In other words, the court may regard as waived the totality of the information which is logically part of the same transaction, for example, other letters which form part of the same correspondence, or other reports which relate to the same subject matter. Unless it can be shown that the further information is clearly severable, much information may be included in the waiver which was not intended to be included [4].

Strictly, privilege applies only to an original communication or document, and there is no objection to a party using other evidence of the same information. It has been suggested, but is far from being conclusively established, that this does not apply where such other evidence has been obtained by means of an obvious error on the part of the privilege holder or his advisers [5] or by means of some deception or ruse which the court should not countenance [6]. But, except in these cases, the use of evidence obtained other than by using the original privileged information is permitted. At the same time, a party may claim injunctive relief to have restored to him privileged documents in the hands of another party who is not entitled to them [7]. This subject is extremely complicated, and reference should be made to the further reading materials suggested at the end of this chapter.

The lawyer's duty to claim a privilege on behalf of the holder may arise in a number of different contexts. In court, it arises whenever the holder is asked a question the truthful answer to which would necessarily result in the disclosure of privileged information. If the holder is not the client of any of the lawyers appearing in the proceedings, because he is simply a witness, the court should investigate the issue of privilege of its own motion, and, if appropriate, advise the holder of his right not to answer the question. It is the duty of the advocates to mention the matter to the court if it does not do so, especially in the magistrates' court in which a lay bench may not appreciate the issue. The duty to claim privilege also arises whenever an opposing party seeks to discover privileged material, for example, by making a request for disclosure of documents, witness statements or expert reports, which remain privileged until a decision is taken to use them for the purposes of trial. All material which is potentially privileged should be kept in separate files, so that it can be readily identified, and produced for the inspection of the court in the event of a dispute.

Consequences of successful claim of privilege   Where privilege is successfully claimed, the result is that the privileged material may not be used in evidence by any party. The holder of the privilege cannot be compelled to answer any question which might result in the disclosure of privileged information, or to produce any privileged documents. Furthermore, no comment may be made on the fact that the privilege is claimed, so that no adverse inference may be drawn against the holder of the privilege simply because he claims it [8]. Any other position would render the privilege of little effect. As we saw in Chapter 6, however, this principle no longer applies to the privilege against self-incrimination to the extent that adverse inferences may be drawn as to the offence charged from the defendant's silence by virtue of ss. 34 to 37 of the Criminal Justice and Public Order Act 1994.

Legal professional privilege

The term legal professional privilege is used to describe two different, though closely related rules. The first is that all confidential communications passing between legal adviser and client, or between legal advisers, are privileged. The second is that all materials prepared for the dominant purpose of being used in litigation are privileged, which may include witness statements and communications with and reports prepared by experts. In the case of witness statements and expert reports, a decision to use these documents for the purposes of trial necessarily requires a waiver of the privilege, but the privilege applies unless that decision is made. The second rule has, however, been the subject of some erosion by the courts. In the case of both rules, it is irrelevant whether the legal adviser is a solicitor or counsel, an employed lawyer, or a foreign lawyer, whether any third parties such as experts are in England or elsewhere, and whether relevant litigation has been or is to be commenced in England or elsewhere [9].

Communications between lawyer and client   This privilege is specific to the relationship between lawyer and client, in the sense that communications, however confidential, between a client and other professional advisers, such as doctors, psychologists, clergymen, accountants or financial advisers, or between a person and that person's spouse or other family members, enjoy no privilege [10], though most courts will respect such confidences unless to do so would conflict with the need to permit evidence to be adduced. This may obviously produce difficulties in the case of professional advisers who are legally qualified but who serve in some business capacity within a company, or who offer other services such as tax or investment advice. The only advice that can be given is to segregate the legal representation functions of such a person from his business functions as far as possible, but obviously, this is not always feasible. The privilege extends to instructions given during an initial consultation the purpose of which is to explore the possibility of representation, even if no representation results from it. It is irrelevant whether any, and if so what fee is paid for the representation.

The lawyer–client communication privilege appears to be absolute, and without limitation of time. This was the view of the House of Lords in *Derby Magistrates' Court, ex parte B* [11], in which it was held that the privilege might be maintained despite the competing interests of any other party in using the privileged information, even (as in the case before the House) where the information might have assisted in the defence of a person accused of murder. Lord Taylor of Gosforth CJ said that this was 'in the wider interests of all those hereafter who might otherwise be deterred from telling the whole truth to their solicitors'.

Communications with third parties   This privilege applies only where the dominant purpose of the communication is actual or contemplated litigation. If the communication is made at a time when no litigation is contemplated, the privilege does not apply, even though the communication may later become relevant to litigation which is then contemplated or in being [12]. The communication need not have been made for the sole purpose of the litigation, but that must have been the dominant purpose. Thus, in *Waugh* v *British Railways Board* [13], where an internal report submitted to the Board following a fatal accident was intended for use during the resulting litigation, but had an equally important purpose in ensuring future safety, it was held that no privilege applied to it.

An important exception to the third-party litigation privilege (but not, it must be emphasised, to the lawyer–client privilege) has been created in cases concerning the welfare of children. In *Re L (A Minor) (Police Investigation: Privilege)* [14], a majority of the House of Lords held that, in proceedings for a care order brought under the Children Act 1989, no privilege prevented the compelled disclosure of the report of a medical expert which dealt with how a child came to ingest methadone while under the care of its mother, who was admittedly a drug addict. The report had been obtained by the mother under leave of the court, and she claimed that it was privileged as pertaining to the litigation. But the majority held that (unlike the lawyer–client privilege) the third-party litigation privilege did not apply to 'essentially non-adversarial' proceedings involving the welfare of children. Lord Jauncey based his view in part on the proposition that, unlike a legal adviser, a third-party expert was compellable to give his opinion on the merits of the case. Although the House did not decide the point, it would seem that this principle would apply to any proceedings in which the welfare of a child is at issue, and not merely to proceedings brought under the 1989 Act. The House also seemed receptive to, but did not adopt a suggestion made in earlier cases [15] that, not only does the litigation third-party privilege not apply to a report made for the purpose of such proceedings, but a party has a positive duty to disclose such a report even though it may be adverse to his case.

Privilege does not protect evidence Legal professional privilege protects a party against the compelled disclosure of communications, but does not, of course, immunise the party against having to disclose items of evidence which are not created within the scope of the lawyer–client relationship, or for the purpose of litigation [16]. To take an obvious example, if a defendant commits a robbery, and, in order to escape detection, rushes into his solicitor's office to hand him the gun used in the robbery, the gun is obviously not privileged. The defendant himself could not object to the seizure of the gun, and cannot better the position by putting it into the hands of his solicitor. (This is not to mention the legal and ethical problems the solicitor would create for himself by attempting to resist the seizure.) But even if the evidence is not evidence of crime, the same principle would apply. Any documents or other pre-existing evidence which a client may give to his solicitor for the purposes of obtaining legal advice or representation can be no more privileged in the solicitor's hands than in the client's hands.

No privilege for communications in furtherance of crime or fraud On a related subject, the privilege does not apply where the communication sought to be protected is one designed by the client to further a crime or fraud. It is irrelevant whether the lawyer is an accomplice of the client in the crime or fraud, or is innocent of the client's intentions [17]. There must be at least a *prima facie* case of furtherance of the crime or fraud before the court overrules the privilege on this ground, but this may appear from the allegedly privileged documents themselves [18]. But if the evidence shows, not a crime or fraud, but merely some civil wrong of a non-fraudulent nature, the privilege must be maintained — the rule is simply one of policy preventing the use of privilege as a front for, or to avoid detection of criminal activity. By virtue of a recent extension of this principle, it now seems that the criminal intent which defeats the privilege may also be that of a third party [19] or even the lawyer [20].

'Items subject to legal privilege' are expressly excluded from seizure pursuant to a search warrant issued under s. 8 of the Police and Criminal Evidence Act 1984. Such items are defined by s. 10 of the Act in accordance with the common law principles described above, and do not include 'items held with the intention of furthering a criminal purpose' (s. 10(2)) [21]. This has occasioned great difficulty for solicitors whose offices are visited by police officers armed with a search warrant. Steps must be taken to preserve material which is privileged, but if material is wrongly withheld, charges of obstruction may result. The situation is fraught with legal danger for the client and with legal and professional danger for the solicitor. It is suggested that, in this mercifully rare situation, the solicitor must immediately obtain independent legal advice and make an application to the Crown Court without delay to resolve the situation. Items subject to legal privilege are not subject to the 'special procedure' established by sch. 1 to the Act, so that an application to the Crown Court *inter partes* is required [22].

Privilege against self-incrimination

The privilege against self-incrimination enables a person to refuse to provide evidence against himself in the form of a confession by answering questions put to him. With respect to offences with which a person is charged, we saw in Chapter 6 that that person enjoys a right to remain silent at every stage of the investigation or proceedings, but that if he chooses to exercise that right, an adverse inference may be drawn against him under ss. 34 to 37 of the Criminal Justice and Public Order Act 1994. But the privilege against self-incrimination applies equally to offences with which that person might be charged in the future. The privilege applies to a question put to a witness in any court or tribunal before which evidence is given under oath. The privilege permits him to refuse to answer any question if the answer would, in the opinion of the court, have a tendency to expose him to any criminal charge, criminal forfeiture or penalty, if the court regards it as likely that proceedings would be commenced against him.

The privilege does not apply where a statute requires that certain questions be answered, and substitutes an alternative form of protection, namely a provision that the answers shall not be used as evidence in subsequent criminal proceedings. There are various statutory provisions of this kind, often connected with the setting up of a special statutory tribunal to investigate some specific matter [23]. In these cases, the extent of the protection afforded to the witness is governed by the statute, although the witness may still claim the privilege if the questions put exceed the scope of those permitted by the statute [24].

It seems also that a civil court may substitute an alternative form of protection by making an order that answers given in proceedings before it shall not be used in evidence in subsequent criminal proceedings. The law on this point, however, is very far from being settled. In *AT & T Istel Ltd* v *Tully* [25] both Lord Templeman and Lord Griffiths strongly expressed the view that the privilege against self-incrimination should not be used to prevent the operation of orders for discovery made in civil cases, for example, orders permitting the search of premises to discover evidence of copyright infringement (which may technically lead to prosecution, though such prosecutions are extremely rare). The judge at first instance in this case had made an order protecting the defendants against the use of any discovered evidence in subsequent criminal proceedings, and had invited the Crown Prosecution Service to intervene to contest this order (which the CPS declined to do). The House of Lords recognised that any such restriction of the privilege would require a statutory change in the law, but the practice of making such orders seems to be becoming more common. It seems, strictly, that the CPS would not be bound by the order, but it is to be hoped that a criminal court would exercise its inherent power to prevent oppressive prosecutions if it were sought to make use of the evidence in breach of the order of the civil court [26].

Before permitting the witness to refuse to answer a question, the court must be satisfied (a) that the answer would tend to expose him to criminal prosecution, and (b) that there is a real risk that criminal proceedings would be instituted as a matter of practical reality. It may well be necessary for the court to sit *in camera* to consider these matters. The court may take into account the rarity of certain kinds of prosecution (for example those for copyright infringement, which is now regarded as an essentially civil matter), the lapse of time since the commission of an apparent offence, or the fact that any offence disclosed may appear to be trivial. But these factors are not determinative. It cannot be assumed that forbearance to commence proceedings is attributable to lack of concern on the part of the prosecuting authority; it may simply be that there has not, thus far, been sufficient evidence to justify proceedings, and the evidence provided by the answer may change that situation [27]. But the court may require an answer if it seems clear that the witness has already compromised his position by answering questions put to him by the police or making some public statement, so that any answer given to the court will not make matters appreciably worse [28].

Section 14(1) of the Civil Evidence Act 1968 provides that, in civil proceedings (a) the privilege against self-incrimination applies also to questions which, if answered, would tend to expose the spouse of the witness to criminal proceedings, and (b) the privilege applies only to exposure to criminal proceedings under the law of any part of the United Kingdom (i.e., including the law of the European Community, but excluding foreign law). The law on these points at common law, which would apply in criminal cases, is unclear, but it seems likely that the same position would now be adopted.

If a witness is wrongly compelled to answer a question in violation of the privilege against self-incrimination, his answer may not be used against him in subsequent criminal proceedings [29].

Without-prejudice communications

The law has an obvious interest in promoting the settlement of civil cases. But a willingness to negotiate and discuss terms of settlement may be regarded as a sign of weakness, so it is essential to provide some protection against the use in evidence of statements made for the purpose of negotiation. The rule is, therefore, that communications made 'without prejudice' are inadmissible in evidence on the issue of liability or the weakness or invalidity of a claim. In *Rush and Tompkins Ltd* v *Greater London Council* [30] the House of Lords reaffirmed that the rule applies to 'all negotiations genuinely aimed at settlement, whether oral or in writing'. Lord Griffiths pointed out the desirability of heading any written communication with the words 'without prejudice', but the rule does not require this, and any communications which clearly fall into this category are protected against use in evidence on liability issues. This would include not only offers of settlement *per se*, but any counter-offers and communications necessary to initiate or continue negotiations [31].

However, without prejudice communications may be admissible on issues unrelated to liability, for example, the question of costs in the light of an unreasonable refusal to settle, or, of course, proceedings brought to enforce a settlement agreement. Whenever possible, a party should protect his position as to costs by making a payment into court. But, where this procedure is not available, the court may take into account a written offer expressed to be 'without prejudice except as to costs' in deciding what order as to costs should be made [32].

Further reading

Murphy on Evidence, 6th ed., ch. 13 and 14; *Blackstone's Criminal Practice 1998*, F9.

Notes

1. *Kershaw* v *Whelan* [1996] 1 WLR 358.
2. *Kinglake* (1870) 22 LT 335.
3. *Re L (A Minor) (Police Investigation: Privilege* [1997] AC 16; *Noel* [1914] 3 KB 848.
4. *Great Atlantic Insurance Co.* v *Home Insurance Co.* [1981] 1 WLR 529; *General Accident Fire and Life Assurance Corporation Ltd* v *Tanter* [1984] 1 WLR 100; *Churton* v *Frewen* (1865) 2 Drew & Sm 390.
5. *English and American Insurance Co.* v *Herbert Smith & Co.* (1987) 137 NLJ 148.
6. *ITC Film Distributors Ltd* v *Video Exchange Ltd* [1982] Ch 436.
7. *Guinness Peat Properties Ltd* v *Fitzroy Robinson Partnership* [1987] 1 WLR 1027; *Goddard* v *Nationwide Building Society* [1987] QB 670; *Lord Ashburton* v *Pape* [1913] 2 Ch 469; *Calcraft* v *Guest* [1889] 1 QB 759; though not in an attempt to restrain a criminal prosecution (*Butler* v *Board of Trade* [1971] Ch 680).
8. *Wentworth* v *Lloyd* (1864) 10 HL Cas 589.
9. *Re Duncan* [1968] P 306.
10. *Attorney-General* v *Mulholland* [1963] 2 QB 477; *K (T.D.)* (1992) 97 Cr App R 342; *Re D (Minors) (Conciliation: Disclosure of Information)* [1993] Fam 231. As to communications between journalists and their sources, see s. 10 of the Contempt of Court Act 1981. As to patent agents and similar representatives, see s. 280 of the Copyright, Designs and Patents Act 1988.
11. [1996] AC 487.
12. *Wheeler* v *Le Marchant* (1881) 17 ChD 675.
13. [1980] AC 521.
14. [1997] AC 16. See also *Oxfordshire County Council* v *M* [1994] Fam 151; *Essex County Council* v *R* [1994] Fam 167.
15. *Essex County Council* v *R* [1994] Fam 167, per Thorpe J; *Re D.H. (A Minor) (Child Abuse)* [1994] 1 FLR 679, per Wall J.
16. *Peterborough Justices, ex parte Hicks* [1977] 1 WLR 1371; *King* [1983] 1 WLR 411.

17.   *Jones* (1846) 1 Den 166; *Cox* (1884) 14 QBD 153.
18.   *Governor of Pentonville Prison, ex parte Osman* [1990] 1 WLR 277, 309; *O'Rourke* v *Darbishire* [1920] AC 581.
19.   *Central Criminal Court, ex parte Francis and Francis* [1989] AC 346.
20.   *Leeds Magistrates' Court, ex parte Dumbleton* [1993] Crim LR 866.
21.   *Central Criminal Court, ex parte Francis and Francis* [1989] AC 346; *Snaresbrook Crown Court, ex parte DPP* [1988] QB 532.
22.   *Guildhall Magistrates' Court, ex parte Primlaks Holdings Co. (Panama) Inc.* [1990] 1 QB 261.
23.   Commonly encountered examples are Theft Act 1968, s. 31; Supreme Court Act 1981, s. 72; Children Act 1989, s. 98; Criminal Justice Act 1987, s. 2. See also *Re G (A Minor) (Social Worker: Disclosure)* [1996] 1 WLR 1407.
24.   *Commissioners of Customs & Excise* v *Harz* [1967] 1 AC 760.
25.   [1993] AC 45.
26.   See also *Re O (Restraint Order: Disclosure of Assets)* [1991] 2 QB 520.
27.   *Rio Tinto Zinc Corporation* v *Westinghouse Electric Corporation* [1978] AC 547.
28.   *Khan* v *Khan* [1982] 1 WLR 513.
29.   *Garbett* (1847) 1 Den 236.
30.   [1989] AC 1280.
31.   South Shropshire District Council v *Amos* [1986] 1 WLR 1271; *Cheddar Valley Engineering Ltd* v *Chaddlewood Homes Ltd* [1992] 1 WLR 820.
32.   See RSC, Ord. 22, r. 14.

Eleven

Presentation of Evidence at Trial

Introduction

This chapter is concerned with the rules of evidence relating to the examination of witnesses and the introduction of evidence at trial. Every witness called is subject to examination by the party calling him, all other parties and the court. The advocate must, therefore, be familiar with the rules governing examination-in-chief, cross-examination, re-examination and examination by the court.

In civil cases, the parties and any witnesses may remain in court throughout the trial, unless otherwise ordered by the judge on the application of any party [1]. Unless there is a serious basis for suspecting that evidence on the other side may be dishonest, it is generally best not to invite the judge to exclude witnesses, since your own witnesses will also be excluded. In criminal cases, on the other hand, with the exception of the defendant and any expert witnesses, any witness waiting to give evidence must remain outside court until called. A bench will almost certainly attach less weight to the evidence of a witness who has been in court listening to the evidence before being called, because of the possibility that his evidence has been tailored to what he has heard. After giving evidence, witnesses must remain in court for the duration of the trial, unless released by the court. Unless there is a substantial likelihood that the witness may be recalled, it is proper and kind to ask that he be released.

Examination-in-chief is the process whereby a party calling a witness seeks to elicit from that witness facts favourable to his case. Examination-in-chief must be conducted without leading questions, and subject to a number of important rules of evidence, which will be considered shortly.

Any witness called is liable to be cross-examined by each other's party. In a criminal trial, the witness is cross-examined by the defendants in the order in which they are named in the charge or charges, and lastly, in the case of a defendant or defence witness, by the prosecution.

Cross-examination has two purposes, the first being to challenge the witness's evidence in chief, in all respects in which it does not correspond with the cross-examiner's instructions, and the second being to elicit or further emphasise facts favourable to the cross-examiner which were either not referred to or insufficiently emphasised in chief. The second purpose suggests, correctly, that a witness is liable to cross-examination once called, even if he has given no evidence in chief, as witness the convenient practice of simply tendering corroborative police officers for cross-examination. Questions may be asked in cross-examination, not only to challenge the substance of the evidence in chief directly, but also to attack the credit of the witness by showing that he is lying, exaggerating, had insufficient opportunity to observe the events about which he is giving evidence, or that his recollection is unsatisfactory. Except in the case of a criminal defendant, a witness may also be discredited directly by cross-examination about his previous bad character.

Re-examination, a much neglected art, is the process whereby a party who has called a witness may seek to explain or clarify any evidence given during cross-examination, which appears to be damaging or unfavourable on the facts or in terms of the witness's credit. Questions in re-examination must be confined to matters raised during cross-examination. But the cross-examiner should be aware that, if a matter is raised during cross-examination, it may be fully explored in re-examination. The cross-examination will have opened the subject up for exploration, even if the evidence would have been inadmissible had the re-examiner tried to introduce it in chief.

The judge or bench (acting through the chairman or clerk) may put questions to a witness, in order to clarify any matter which is unclear to them. Courts vary a great deal in the number of questions they ask. Some will even interrupt an advocate to ask them. Disconcerting as this may be, it is inadvisable to object, unless the witness is your client and the interruptions are making examination of him practically impossible to conduct, or the questions seem to be having the effect of harassing, intimidating or upsetting your client. This is relatively unusual, but where it occurs, you must explain to the court the difficulties which the interruptions are causing for you or your client, and politely suggest that the court defer its questions until the end of your client's evidence.

It is proper and advisable to ask leave to put further questions arising from any answers given in response to the court.

We now proceed to examine in more detail a number of important rules of evidence concerning examination-in-chief, cross-examination and re-examination.

Examination-in-chief

Leading questions The use of leading questions is improper in examination-in-chief and in re-examination, and evidence elicited by means of leading questions, while not inadmissible, is of very slight weight [2]. This basic rule is easy to state, but far from easy to apply. The story is told of counsel who, when representing a client charged with larceny (it is quite an old story) of a pig, placed his client in the witness-box, and asked him: 'Mr D, is it right that you were walking down the road, when you found the pig, the subject of this indictment?' Counsel for the prosecution was ungracious enough to object to this as a leading question, and the judge ordered it to be rephrased. After some thought, counsel asked his client: 'Mr D, by what means were you proceeding down the road, when you found the pig?'

Up to a point, all the characters involved in the story were correct. Counsel for the prosecution was correct in his objection that the question was leading, and the judge was correct to rule that it must be rephrased. Counsel for the defendant correctly identified one of the two areas in which his question was leading. His rephrasing was partially successful, in that it offered the witness a free hand to describe his method of progress along the road. This, however, did nothing to legitimate the form of the question, insofar as it related to the far more important issue of how the defendant had come by the pig. In this respect, the question was not improved at all.

What was counsel's error in posing these questions? It was that they tended to put words into the witness's mouth, or to suggest directly to the witness the evidence that counsel expected to receive. To present evidence by means of a series of leading questions is to do no more than use the vocal cords of the witness to make a prepared speech to the court, whereas the court is concerned to hear the evidence in the words of the witness, not of the advocate. In the example given, the witness was being invited merely to assent to counsel's statement of how he came by the pig.

It is not easy to avoid leading questions, and experience, including time spent listening to how other advocates bring out evidence without them, is the best teacher. As a general guide, the 'two-for-one rule' is useful. This rule draws attention to the fact that leading questions are defective primarily because they are too specifically worded. To avoid this, ask two questions instead of one, to get at the same fact. The first question takes a step back from the desired result, and will be phrased in general terms. You will ask whether something happened, whether the witness went somewhere, or the like, inviting a yes-or-no answer. Having got the answer to that, your second question will invite the specific detail implied in the answer to the first question, but still without actually putting the answer into the witness's mouth. Using the two-for-one rule, let us see how counsel should have elicited the fact that his client's possession of the pig was innocent. The examination-in-chief might proceed as follows:

Q   Mr D, did there come a time on the day in question when you went out?
A   Yes.
Q   Where did you go?
A   I walked down Lover's Lane.
Q   While you were in Lover's Lane, did anything come to your attention?
A   Yes.
Q   What was that?
A   I saw a pig coming towards me in the middle of the road.
Q   As a result of seeing the pig, did you do anything?
A   Yes.
Q   What did you do?
A   I got hold of the pig and began to walk along the road with it, so that I could return it to a field.
Q   At that time, was any other person on the scene?
A   Not at that time. But a minute or so later, a policeman came and accused me of stealing the pig.

Notice that counsel has asked two questions rather than one, to establish where the defendant went, what he did, and how he came by the pig. The court has now heard the evidence in the language of the witness, yet counsel retained control throughout by leaving the witness in no doubt of the answer which should be given. This is the essence of good examination-in-chief.

For reasons of practical convenience, leading questions in chief are permitted in the following limited circumstances, because there can be no objection to them:

(a)   On purely preliminary matters not directly related to the facts in issue. Usually, but not invariably, such matters as the witness's name, address and occupation would fall under this head.

(b)   On any matters not in dispute.

(c)   Where a witness is going to deal with a fact which has already been established by other evidence, he may be asked directly about that fact.

(d)   In any case where all advocates in the case agree that leading questions shall be permitted in certain areas. This is a helpful practice, which saves time and facilitates the examination-in-chief, though care must be taken to define the areas in which leading is to be permitted, and you should not hesitate to object if leading questions are asked on other subjects not covered by the agreement.

(e)   Where leave has been granted to treat a witness as hostile, in which case the examination-in-chief partakes of the nature of cross-examination. This topic is dealt with later in this chapter.

Memory-refreshing documents   In criminal cases, it is a common sight to see a police officer, who has just been sworn, reach into his pocket and produce a notebook, to which he asks to refer, in order to refresh his memory while giving evidence. Almost always, the court agrees, and the officer refers to, or even reads from, the notebook while giving evidence. This is a perfectly proper procedure, but not because it is a criminal case, or because the witness happens to be a police officer, or because the document happens to be a notebook.

In civil and criminal cases alike, any witness may, with leave of the court, refresh his memory while giving evidence, by reference to any document which was made or verified by the witness, contemporaneously with the events to which it relates. It is important to note that the requirements of contemporaneous making or verification, which will be examined below, apply only where the reference is made in the witness-box and while giving evidence. A witness may look at any material outside court, for the purpose of refreshing his memory [3], and it is usually good practice to show your witness a copy of his proof of evidence or statement before he goes into court, so that the giving of evidence is not reduced to a test of memory. Even though the witness would not be permitted to refer to such non-contemporaneous documents while in the witness-box, there is absolutely no objection to his doing so before giving evidence.

Once the witness steps into the box, the rules come into play. The first rule is that the document must have been made or verified by the witness. The best type of document is one, which, like the police officer's notebook, was made for the express purpose of later reference. But this is not a requirement. Literally any document, however made, will suffice, for example, the cigarette packet on which the witness scrawled the number of the car. The witness need not even have made the document personally, provided that he verified it, that is to say that he either saw it being made, read it or even had it read to him soon enough after another had made it to be 'contemporaneous', and in either case, that he checked its contents at that time and acknowledged them to be accurate. Hence the practice whereby a police officer makes a note reflecting the joint recollection of himself and his colleague, while the colleague verifies the note, and both thereafter refer to it while giving evidence.

The second rule is that the making or verification of the document must have been 'contemporaneous' with the events to which the document refers. The word 'contemporaneous' cannot, of course, be construed literally. Although a literally contemporaneous note can sometimes be made, for example, where a record is made of an interview as it proceeds, many events leave no leisure for the making of notes as they actually occur. The rule is, therefore, that the note must have been made at the first practicable opportunity, and while the events were fresh in the mind of the witness. This is a matter of fact and degree in every case, and there is no set time beyond which a document is no longer contemporaneous. The purpose of the requirement is to confine reference to presumptively accurate records, and any unexplained delay in making a note is to be regarded with some suspicion. In very exceptional cases, even two weeks has been held to be 'contemporaneous', but in the absence of a good explanation for the delay, even a few hours may be fatal.

Although in many cases, defence advocates allow the officer's request to go unchallenged, it is a matter for the court to be satisfied that a reference in the witness-box is proper. A prosecutor should in every case ask preliminary questions of the witness to establish whether the document falls within the rules, and these should not be put in the leading form all too often heard, such as 'Were the events fresh in your mind when you made the note?' A defence advocate can and should object both to a failure to lay a foundation for the note, and to any attempt to lead in the foundational questions. The defence may cross-examine the witness solely on the issue of whether reference to the document is proper before any evidence in chief is given. Although in almost every case, the witness will be allowed to refresh his memory — rightly so, since the giving of evidence should be a test of honesty and accuracy, rather than of memory — your cross-examination is far from pointless. You will, if you wish, get an early look at the document. And if the contemporaneity of the document is marginal, you will have cast doubt on the witness's evidence before it is even given. This doubt will increase if it transpires that the witness has no or little independent recollection of the events, and is relying entirely or substantially on the document. You will then start your main cross-examination at quite an advantage.

It not infrequently happens that a police officer's notebook, or other contemporaneous document is lost before trial. If, before the notebook is lost, the officer has made a copy of the note, or has compiled a statement by copying the note out, there is no reason why he should not refresh his memory from what he has copied, since the original was made contemporaneously: *Cheng* [4]. And in *Attorney-General's Reference (No. 3 of 1979)* [5], it was held proper for an officer to refresh his memory from a note compiled partly from a literally contemporaneous rough note of an interview, and partly from his own recollection, even though the finished note was not identical to the rough note.

There are signs that courts are becoming more lenient in their approach to the memory-refreshing rule, conscious that it is undesirable to turn the giving of evidence into a test of memory, rather than a test of honesty and reliability. In *Da Silva* [6], the Court of Appeal held that the trial judge has a discretion to permit a witness to refresh his recollection, either in or outside court, from a document which does not satisfy the strict test of contemporaneity, if the witness cannot recall the events because of the lapse of time and if it seems necessary in the interests of justice. And in *South Ribble Magistrates' Court, ex parte Cochrane* [7] it was held (contrary to a suggestion in *Da Silva*) that this may be done even in a case where the witness has read the document before giving evidence, though the witness in *South Ribble* had stated that, while he had read the document, he had not 'digested' it. Clearly, the weight of a witness's evidence may be adversely affected if it is seen that his recollection has to be supported to this extent, so that, though the approach of the courts may be becoming more liberal, it is by no means desirable that the witness take full advantage of it.

At common law, a memory-refreshing document is not evidence of the truth of the facts recorded in it, because it is hearsay and inadmissible for that purpose. By referring to the document, the witness does not make it evidence. The evidence is what the witness states from the witness-box, not what is contained in the document. Although this may seem an academic distinction, especially where the witness apparently has no independent recollection and reads word for word from the document, it has important consequences in cross-examination. Cross-examination using memory-refreshing documents will be dealt with later in this chapter. In civil cases, as we saw in Chapter 3, the effect of s. 6 of the Civil Evidence Act 1995 is that, while the common law rules regarding the admissibility of such a statement are left unaffected, such a statement, if admitted, is evidence of the truth of any matter stated in it in addition to its value on any issue affecting credibility.

Previous consistent statements   A witness may not seek to enhance his evidence by relating to the court what he himself has said on the same subject on another occasion. Such statements, known as previous consistent or self-serving statements, are in reality a form of hearsay, and do not add anything of value to the evidence of the witness. They were inadmissible at common law. In *Roberts* [8], the defendant was charged with murder. His defence was that the killing had been accidental. It was held that the defendant was not entitled to state in evidence that, two days after the killing, he had told his father that it had been an accident. Nothing in s. 23 or s. 24 of the Criminal Justice Act 1988 renders such statements admissible in criminal trials in the magistrates' courts.

In civil cases there would seem to be no reason why previous consistent statements should not be admissible as evidence of the facts stated by virtue of the Civil Evidence Act 1995 although the weight of such statements would generally be slight, except in the following cases in which they enjoy a specific relevance. In these exceptional cases, previous consistent statements are admissible even at common law. These cases are as follows:

(a)   In a few unusual cases, a witness may relate to the court an excited utterance or spontaneous exclamation which he (or another) made in the excitement of the event which he is describing in evidence. This is a common-law exception to the hearsay rule, which applies to previous consistent statements, and is dealt with in detail in chapter 2. It applies only where the utterance is so closely related in time and circumstances to the event itself as to be part of that event, and where the court can be satisfied that the utterance was not calculated by the witness for his own advantage. In other words, the statement must not have been deliberately self-serving. For a thorough discussion of this rule, see *Andrews* [9].

(b)   Where a witness has identified the defendant as the perpetrator of the offence charged, the witness may state that he previously made an out-of-court identification of the defendant. Although such a statement is self-serving, assuming that the witness maintains in evidence that the defendant was the perpetrator, it is in the interests of the defendant, no less than of the prosecution, that a witness should be given the chance to identify a suspect at an early stage, preferably on an identification parade, and the results of such identification are held to be admissible for reasons of obvious practicality.

(c)   Where the charge is one of a sexual offence, the complainant may give evidence that he or she made a 'recent complaint' about the offence. This complaint must have been made at the first reasonably practicable opportunity, so that there is a reasonable inference that it is not deliberately self-serving. This principle, however, need not be taken to absurd lengths. It may be reasonable for the complainant to wait a short time for the opportunity of speaking with a friend or relative, rather than confiding in the first person she may meet [10]. The evidence of the complaint may include any statement of the identity of the offender. The evidence of the complaint has a strictly limited value, and is admissible only to confirm the complainant's evidence (insofar as consistent) or to rebut or disprove consent on the part of the complainant, if consent is an issue in the case. The complaint is not evidence of the truth of the matters complained of.

(d)   Where a witness is cross-examined in such a way as to suggest that he has, within a specific period of time, fabricated his evidence, the witness may rebut this suggestion by relating that he made a statement consistent with his evidence at a time prior to the alleged fabrication. This is known as rebutting an allegation of recent fabrication, and although it arises generally in re-examination rather than examination-in-chief, may properly be dealt with here.

The right does not arise merely because it is suggested to the witness that he is not telling the truth. There must be a suggestion, made expressly or by necessary implication, that there was a fabrication of evidence at or after some time, so that the timing of the prior statement has evidential value in rebutting the suggestion. In *Oyesiku* [11], the defendant's wife gave evidence on his behalf. It was suggested to her in cross-examination that she had prepared her evidence in collusion with her husband. In rebuttal of this suggestion, it was admissible for the wife to give evidence that, after the defendant's arrest and before she had had any opportunity to speak with him, she had made a statement to the defendant's solicitor consistent with her evidence in chief. A previous consistent statement tendered to rebut a suggestion of recent fabrication in a criminal trial in the magistrates' court is, by virtue of common law, admissible only to rebut the suggestion, and is not evidence of the facts contained in the statement. In civil cases, such a statement is also admissible as evidence of the facts stated by virtue of s. 6 of the Civil Evidence Act 1995 (see Chapter 3).

Unfavourable and hostile witnesses   Witnesses who fail to come up to proof, who in other words prove to be unfavourable, or less favourable in their evidence than might have been anticipated, are one of the hazards of litigation. Whatever care has been taken in interviewing witnesses and in preparing proofs of evidence, it is inevitable that occasionally some disastrous departure from the anticipated evidence will occur. There is sometimes a lesson to be learned here, namely never to call a witness merely because the witness is available. However much your client may believe in the witness, offer to produce the witness at court and try to pressure you into calling the witness, you should always rely in the end on your professional judgment of the witness and of the anticipated evidence. Avoid calling a witness from whom you do not have a signed proof of evidence, unless it appears really necessary. However, the disaster of the witness who fails to come up to proof is not necessarily a question of failure to learn these lessons, but can strike the most careful advocate in almost any situation, and without warning. What can be done to salvage the case?

    As in many situations in advocacy, the most effective solution is the simplest, and is often overlooked. This is to call any other evidence at your disposal, having got the witness out of the witness-box as quickly as possible. It may be that the remaining evidence will be sufficient to win the case. The fact that you have had the misfortune to call an unfavourable witness is not always fatal, especially if the points of inconsistency are not of the most material kind, and other witnesses may be able to convince the court to disregard the unfavourable parts of the evidence. Remember, however, to be ruthlessly honest and realistic in your closing speech. Face, and do not try to fudge the fact that there is evidence against you which you yourself have called. The court will know this anyway, and to try to conceal it is a dreadful error of judgment. Face the problem and then work to overcome it by stressing the other available evidence.

In some cases, of course, you will have no other evidence, or the effect of the unfavourable evidence will be irreparable. In such a case, you may wish to impeach, or in other words directly discredit your own witness. This you can only do if the court adjudges the witness to be hostile, instead of merely unfavourable. It is obviously embarrassing and undesirable that a party should be permitted to impeach a witness whom he has tendered to the court as a witness of truth. However, where the witness is hostile, this is allowed in order to protect a party against deliberate sabotage of his case. A hostile witness, for this purpose, is one who displays an inimical animus towards the party calling him or evinces no desire to give evidence fairly or to tell the truth. Hostility may stem from malice, bribery, intimidation or from a mere indisposition to cooperate. In dealing with such a witness, you can pray in aid s. 3 of the Criminal Procedure Act 1865, which provides rather inelegantly that:

A party producing a witness shall not be allowed to impeach his credit by general evidence of bad character; but he may, in case the witness shall in the opinion of the judge prove adverse, contradict him by other evidence, or, by leave of the judge, prove that he has made at other times a statement inconsistent with his present testimony; but before such last-mentioned proof can be given the circumstances of the supposed statement, sufficient to designate the particular occasion, must be mentioned to the witness, and he must be asked whether or not he has made such statement.

The section applies, despite the name of the statute, to civil and criminal cases alike. It provides two weapons for use against the 'adverse' (which has been interpreted judicially to mean 'hostile') witness. Both require leave of the court, which must be applied for in every case, by submitting to the court frankly that the witness is hostile and not just unfavourable. This involves jettisoning the witness, and therefore requires a crucial exercise of judgment on how bad the damage is, the likelihood that your case may be totally sabotaged if you do nothing, and whether or not you can prove your case without the witness. In the case of the prosecution, it is the duty of the prosecutor to show to the bench the statement of any witness who proves to be hostile, and to ask leave to treat the witness as such [12].

Having obtained leave, you may either call evidence to discredit the witness directly (contradicting the witness rather than merely proving your case by other evidence) or cross-examine the witness about any previous statement (such as his witness statement, deposition, evidence in former proceedings or proof of evidence) which is inconsistent with his present evidence. Note that what you are doing is designed to discredit the witness, not prove facts. At common law, and therefore in criminal trials in the magistrates' court, evidence of such a prior inconsistent statement is evidence only of the inconsistency of the witness, and is not evidence of the facts contained in the previous statement. In civil cases, s. 6 of the Civil Evidence Act 1995 (see Chapter 3) permits previous inconsistent statements to be used for either or both purposes, but their weight as evidence of the facts previously stated is generally only substantial where it can be shown that the previous statement was made prior to the time when the malice, bribery or intimidation of the witness commenced, and is therefore apparently reliable.

Note also the procedural requirements of the section, in terms of identifying the previous statement to the witness and asking him to admit that he made it. There is nothing in the section which prevents reference to a previous verbal statement, but if the witness denies making it, there is not much you can do except call someone who heard it, and hope for the best. It will not be very convincing. This amply illustrates the rule that signed proofs should be obtained whenever possible.

In *Thompson* [13], the victim of an alleged offence of incest was called for the prosecution, but refused to give evidence. The trial judge permitted her to be treated as hostile. It was argued on appeal that this was improper, because the witness having given no evidence, there was no 'present testimony', with which the previous statement could be said to be inconsistent. While accepting that this was a sound argument in terms of s. 3 of the 1865 Act, the Court of Appeal held that the trial court retained power at common law to satisfy the ends of justice by treating a silent, uncooperative witness in the same way as a vocal one.

Identification cases   Cases in which the evidence for the prosecution depends wholly or substantially on the visual identification of a person by witnesses pose great difficulties. It is now recognised that there are many obstacles to accurate visual identification, including the most obvious ones, such as bad lighting or an opportunity for only a fleeting glance. Identification may be confirmed, wrongly, in the mind of the witness, by the presence of the defendant at the police station, or later in court.

The Court of Appeal in *Turnbull* [14] laid down guidelines for the treatment of such cases in trials on indictment, and what the court had to say can be applied sensibly to any criminal trial. These guidelines may be summarised and adapted for use in summary trials as follows. The bench should always scrutinise all the evidence surrounding an identification, including the conditions under which it took place, the length of time available to observe, whether or not the witness knew the defendant before the identification, whether there is any reason why the witness would be likely to remember the person who committed the offence and how soon after the event the witness gave a description to the police. The court should consider carefully any weaknesses in the identification evidence, and should be open to dismissing the charge if the weaknesses are significant, and there is no or little evidence tending to support the identification. If the defendant puts forward an alibi, which the bench believe is not only false, but put forward with the object of deceiving them, this may constitute some support.

Many courts since *Turnbull* have commented on the need for care in identification cases, especially where the identifying witness had the opportunity for no more than a fleeting glance [15]. It has been held that a police officer may be assumed to be a somewhat more reliable identifying witness than an ordinary member of the public [16], but even if this may generally be true, care must be taken in any case where the officer's purported identification may be invalidly reinforced by some subsequent contact with the suspect, for example, at the police station [17]. Cases of personal recognition, where the witness knows the suspect before making the identification, cause less difficulty, but in these cases too there is authority that the bench should advise itself of the possibility of mistakes or deliberate dishonesty (*Shand* v *R* [18]).

Ideally, of course, identification should be made at a properly controlled identification parade conducted in accordance with Code of Practice D. It is undesirable that a witness should be asked to identify a person in court for the first time, and it is quite proper to object to the evidence of identification on this basis [19]. The detailed provisions of the code, and the law relating to identification parades, and other forms of identification by confrontation, photographs, samples and the like, are dealt with in the current edition of *Blackstone's Criminal Practice* at F.18.

Evidence of children in youth courts

Section 32 of the Criminal Justice Act 1988 as amended provides that in certain criminal proceedings, including proceedings in youth courts and appeals to the Crown Court therefrom (but not summary trials in magistrates' courts) a witness other than an accused who is either outside the United Kingdom, or is a child, may give evidence via live television link. This procedure requires leave of the court, and is applicable, in the case of a child witness, only where the offence charged is one referred to in s. 32(2). These offences are essentially offences involving injury to or sexual offences against a child.

Section 32A of the Act, added by s. 54 of the Criminal Justice Act 1991, provides that, in the same cases, a video recording of an interview between a child (other than an accused) and an adult may, with leave of the court, be admitted in evidence. Section 32A(3) requires the court to give leave unless some prejudice will be caused to the defendant, either because the child is not available for cross-examination, or because there has been a failure to comply with applicable rules, or because to give leave would, for some reason, be against the interests of justice. The cross-examination of the child witness may be ordered to be carried out by live television link under s. 32.

In the case of both sections, once leave has been given, the child's evidence may not be given in any other manner unless the court, on application by any party based on a change of circumstances, rules otherwise (s. 32(3C), (3D) and (3E) and s. 32A(6A) to (6D) added by the Criminal Procedure and Investigations Act 1996).

The text of these sections is given in the appendix to this book, and should be studied carefully. Despite the safeguards provided for the defendant, it is obvious that these provisions cause significant problems in terms of challenging the evidence of a child. The prosecution should, of course, always consider their use when applicable, in order to minimise the ordeal experienced by children when giving evidence about offences of which they are the victims. From the defence point of view, they compound the always-present difficulty of cross-examining effectively without alienating the sympathy of the court.

The video recording of interviews, of course, presents the greater danger. The main danger with the live television link lies in the reduced ability of the court to assess the demeanour and credibility of the witness. While serious, this can be addressed effectively in a closing speech, and may sometimes operate to the advantage of the defendant. The video-recorded interview, on the other hand, will usually be conducted by an adult who is not a lawyer, and who has a natural (though possibly sometimes misguided) sympathy for the child. This can create a far more substantive imbalance in favour of the witness. The only means of redressing this imbalance, in addition to taking full advantage of the opportunity to cross-examine, is to remind the court forcibly in the closing speech of the potential dangers of such evidence. It should also be emphasised that only matters admissible in evidence may be presented in the recording, and any inadmissible material must be excluded. Moreover, the court may, as always, exclude evidence tendered by the prosecution in the exercise of its discretion.

Evidence given by written witness statement in civil cases: CCR Ord. 20, r. 12A

In civil cases in the county court, the court may, during pre-trial review, direct the exchange of written witness statements dealing with any issues of fact to be decided at the trial, or dealing with such facts as may be specified in the order. The detailed procedural rules governing this exchange are to be found in CCR Ord. 20, r. 12A, and are discussed further in Chapter 12. Where a party calls a witness at trial whose statement has been exchanged, the judge may (except in the rare case of a jury trial) order that the witness statement serve as the evidence in chief of that witness. The party calling the witness may not adduce evidence of facts which were not included in the substance of the witness statement, unless

(a) the order specified that the statement should deal only with some particular facts and the witness can give relevant and admissible evidence also of other facts, or

(b) all other parties agree, or

(c) the judge gives leave in his discretion.

If the witness is not called, however, no other party may adduce the statement. The purpose of this provision is to save time and costs. It should be noted, however, that this rule does not make admissible evidence which is not admissible; the statement must be confined to relevant and admissible facts. The statement may, of course, be used in cross-examination of the witness. It is useful to note the observations of the Court of Appeal in *Mercer* v *Chief Constable of the Lancashire Constabulary* [20] as to the giving of directions relating to witness statements.

Cross-examination

Cross-examination has two purposes: to challenge the evidence in chief insofar as it conflicts with your instructions; and to elicit facts favourable to your case which have not emerged, or which were insufficiently emphasised in chief. In Chapters 12 and 13, we shall see how these objectives should be borne in mind when preparing a cross-examination. This chapter will examine the rules of evidence which underlie the conduct of cross-examination.

The main evidential reason for cross-examining any witness is that a failure to cross-examine may be taken by the court as an acceptance of any part of the examination-in-chief which is not challenged: *Bircham* [21]. This means that the cross-examiner should cross-examine the witness about any matters on which his instructions differ from the evidence in chief, and about any parts of his case with which the witness can reasonably be expected to deal. Although facts about which the witness has not given evidence in chief are excluded from this rule, the court may draw an adverse inference from failure to cross-examine about a relevant matter with which the witness could have dealt.

It is regarded as unfair to a witness to deny him the opportunity to answer challenges to his evidence, where an advocate intends to invite the court to disbelieve or disregard the evidence of the witness. Accordingly, it is the duty of a cross-examiner to 'put his case' to the witness, or in other words, to question the witness directly on the points on which his evidence diverges from the cross-examiner's instructions. This means that you must fairly put the substance of your case, not that you must harp on every tiny detail. As an advocate, you are trusted to distinguish the essential from the inconsequential. Moreover, it is quite proper to forbear from putting to an exactly corroborative witness everything which you have put to one witness already. It is a safe and good practice to tell the court that, in order to save time and to avoid repetition, you are exercising this discretion. There is authority to the effect that the rule requiring cross-examination on all points of difference does not apply to proceedings in magistrates' courts [22], but, from a tactical point of view, it is unsafe to rely on it. It is simply better to put your case.

All advocates are human, and from time to time, you will forget to put something which should be put. When this happens, ask the court to have the witness recalled, if necessary, at the first possible opportunity. Although this can cause delay and inconvenience, it is better than omitting an important aspect of your case. Recall of a witness is within the court's discretion, and although the court may express some disapproval, it will realise that occasional inadvertence is a fact of life. Unless you habitually omit matters and exude a general air of incompetence, you are unlikely to be refused.

Because cross-examination is designed to probe the accuracy of evidence in chief, and to expose dishonest or unreliable evidence, leading questions are always permitted, although many advocates prefer a blend of leading and non-leading questions, in the interests of cultivating a restrained and moderate style.

The rules of evidence apply to cross-examination, as they do to examination-in-chief, and accordingly questions which invite irrelevant or inadmissible answers may not be asked: *Thomson* [23]. However, it is important to take account of a crucial distinction. Although inadmissible evidence may not be elicited in cross-examination, the cross-examiner may freely introduce issues which were not raised, and which perhaps could not have been raised in chief. If such issues are raised, evidence which is relevant to them may become admissible in re-examination, even though it could not have been admitted in chief. Thus, if a witness is asked for the first time in cross-examination about a conversation he had with a third party, the conversation becomes admissible, and the re-examiner may elicit the whole conversation, even though only part of it was introduced in cross-examination. This is a trap into which inexperienced cross-examiners often fall. The conversation may have been wholly inadmissible in chief, but admissible in cross-examination as affecting the credit of the witness. The effect is to allow a full-scale re-examination. A skilled cross-examiner will always consider whether he is letting in evidence on which his opponent may capitalise in re-examination.

In *Rowson* [24] the Court of Appeal held that it was permissible for a defendant to cross-examine a co-defendant about a statement made by the co-defendant to the police, and to use the statement as a previous inconsistent statement to contradict the co-defendant's evidence, even though the judge had ruled that the statement would be excluded when tendered by the prosecution because of a breach of the Judges' Rules. There is some reason to doubt whether this decision was desirable, and it certainly contrasts starkly with the position where only one defendant is being tried, in which case the statement would have to be excluded for all purposes [25]. But it is worth bearing in mind if you are defending in a case with more than one defendant.

In order to minimise the trauma of cross-examination on child witnesses, s. 34A of the Criminal Justice Act 1988 (inserted by s. 55(7) of the Criminal Justice Act 1991) limits the right of an unrepresented defendant to cross-examine a child witness. In the case of the offences referred to in s. 32(2) of the 1988 Act (offences involving injury to or sexual offences against a child) a defendant may not cross-examine in person a child witness who is the alleged victim of the offence or who witnessed it, including a child whose video-recorded evidence has been admitted under s. 32A. There is, of course, no bar to cross-examination by the defendant's advocate, which indicates that it is essential for the defendant to be legally represented in all such cases.

Cross-examination on memory-refreshing documents The hazards described above are well illustrated by looking at what happens when a cross-examiner cross-examines on a document which a witness has used to refresh his memory while giving evidence. Clearly, such a document is inadmissible as evidence during examination-in-chief, since it is a self-serving document. We have already used the police officer's notebook as a typical example, and it will be convenient to continue to do so, though we have noted that it is in no way distinct from any other contemporaneous document used by any other witness.

The cross-examiner is entitled to inspect in court any memory-refreshing document, but is not obliged to introduce it into evidence. He may forbear from cross-examining on the notebook at all, or cross-examine only on those parts of the notebook used by the officer to refresh his memory, and in neither case does the notebook become evidence. However, once the cross-examiner strays into an area of the notebook to which the officer has not referred to refresh his memory, quite different principles apply. The cross-examination has ceased to be concerned with the memory-refreshing document, and has become concerned with a new documentary item which has not so far formed part of the case. It is just as though the cross-examiner had introduced a document from his own custody and cross-examined the witness about it. The document must go into evidence and be put before the court as a document produced for the purpose of cross-examination, and of course the court may examine the entire document.

For this reason, if there is nothing suspicious or inconsistent on the face of the notebook, the best course is to hand it back to the witness and ask no questions about it. If you do see something which prompts cross-examination, bear the above rule in mind. Ask yourself whether you can exploit any inconsistency without cross-examining on those parts of the notebook to which the officer has not referred. If you cannot avoid this, consider whether the evidential points to be scored by demonstrating the inconsistency are strong enough to justify allowing both the consistent and inconsistent parts of the whole document to go before the bench in evidence. There may be cases in which you are prepared to take this undoubted risk. If the discrepancy between the officer's evidence and the contents of the notebook is substantial and damaging, you may not care that the remainder of the note, which is consistent with his evidence, also goes before the bench. But in the case of an inconsequential or minor discrepancy, you would probably not want to take the risk of having a largely consistent note go before the bench, to provide a permanent record of the officer's evidence.

If the notebook is admitted in evidence as a result of cross-examination, by inadvertence or design, you should still not lose sight of the fact that you are dealing with a memory-refreshing document, and not with a document whose contents have evidential value. At common law, and therefore in criminal cases in the magistrates' court, where a memory-refreshing document is admitted in evidence, it is evidence affecting only the credit of the witness, and is not evidence of the facts contained in the document. In other words, the contents have no evidential value to prove the facts which they record. In *Virgo* [26], the conviction was quashed where the trial judge directed the jury that the diary of a prosecution witness, which the witness had used to refresh his memory, might be regarded as evidence of the truth of facts contained in the diary. Although the diary had rightly been admitted in evidence, because it had been cross-examined upon extensively, the jury were not entitled to substitute the diary for the evidence of the witness. The diary was evidence affecting only the consistency, and therefore the credit of the witness. In civil cases, s. 6 of the Civil Evidence Act 1995 (see Chapter 3) makes a memory-refreshing document evidence of the truth of facts stated in it, as well as evidence of consistency, but its weight on the former issue is generally not great, unless the document is clearly reliable when judged in the light of the circumstances in which it was made, and when compared to the oral evidence of the witness at trial.

As a matter of fact, you have a right to call for and inspect any document in the possession of an adverse witness when giving evidence at trial, even if the witness has not used it to refresh his memory: *Stroud* v *Stroud (No. 1)* [27]. However, in the case of a document not used to refresh the memory and simply in the possession of the witness, your opponent is entitled to require you to put the document in evidence, even if you merely inspect it, and irrespective of the scope of your cross-examination on it. It will, therefore, be obvious that you should call for such a document only where it seems clear that it will be favourable to your case. In a civil case in which exchange of documents has taken place, there should generally be a reduced risk of surprise arising from such documents. But in a criminal case, you may learn of the document's existence only through cross-examination, in which case you will need to weigh the situation very carefully. It may be advisable to seek a short adjournment to take instructions about what the document is likely to contain.

Cross-examination concerning credit   The credit, or credibility, of a witness is a factor in the determination by the court of the weight which should be given to his evidence, and will depend on the view which the court takes of his knowledge of the facts, his impartiality, his truthfulness, his respect for his oath or affirmation and his general demeanour. The cross-examiner is entitled to test and to challenge each of these qualities, and is therefore not confined to the facts of the case. The cross-examiner may equally attack the witness in terms of his character, bias or unreliability. The only exception to this is in the case of the defendant in a criminal case, who, as discussed in chapter 7, is (within certain limits) protected against cross-examination about his previous convictions and bad character by s. 1 of the Criminal Evidence Act 1898.

Although cross-examination may be directed to discreditable acts committed by the witness, it is improper to cross-examine about mere allegations. For example, the court should not permit cross-examination of a police officer regarding pending criminal charges or disciplinary complaints against him which have not yet been adjudicated upon: *Edwards* [28]. In the same case, the Court of Appeal disapproved of the practice of cross-examination of an officer about alleged misconduct of other officers attached to the same squad. Where police misconduct can be demonstrated to have led to a finding or verdict of not guilty or the reversal of a conviction on appeal in an another case, the court may allow cross-examination on that subject. However, this will be very difficult to demonstrate, because it is usually impossible to tell what lies behind a general finding or verdict of not guilty, which may be based simply on the failure of the prosecution to prove a case beyond reasonable doubt. In *Y* [29], the defendant was charged with three counts of indecency with a child. He was acquitted on the third count, and a retrial took place on the first two. It was held that the acquittal was irrelevant to the credit of the complainant at the retrial, because it could not be demonstrated that the acquittal had been based on a rejection of the complainant's evidence.

Even when unrestrained by the rules protecting defendants, it is a good rule of advocacy to refrain from making attacks on the character of witnesses when it can be avoided. In a criminal case, there are specific reasons for this, related to loss of the shield, although cross-examination which exposes the serious bad character of a witness does undoubtedly affect the credit of that witness adversely, and is an accepted, if somewhat over-used weapon. In a civil case, it is almost always a mistake, because a county court judge seeking to decide a case on the balance of probabilities will prefer to avoid viewing character in terms of black and white, and will prefer to find that a witness is mistaken rather than dishonest. A brash attack on the witness will usually forfeit the sympathy of the court. This is especially true where the damage to the witness's credit could equally well have been done by means of demonstrating his unreliability or partiality.

In a criminal case, the court may, as a matter of discretion, restrain and disallow excessive cross-examination concerning credit: *Sweet-Escott* [30]. The judge in a civil case probably has the same power, but is more likely to let you carry on and let your forfeiture of his sympathy count against you.

Previous inconsistent statements A most effective way of attacking the credit of any witness is the use of previous inconsistent statements made by the witness. The use of previous inconsistent statements against one's own hostile witnesses, as permitted by s. 3 of the Criminal Procedure Act 1865, has been examined in this chapter under the heading 'Unfavourable and hostile witnesses'. Sections 4 and 5 of the same Act make available the same weapon against the other side's witnesses, for which no leave is needed, since one's opponent's witnesses are always deemed to be hostile. These sections, which like s. 3 apply to civil and criminal cases alike, provide as follows:

4. If a witness, upon cross-examination as to a former statement made by him relative to the subject-matter of the indictment or proceeding, and inconsistent with his present testimony, does not distinctly admit that he has made such statement, proof may be given that he did in fact make it; but before such proof can be given the circumstances of the supposed statement, sufficient to designate the particular occasion, must be mentioned to the witness, and he must be asked whether or not he has made such statement.

5. A witness may be cross-examined as to previous statements made by him in writing, or reduced into writing, relative to the subject-matter of the indictment or proceeding, without such writing being shown to him; but if it is intended to contradict such witness by the writing, his attention must, before such contradictory proof can be given, be called to those parts of the writing which are to be used for the purpose of so contradicting him: Provided always that it shall be competent for the judge, at any time during the trial, to require the production of the writing for his inspection, and he may thereupon make such use of it for the purposes of the trial as he may think fit.

It is important to follow the procedure laid down by the section. It is necessary to bring to the witness's attention the specific circumstances of the alleged statement, and give him an opportunity to admit or deny making it. If the witness admits to having made the statement, you can then ask why the statement is different from his present evidence. If he denies making the statement, you may prove that the statement was, in fact, made and you can deal with the inconsistency during your closing speech.

Section 5 also calls for more than one step. The first step is to cross-examine the witness without showing him his previous written statement. A frequent error of inexperienced cross-examiners is to rush in and thrust the statement at the witness without preliminaries. You can and should reserve that step until you have obtained an answer to the question whether he made a statement on that occasion or not. Only if you go on to contradict the witness, that is to say, to suggest that his previous statement is true in contradistinction to his evidence at trial, are you obliged to show the witness the statement.

This requires an exercise of judgment on whether you want to go that far, since the court will then see the statement also. Before beginning your cross-examination, you should decide whether you are going to ask the witness to admit that the contents of the previous statement are true, or whether you are content to submit to the court that the witness appears incapable of giving a consistent account of the facts. Always bear in mind that the re-examiner may introduce the whole of the statement for the purpose of re-establishing the credit of the witness, even if you have made use only of part. Make sure that the inconsistency is substantial enough to justify the risk that an otherwise consistent document may be placed before the court. You must, of course, have the written statement available in court for the use of the court, if required.

Despite the reference in s. 5 to the judge making 'such use of [the statement] for the purposes of the trial as he may think fit', the rule at common law for statements adduced under s. 4 or s. 5 is that such statements are evidence affecting only the credit of the witness, and are not evidence of the truth of the facts stated in them. This rule applies to criminal cases in the magistrates' court. In civil cases, s. 6 of the Civil Evidence Act 1995 (see Chapter 3) allows such a statement to be used for either purpose, but in keeping with our observations on other analogous situations, it should be noted that the weight of the statement as evidence of the truth of the facts stated in it will not necessarily be very great.

Impeachment of the maker of an admissible hearsay statement

Both the Civil Evidence Act 1995 and the Criminal Justice Act 1988 make provision for similar weapons of impeachment in cases in which hearsay evidence is admitted, and the maker of the hearsay statement is not called as a witness. In such cases, evidence akin to that which might have been employed if he had been called are made available. Section 5(2) of the Civil Evidence Act 1995 provides:

Where in civil proceedings hearsay evidence is adduced and the maker of the original statement, or of any statement relied upon to prove another statement, is not called as a witness—

(a)   evidence which if he had been so called would be admissible for the purpose of attacking or supporting his credibility as a witness is admissible for that purpose in the proceedings; and

(b)   evidence tending to prove that, whether before or after he made the statement, he made any other statement inconsistent with it is admissible for the purpose of showing that he had contradicted himself.

Provided that evidence may not be given of any matter of which, if he had been called as a witness and had denied that matter in cross-examination, evidence could not have been adduced by the cross-examining party.

The Criminal Justice Act 1988, sch. 2, para. 1, provides:

Where a statement is admitted as evidence in criminal proceedings by virtue of Part II of this Act—

(a)   any evidence which, if the person making the statement had been called as a witness, would have been admissible as relevant to his credibility as a witness shall be admissible for that purpose in those proceedings;

(b)   evidence may, with leave of the court, be given of any matter which, if that person had been called as a witness, could have been put to him in cross-examination as relevant to his credibility as a witness but of which evidence could not have been adduced by the cross-examining party; and

(c)   evidence tending to prove that that person, whether before or after making the statement, made (whether orally or not) some other statement which is inconsistent with it shall be admissible for the purpose of showing that he has contradicted himself.

There is an important difference between these two sections. In criminal cases, the court may give leave for evidence to be given as relevant to credibility, even though the evidence is collateral, and, therefore, could not have been adduced if the maker of the statement had been called as a witness. The corresponding provision of the Civil Evidence Act 1995 expressly precludes this. The requirement for leave is a prudent one, because a prolonged exploration of collateral issues frequently diverts the attention of the court from the real issues, but the rule is nonetheless desirable because of the greater prejudice which may accrue to the defendant in criminal cases where the maker of an admissible hearsay statement is not called as a witness.

Re-examination and evidence in rebuttal

There are really only two rules of evidence pertaining to re-examination. The first is that leading questions are not permitted. This is for much the same reason as in examination-in-chief, that an advocate should not put words into the mouth of his own witness. The second is that re-examination must be confined to matters raised during cross-examination. This rule is designed to prevent the proliferation and repetition of issues. The art of re-examination, however, as opposed to the rules which govern it, calls for great skill and is much neglected. If you have studied the preceding section dealing with cross-examination, you will probably have begun to appreciate that, when the other side have taken full advantage of the weapons of cross-examination against your witnesses, a certain amount of repair work is necessary. Re-examination is basically a remedial process, but it can also be employed to good effect to emphasise some positive aspect of the witness's evidence, which perhaps was not previously apparent.

This means exploiting every opportunity to put into evidence documents or conversations which were raised for the first time in cross-examination, and knowing when evidence which was inadmissible in chief has become admissible in re-examination. It also requires the advocate to evaluate the damage done to a witness in cross-examination, for example by an attack on character, and to know how to rehabilitate the witness by exploring the facts of previous convictions, or by eliciting mitigating circumstances. If some inconsistency has been exposed by use of a previous inconsistent statement, or some passage in a memory-refreshing document, there is no need to give up altogether. Very often there is some explanation which removes the sting from the cross-examination, and renders innocuous an apparently damaging circumstance. It is your duty as an advocate to monitor the cross-examination of your witnesses with a view to finding such avenues of re-examination. During cross-examination, you should be thinking constantly: 'That sounds bad, but it is not quite like that; why, and what questions can I ask to make the court understand why?'

Evidence in rebuttal is evidence which tends to contradict some evidence called for the other side, but which was not presented during the case of the party calling the evidence. It is a general rule that every party must present all the evidence on which he intends to rely before closing the case. Mere inadvertence does not permit a party to reopen his case once it has been closed, because the other side are entitled to base their conduct of the case on the way in which yours has been presented. This suggests, rightly, that you should draw the attention of the court to any inadvertent omission of relevant evidence at the earliest possible opportunity.

However, the court will allow evidence in rebuttal where any party is taken by surprise by some development during the trial, which necessitates the calling of evidence that could not have been foreseen as necessary at the outset of that party's case. In older cases, such as *Frost* [31], it was said that such evidence in rebuttal could be given only if 'any matter arises *ex improviso* which no human ingenuity could foresee'. More modern authority has defined the test as one of reasonable foreseeability, and it seems that evidence may now be introduced to rebut any matter which has genuinely taken a party by surprise. In civil cases, this may often be gauged by what is reasonably to be anticipated on the pleadings, whereas in criminal cases, the question is more one of the court's duty to ensure a fair trial by preventing one side or the other from profiting unfairly by the element of surprise. Leave to call evidence in rebuttal is always required, and will not be granted unless appropriate circumstances can be demonstrated. In *Day* [32], a conviction was quashed where the prosecution were permitted to call a handwriting expert, not only after the close of their own case but after the defendant had given evidence, and where it should have been obvious from the outset that such evidence might well be required. Nonetheless, leave should be granted readily where the evidence in question is essentially formal in nature, and cannot reasonably be disputed, e.g., *Palastanga* v *Solman* [33], in which formal proof of a regulation by adducing an HMSO copy was inadvertently omitted, or even in a case such as *Francis* [34], in which the omission of more substantive evidence was caused by a reasonable misunderstanding about what facts were in dispute.

Evidence in rebuttal does not, however, always fall into the category of evidence which might have been introduced during a party's own case. It is sometimes required to rebut answers given during cross-examination, and may have been inadmissible during the cross-examiner's own case. The rule in such cases is that evidence in rebuttal may be called, except in relation to 'collateral issues'. In relation to collateral issues the cross-examiner must accept the answers of the witness as final, not of course in the sense that he cannot challenge them in cross-examination, but in the sense that he cannot introduce evidence in rebuttal to contradict the witness. The rule exists for the purpose of limiting the proliferation of secondary issues which often arise during cross-examination. A collateral issue is one relating to the credit of a witness, which is not of direct relevance to the outcome of the case. In *Burke* [35], an Irish witness, giving evidence through an interpreter, asserted that he was unable to speak English. He denied in cross-examination that he had spoken English to two persons while in court. This was held to be a collateral issue, and the cross-examiner was not permitted to call evidence in rebuttal to prove that the witness had spoken English. However, the position would have been different if the witness's command of the English language had been directly relevant to some issue in the case, for example, his authorship of a material document or of an alleged confession.

To this so-called rule of finality on collateral issues, there are five exceptions, which should always be borne in mind. These are as follows:

(a)   Where a witness denies making a previous inconsistent statement, the statement may be proved, subject to certain procedural requirements (Criminal Procedure Act 1865, ss. 4 and 5).

(b)   By s. 6 of the Criminal Procedure Act 1865, if a witness denies having been convicted of a criminal offence, or refuses to answer a question on that subject, the conviction may be proved in rebuttal.

(c)   Any fact tending to prove bias or partiality on the part of a witness may be proved if denied in cross-examination. Bias or partiality requires a suggestion not just that the witness's evidence is challenged, but that there are specific facts which indicate that the witness is prepared to give evidence untruthfully or unfairly. This may arise from the relationship of the witness to one party or another (for example a mistress: *Thomas* v *David* [36]) or from malice or bribery. But there must be some positive fact; a mere allegation that the witness's evidence is inaccurate, or even untruthful, will not suffice. There must be some positive disposition to favour one side as against the other.

In any event, there is often a very fine line between evidence of bias and partiality on the one hand, and evidence which is directly relevant to the case on the other. Thus, an allegation that witnesses have been instructed about what to say against a defendant who denies their evidence [37], or an allegation that the police have kept a defence witness out of the way by threats [38], are allegations affecting the substance of the case being tried, and evidence in rebuttal will always be allowed in such cases. But an allegation that a witness has behaved improperly in another case affects only his credibility [39]. The test may be whether or not the conduct is designed to affect directly the outcome of the instant case, as opposed to being merely evidence of the way in which the witness was prepared to behave in relation to another case.

(d)   A witness may be called in rebuttal to show that, in the opinion of the witness, a witness called on the other side should not be believed because of his reputation for being unworthy of belief: *Richardson* [40]. Such evidence is rarely used, and probably rarely available, but there is no objection to it. Indeed, the rebutting witness may even state his opinion of the credibility of the opposing witness, provided that the opinion is based on facts within his personal knowledge.

(e)   Where evidence is available that, for medical reasons, the reliability of a witness is open to doubt, such medical evidence may be given in rebuttal of the witness's evidence. In *Toohey* v *Commissioner of Police of the Metropolis* [41], the House of Lords held that it was permissible to ask questions of a doctor tending too show that the victim of an alleged offence was abnormally prone to hysteria, and that such hysteria might have been induced by alcohol.

Presentation of documentary and real evidence

Many advocates assume that the presentation of documentary and real evidence involves no more than remembering to bring it to court, together with sufficient copies for the court and other parties. While this is certainly an important consideration, there are less mundane things to think about.

In the case of an evidential document, you must prove, unless admitted, both the contents and, where required, the due execution of the document. Such proof is important in civil cases more often than in criminal, but the rules are the same in either case. Very often, the required proof can be dispensed with by agreement, and you should always invite all other parties to enter into such an agreement in good time before trial.

It is a fundamental and too-often overlooked rule of English law that, in order to prove the contents of an evidential document, primary evidence of those contents must be adduced [42]. In almost all cases, this means producing the original document. An admission by all other parties of the contents of a document is also regarded as primary evidence. In the county court, notice to admit in respect of all evidential documents on which you propose to rely at trial should be served, as provided for by CCR Ord. 20, r. 3(1). Failure of another party to respond with a notice of non-admission will result in such party being deemed to have admitted the authenticity of the documents set forth in your notice. Also regarded as primary evidence is the official copy of a document, the original of which is required by law to be enrolled in a court or other public office. On the other hand, a copy, however produced, and oral evidence about the contents of a document are secondary evidence.

Despite older views to the contrary, it is now clear that although film, videotape and the like are regarded as documents, they are not subject to the rule requiring primary evidence [43]. The courts have simply been unwilling to encumber these newer media of communication with the technicalities of a rule which arose centuries ago to deal with the practicalities of preventing fraud and error arising from the copying by hand of written documents.

Secondary evidence is admissible to prove the contents of an evidential document only in the following exceptional cases:

(a)   If your opponent fails, after notice to produce, given pursuant to CCR Ord. 20, r. 3(4), to produce at trial the original documents called for, you may prove the contents of such documents by any secondary evidence.

(b)   Secondary evidence may be used to prove the contents of a document where the original is in the lawful possession of a stranger to the proceedings, who refuses and cannot be compelled to produce it. However, if the stranger's possession or refusal to produce is unlawful, the procedure is to compel production of the original, and secondary evidence will not be admissible. For similar reasons, secondary evidence may be admitted where production of the original is physically impossible (for example where it is a tombstone) or legally impossible (for example where the original is required by law to be kept in or affixed to some public place).

(c)   Where the original has been lost, and cannot be found after all reasonable steps have been taken to search for it (the proof of which lies upon the party asserting the fact) secondary evidence will be admitted.

(d)   The Bankers' Books Evidence Act 1879 provides that a copy of an entry in a banker's book may be admitted as evidence of the contents without production of the original, on certain conditions set forth in the Act designed to ensure the authenticity of the contents and the copy.

Where due execution of a document must be proved, this may be done by direct or percipient evidence of the execution, by the evidence of attesting witnesses, by scientific comparison of the document with a known sample of the handwriting of the purported executer or even by the opinion evidence of a witness familiar with the handwriting of the executer. A document which is, or purports to be more than 20 years old and comes from proper custody, is presumed to have been duly executed. Any document is presumed to have been executed on the date it bears, and except in the case of a will (when the reverse is presumed) it is presumed that any alteration was made before execution.

Where real evidence, such as photographs, tapes and the like, is produced, the party producing it must show a *prima facie* case that the proposed exhibit is original and authentic. This is a rule of some importance in criminal cases, since the prosecution are often unable, if pressed, to demonstrate a continuous chain of possession of an exhibit such as a tape recording. Since the prosecution must show a *prima facie* case that the exhibit is the original and has not been tampered with, the court should exclude it if a proper chain of custody cannot be shown and if there is any real possibility of tampering having occurred [44]. This opens up excellent fields of cross-examination, which often reduce the weight of an exhibit, even if the court decides to admit it.

Further reading

Murphy on Evidence, 6th ed., ch. 16, 17 and 19; *Blackstone's Criminal Practice 1998*, F6–F8; D19.

Notes

1. *Moore* v *Registrar of Lambeth County Court* [1969] 1 WLR 141; *Tomlinson* v *Tomlinson* [1980] 1 WLR 323.
2. *Moor* v *Moor* [1954] 1 WLR 927.
3. *Richardson* [1971] 2 QB 484.
4. (1976) 63 Cr App R 20.
5. (1979) 69 Cr App R 411; *Chisnell* [1992] Crim LR 507.
6. [1990] 1 WLR 31.
7. [1996] 2 Cr App R 544.
8. [1942] 1 All ER 187.
9. [1987] AC 281.
10. *Valentine* [1996] 2 Cr App R 213.

11. (1971) 56 Cr App R 240.
12. *Fraser* (1956) 40 Cr App R 160.
13. (1976) 64 Cr App R 96.
14. [1977] QB 224.
15. See, e.g., *Oakwell* [1978] 1 WLR 32; *Reid* v *R* [1990] 1 AC 363.
16. *Ramsden* [1991] Crim LR 295.
17. *Powell* v *DPP* [1992] RTR 270.
18. [1996] 1 WLR 511.
19. *Cartwright* (1914) 10 Cr App R 219. But the practice is not always undesirable: see *Creamer* (1984) 80 Cr App R 248; *John* [1973] Crim LR 113.
20. [1991] 1 WLR 367.
21. [1972] Crim LR 430
22. *O'Connell* v *Adams* [1973] RTR 150.
23. [1912] 3 KB 19.
24. [1986] QB 174. See also *Lui Mei Lin* v *R* [1989] AC 288.
25. *Treacy* [1944] 2 All ER 229.
26. (1978) 67 Cr App R 323.
27. [1963] 1 WLR 1080.
28. [1991] 1 WLR 207.
29. [1992] Crim LR 436.
30. (1971) 55 Cr App R 316.
31. (1840) 9 C & P 129, as reported in 4 St Tr NS 85, 386.
32. [1940] 1 All ER 402.
33. [1962] Crim LR 334.
34. [1990] 1 WLR 1264.
35. (1858) 8 Cox CC 44.
36. (1836) 7 C & P 350.
37. *Phillips* (1936) 26 Cr App R 17.
38. *Busby* (1981) 75 Cr App R 79.
39. *Edwards* [1991] 1 WLR 207. See also *Funderburk* [1990] 1 WLR 587.
40. [1969] 1 QB 299.
41. [1965] AC 595.
42. *Garton* v *Hunter* [1969] 2 QB 37; *Taylor* v *Chief Constable of Cheshire* [1986] 1 WLR 1479.
43. *Kajala* v *Noble* (1982) 75 Cr App R 149
44. *Maqsud Ali* [1966] 1 QB 688; *R* v *Stevenson* [1971] 1 WLR 1.

Twelve

Preparing and Presenting a Civil Case*

Introduction

The task of the advocate is to persuade and this task calls for a high degree of sensitivity: unfortunately the greater the degree of sensitivity the advocate possesses, the greater is the likelihood of his being nervous at the prospect of advancing his case in court. It is a commonplace at the Bar that many excellent advocates suffer from a high degree of nervousness before going into court. Now a certain degree of nervousness on the part of the advocate is a good thing — in the same way that the good actor will experience such a feeling before going out on to the stage. But every advocate has experienced on some occasion a very different form of nervousness — the panic which destroys what should be a confident performance. In this chapter I intend to suggest how such a failure of confidence can best be avoided; our theme is that even apparently simple litigation merits a great deal of preparation, and that the key to successful advocacy lies not in acquiring some hidden key to eloquence, but in preparing one's case so thoroughly that by the time one arrives at court, a confidence in one's own ability to put over the case will have developed.

Before the hearing

One of the most important matters to consider before trial is the exchange of witness statements. By CCR Ord. 20, r. 12A, the court may, during pre-trial review, direct the exchange of written witness

---

* This chapter was originally written by David Barnard.

statements dealing with any issues of fact to be decided at the trial, or dealing with such facts as may be specified in the order. The exchange must be made within ten weeks or such other period as the court may specify, and will usually be ordered to be accomplished simultaneously by all parties. The witness statement must be dated, and (except for a specified good reason) signed by the witness. It must state that the facts contained in it are true to the best of the witness's knowledge and belief. It must also sufficiently identify any documents referred to.

The preparation of witness statements is a vital part of your trial preparation for many reasons. The most immediately compelling reason is that failure to comply with the court's order will probably result in your being unable to adduce evidence from any witness whose statement is not exchanged without leave of the court, and, as the purpose of the order is to save time and costs, the giving of leave cannot be anticipated in most cases. Another important reason is that, where you call a witness whose statement has been exchanged, the court will usually order that the witness statement serve as the evidence in chief of that witness. It is, therefore, essential that the statement include all relevant and admissible facts with which you want the witness to deal, and that it be phrased as persuasively as possible (though it must be factual, and not consist of opinion or argument). The rule does not render admissible any evidence which is otherwise inadmissible, so the statement must contain only relevant and admissible factual evidence.

It must be noted also that a witness statement is not a sufficient notice of an intention to adduce hearsay evidence under the Civil Evidence Act 1995 and CCR, Ord. 20, rr. 14–17 (see Chapter 3). If you intend to do this, you must also serve the appropriate Civil Evidence Act notice. This is dealt with in Chapter 3.

Preparing for trial

We start with the preparation the advocate should be making in good time before presenting a client's claim in a disputed and somewhat involved case. A good starting-point is to write out a chronology of the relevant events; in a contract case, for example, the negotiations leading up to the agreement, the relevant letters passing between the parties and the meetings when it was appreciated that something was going wrong should all be set out in a logical order of events.

Once the chronology has been prepared the next step is to tie it up with the relevant documents. So, perhaps in a different colour ink, go back over the chronology inserting into it references to the relevant documents. It is worth remembering that many civil cases are won on documents: a judge faced with a conflict of testimony may well decide the case in favour of the party whose account most closely fits in with what is set out in the documents. Therefore at this stage in the preparation of a case, the advocate should be checking that the documentary evidence has been properly prepared. Are the original documents available? If not, have copies been agreed or can it be proved that the original has been destroyed or is missing and reasonable steps have been taken to trace it? There should, of course, have been prepared a bundle of original documents for the use of the witnesses and bundles of paginated copies for the judge and the advocates. It is the responsibility of the plaintiff's solicitor to prepare the bundle for the use of the court; but if you are acting for the defendant and no bundle has been supplied, it may be worth preparing your own; otherwise the plaintiff may profit by the confusion he has created by not putting in a bundle of relevant documentation.

The next step is to read again the proofs of evidence you have taken. Tie up the proofs to the documents. In particular, see whether there is any point at which the evidence of the witness does not appear to tally with the documents; if you find such a point you must take instructions on it. Consider also what passages seem unclear in the proofs — often it is the matter set out in these passages which will be the turning-point of the case, and in these parts of the proofs, the witnesses may seem vague because they have not been totally frank when the proofs were taken.

You will, of course, already have checked that all the relevant witnesses are willing to attend court; if there is any doubt about the matter, you should have issued a witness summons. It is sometimes said that a reluctant witness is not worth calling but this is an exaggeration: in truth, there are often many reasons why witnesses who can support your case may be unwilling to attend court and yet, if they do attend, they may give evidence which materially helps you to establish your case. Where, therefore, a witness whose testimony is important is reluctant to attend, often the best course is to issue a witness summons and then check his evidence with him when he arrives at the court. If it is clear at that stage that he is going to be adverse to you, then you can decide not to call him; but if you have not taken this step you may have done your client a great disservice because it may be that if the witness had been prevailed upon to attend he could have won you the case.

We have already discussed the problems peculiar to expert witnesses. By now you must be sure you have understood the evidence your expert will be giving. In particular, you must understand why he says the other side's expert is wrong. Check in this final preparation of the case that your expert has provided you with the necessary outlines for a cross-examination. You will already have seen that a copy of his report, together with the relevant plans and diagrams, is available for the judge. It sometimes happens that in this stage of final preparation of a case your attention is drawn to points in the expert testimony which you have not clarified. Make a written note of these points so that you will be able to check them quickly with your expert before going into court. It is always worth attending court well in advance of the time of the hearing; one reason is that this provides you with a chance of going over these points of evidence, which on a careful final consideration of the case, have suddenly assumed a greater significance than they did earlier on.

The next stage in preparing your note is to consider very carefully what orders you are asking the judge to make. If your case is a claim for damages, are you in a position to prove your loss? It sometimes happens that an advocate will prepare a case perfectly so far as liability is concerned yet fail to do the best for the client, through not taking sufficient trouble in proving the full extent of the client's loss. The law on damages is complex; you should check, particularly in a contract case, that you understand the measure of damages which is appropriate to the particular claim you are bringing. Never forget the necessity of proving the items of special damage; usually it will be possible to agree these in advance, but where there is no agreement then you should prepare a schedule showing how the relevant sums are calculated. In preparing that schedule, check how you intend to prove each and every item.

If your claim is for damages for personal injuries then go to court with the relevant quantum flagged in Kemp and Kemp on *The Quantum of Damages* and in *Current Law*. Most judges nowadays are prepared to hear an advocate refer to similar cases in order to give the court guidance on the amount to award; there is still, however, a convention that you do not yourself state the sum which you wish the judge to award.

Where you are claiming an order from the court, for example, for an injunction, it is essential that you draft the precise terms of the order so that you can place your draft before the judge.

It is only at this final stage in preparing your note that we recommend you turn to the law. It should have become clear to you what are the points upon which a legal question might arise. Set out in your note references to the appropriate textbooks and statutes and have those books or copies available at court. If it will be necessary for you to refer the judge to a law report or a textbook, make sure that you have a copy available for the judge to read; do not assume that the court will have copies of anything other than the standard official law reports. Nothing is more senseless than reading a report to a judge who has not got a copy and so is not able to follow word by word what you are saying.

At the hearing

It is always a good rule to arrive very early at court — at least three-quarters of an hour before the case is due to be heard. This gives you time for a last conference with your client. It is remarkable how much new material is likely to emerge at this stage — actually arriving at the court door concentrates the client's mind wonderfully. There is another reason why you should arrive early: you must anticipate that at the court door there will be proposals for settlement emanating from the other side; or you yourself may wish at this stage to make proposals to the other side. You must leave yourself ample time to discuss such matters both with your opponent and with your client; many judges are prepared to grant a degree of indulgence to advocates who wish the court to adjourn while terms of settlement are discussed. You should never assume, however, that this will happen and that is why it is worth arriving in time to have these matters sorted out as far as possible before the judge actually sits. It is a very good idea to work out before you arrive at court the minimum terms upon which you would prepared to settle the case; if these terms are likely to be at all complex, then have them drafted out on paper so that you can discuss them with your opponent and with your client.

Dress correctly for court. It is difficult to persuade a judge to concentrate on your advocacy when he is really thinking with irritation that you have not troubled to dress properly for court. For men, proper court dress involves a dark suit with a waistcoat, a stiff wing-collar and starched clean bands. For women, a dark suit or dress and again starched bands are *de rigueur*. You may think these conventions are outdated and senseless but you cannot afford to do anything which could in any way deflect the court's attention from your presentation of your case, and therefore you must accept these rules until at least you are of sufficient seniority for the court not to care whether you have developed eccentricities of dress.

If your case is not the first in the list it is often a good idea to go into court and listen to the earlier cases. If you have not appeared before the judge before, this gives you a chance of forming some assessment of his character. But even if you know the judge well, it may be worth sitting in court for some time just to see what mood he is in today. Judges — even the best judges — are human and like all of us vary from day to day in their temperament. One other point to note; if you do go into the courtroom never be tempted to chatter with the other advocates while another case is going on; judges notice what is happening at the Bar and the sight of advocates talking to each other while waiting for their cases to come on is apt to infuriate them.

At last your case is called on; we will assume that you are acting for the plaintiff and therefore you now rise to make your opening. A good opening can set the tone for the whole case; equally a bad opening may destroy the case before it has even really begun. This is where the value of good preparation becomes apparent. If you have made a note of the sort suggested earlier in this chapter you will have constructed a good opening for your case.

You will start by telling the judge what sort of case this is and what you are claiming; for example, you will say: 'May it please your Honour, this is a claim for damages for breach of contract' or 'This is a claim for possession of a dwelling-house on the grounds of forfeiture for non-payment of rent'. Then move into the chronology of the relevant events.

Imagine, for instance, you are appearing in a simple building dispute. The sensible course is to hand the judge at this stage the bundle of agreed documents and then take him through the chronology tying up each relevant date with the document to which it relates. Thus, for example, you will tell him that on such and such a day the defendant delivered an estimate to the plaintiff, and you will ask the judge to look at the estimate. You will then go on to refer to the dates of the letters which you say together constituted the offer and acceptance of that estimate. You will then go on to give the date when building works began, and then you will itemise the 'extras' by referring to the work which was to be done and the dates, and so you will build up for the judge a chronological picture of the events which he is going to consider in the case. Go slowly at this stage because the judge may well wish to take a note of this chronology of events. When you have completed your outline of the facts and your survey of the documents then turn to the pleadings and any schedule of defects. You can preface your remarks by indicating what you say are the basic issues in the case, for example, whether certain extra work is properly chargeable or whether there has been a breach of certain contractual terms relating to the manner in which various items of work should be done, or whatever it may be. Now ask the judge to look at the pleadings which should set out formally what the issues are. Refer the judge also to any orders that have been made on a pre-trial review or at any other stage in the case, and give the judge the date upon which such orders have been complied with.

It may be at this point in time you will want to amend your pleadings. If so, have a draft of the amended pleading ready to put before the court, and you would be wise to flag in the *County Court Practice* the relevant paragraphs relating to the principles upon which the court gives leave to amend pleadings.

One last word about the opening speech; it is a mistake to write out one's opening verbatim but, since many advocates find that the greatest hurdle to get over is the first words which have to be spoken, there is no reason why you should not write out the first few sentences of your opening remarks and then develop the rest of your opening in note form.

Once the opening is concluded it will be for you, if you are acting for the plaintiff, to call your own client and then the witnesses who support your case. There will be a bundle of original documents before your witness: make sure that at the appropriate moment he produces each of the documents which he can speak about. Remember that if the original is missing, a copy can only be produced if the original has been destroyed or lost (and all reasonable enquiries can be shown to have been made to trace it). When the original is held by the other side you must serve notice on your opponent to produce it.

As we have already seen, in many civil cases, it will be unnecessary to conduct an examination in chief of a fact witness, because the court will have ordered that his witness statement serve as his evidence in chief. However, because the court may not prefer that method in a particular case, and because the witness statements may not have been ordered to contain all the relevant evidence which the witnesses may give, you must know how to conduct a competent examination in chief.

The following observations, read together with the evidential rules discussed in the last chapter, may help.

There are two important rules where one is calling one's own client or one's own witnesses; in taking the client or witnesses through the evidence in chief the advocate is not entitled to lead the witness on any contentious matter. This means the advocate must not ask questions of the witness which suggest the answer the advocate wishes to receive. Thus for example, if it is in dispute that a party agreed to a particular term, it would be quite wrong to lead one's client by asking him, 'Did Mr X say to you such and such?' The proper course when one comes to the matters which are in controversy is simply to ask the witness to explain in his own words what happened or what was said.

The other rule in examining your own client or witnesses is that, unless witnesses become 'hostile', you are not allowed to contradict their testimony by referring them to any earlier statements they may have made. It will sometimes happen that a witness will depart radically in giving evidence from the proof you have in front of you; you are not in these circumstances entitled to put the witness's proof before him and ask him why he is now saying something different, nor are you entitled to cross-examine him in order to get him to change his testimony. Most advocates in these circumstances will try to ask the question again in case the witness has simply misunderstood them, but once the answer has been clearly given then the advocate must accept that answer and move on to some other point.

For more detail on the examination of witnesses, see Chapter 11.

Brown's rules

There is a great art in producing the evidence upon which you rely, and many writers on advocacy have said that adducing evidence in chief is a more difficult art than cross-examination. Whether or not that is true, it certainly pays to take great care in the way in which your own evidence is put forward. An American advocate called David Paul Brown formulated in the 19th century certain 'golden rules' for taking a witness through his evidence in chief [1]. These rules contain so much good sense that it is worth repeating some of them here.

Brown's first rule relates to the witness who is forward or impertinent; this witness can ruin the presentation of one's case. He demeans the dignity of the court and he may annoy and upset the judge. You as the advocate have to control the witness and prevent him from being forward or impertinent. Brown's suggestion is that you should be very serious and very grave with him; after a few moments he will realise that his impertinence is out of place and is certainly unacceptable to you, and in the vast majority of cases this will affect him sufficiently for his testimony to be given properly. What you must never do is to go along with such a witness and in any way seek to encourage him.

The second rule that Brown formulated related to the witness who was timid or nervous, and this is a much more common type. Lawyers tend to forget how intimidating it is to a lay person to appear as a witness in a court of law, and your task as the advocate is to make sure that any timidity or nervousness on the part of your witness does not prevent him from giving the testimony for which you have called him. Therefore, says Brown, it is worth beginning by asking the witness about familiar matters and lead him only gradually to the questions which are contentious and upon which you expect he will later be cross-examined. So, for example, if in a case involving a factory accident you were calling a particular workman, it would be worth asking him about his job, his duties and about how long he had been employed before you turn to the facts of the accident. Most judges understand why this is done and will not criticise the advocate for attempting shortly to make the witness feel at home.

The third witness identified by Brown was the witness who was unfavourable; by that is meant the witness who says something which strikes against the case you are trying to build up. It is an important rule that one should not at this stage appear to be taken aback. This is particularly true where the tribunal consists of lay persons, for example, an industrial tribunal or magistrates, but it is also true of the judge; all tribunals watch the advocate and all advocates therefore have to develop devices of their own for concealing the fact that a witness's testimony may have come as a very unpleasant shock to them.

The fourth type of witness, says Brown, is the witness who is prejudiced. By this he means the witness who is obviously hostile to your client. Normally in such a case the only advice that can be given is not to call that witness, but sometimes the witness has to be called, and you have no alternative, because he is going to give some item of evidence which is essential so far as your case is concerned. The advice in such a case is to get rid of him from the witness-box as quickly as possible; certainly do not think that you will be able to charm him while he is in the witness-box into helping your case. The only safe course is to ask him shortly the matters upon which he gives vital testimony and then sit down.

Brown's fifth rule relates to the witness whom your adversary must call. You should never call such a witness, the reason being that if you let the other side call him you will be able to cross-examine him, and cross-examination, particularly of a witness who is not hostile to your case, is a far easier method of eliciting the evidence that you want to present before the court than examination-in-chief.

Brown's sixth rule is never to ask a witness a question without some object. I would also suggest that you should consciously try not to ask questions which can be objected to. Of course this is a counsel of perfection because every advocate from time to time will make a mistake, but one should think about the admissibility of the evidence that one proposes to adduce, and although a court will forgive one or perhaps two mistakes, the advocate who is constantly asking improper questions will forfeit the confidence of the court.

I would add to Brown's rule the suggestion that you should not object to your opponent's questions unless the matters involved are crucial to the case. There is nothing which irritates the tribunal more than the advocate who keeps on taking points of evidence where the matters in question are not of any great significance. Therefore confine your objections to the occasions when the other side have asked the witness to give inadmissible evidence about matters which are really crucial to the case. When such a matter does arise and you have made your objection, you must then be prepared to argue distinctly and without hesitation why the evidence is not admissible. This is why a thorough and readily accessible knowledge of the basic rules of evidence is of such great assistance to the advocate. Questions of the admissibility of evidence arise suddenly during the course of a case and cannot always be anticipated. The good advocate knows this and is able to explain clearly and distinctly why it is that he objects to any matter of evidence.

The last of Brown's rules seems almost self-evident, and yet it is often seen to be broken in practice. Brown says that the advocate must speak clearly and distinctly as if he is awake and engaged in a matter of interest. There is nothing more unattractive than the advocate who appears to be bored with the case upon which he is engaged, and yet many advocates affect such a lack of interest. This is an unattractive approach to advocacy and we would suggest that the good advocate is the advocate who is seen to be clearly concerned and interested in the case which he is advancing.

I would add to Brown's rules one overriding principle, and that is that the advocate should be polite. It sometimes seems to a lay person that lawyers are unduly obsequious in court. In truth, they are taking part in a highly organised ritual, where the use of language is important, and where deference to the tribunal expressed in the language used actually assists in making the process work. It may be very difficult to restrain one's temper in the face of a witness who is being hostile or rude, and indeed every advocate has come across the occasion when judges have been less than courteous to him; nonetheless we believe that it is of paramount importance that the advocate should always be seen to be courteous and polite both to the witnesses and to the tribunal.

During your opponent's cross-examination

When the examination-in-chief is concluded you sit down and your opponent begins to cross-examine your witness. You must take a very full and careful note of the cross-examination. Take down as much as you possibly can because it is often not apparent at any given moment whether or not the particular passage of evidence will subsequently appear to be important. The judge will himself take a note of both the evidence in chief and cross-examination, and most judges like the advocates to refer to the evidence by referring to a note; one only has to sit in a county court for a day to see the number of occasions in a contested trial in which the judge will refer back to the notes he has taken, and ask the advocates to refer to the notes they have of the relevant passages. Quite apart from this it must be remembered that many cases in the county courts are adjourned either for further evidence or for argument, and it is of great help to the advocate to have a full note of evidence when days or weeks later he comes to prepare the case again for the next stage of the hearing.

Your own cross-examination

The rules of evidence so far as cross-examination are concerned are straightforward; the advocate is entitled to ask as many leading questions as he wishes in cross-examination and he is entitled to put to the witness any letter or note or other document in which the witness has earlier said something different from the testimony he has given in the witness-box. Although the rules of evidence are straightforward, the actual technique of cross-examination is difficult and sometimes, to the beginner, extremely difficult. I offer some suggestions. The first thing to do is to determine whether the witness who has given evidence which is adverse to your client is merely mistaken or is deliberately fabricating the evidence. In 90 per cent or more of all cases (particularly in civil courts) witnesses are in fact mistaken and not lying when they give evidence which is subsequently rejected by the court. It is much easier to persuade a judge that a witness is mistaken than that he is lying. Now if you come to the conclusion that the witness who has said something adverse to your client has made a genuine mistake, the right course in cross-examining him is to indicate to him at the very beginning of your questioning that you are not suggesting that he is lying; this often comes as a great relief to the witness who, on the basis of television dramas and novels, will have an exaggerated idea of what is likely to happen to him in the witness-box. Once you have made it clear to the witness that it is not part of your case that he is in any way dishonest, he will automatically be relieved and more amenable to the suggestions that you put to him.

There is not much point at this stage in putting it squarely to the witness that he is wrong, because all of us have a natural pride in our memory and in our ability to comprehend what has been going on and would resent such a frontal attack. The best technique with such a witness is to explore with him in more detail the surrounding circumstances of the disputed matter upon which he has given evidence, and in exploring those circumstances see if in his account of the detail of the events in question he is putting forward a version of events which contains inconsistencies, or which is simply on a balance of probabilities unlikely to be true. Often it will be very relevant to see if his detailed account under cross-examination ties up with what has been recorded at the time in relevant documents.

When, as will be rare in a civil case, you come to the conclusion that the witness is lying, then the technique of cross-examination will be rather different. You should out of fairness make it clear to the witness that you do not accept his testimony is truthful. That does not, however, mean that you should cross-examine crossly or in an impolite manner. The method of cross-examination is to keep testing his story by making him repeat the evidence that he has given in the witness-box and asking for details. Many a man can invent a simple story but few have the imagination to be able to colour it with detail, and one of the techniques of cross-examining a lying witness is to demonstrate, by pressing him for the detail of his story, that his evidence cannot be true. Expect in such a case the witness to become evasive. If he does so, you must not allow him to avoid answering the question. One characteristic of untruthful witnesses is that when they see a question which they think might expose their dishonesty they will answer some other question, or embark upon a long involved story which detracts from the question that has been put to them. Be careful to watch out for such behaviour.

Final speech

At the end of the evidence you will be called upon to make your final speech. Now in a civil action this is more difficult to prepare than in a criminal case; you will be addressing a professional lawyer who will not be at all interested in any sort of flight of rhetoric; he will also expect something more than a prepared statement of your case. In the final speech you have to be flexible and you have to look back at the evidence that has been given. Remember of course that in a civil case the party wins whose version of events is more likely to be correct than incorrect — i.e., he succeeds on a 'balance of probabilities'. You are arguing therefore that your account is more likely to be true than not true. The speech will therefore be very different from that of a criminal advocate seeking to show there is a reasonable doubt about the matter.

It is often a sensible starting-point to ask the judge to look at the facts which are not in dispute and to show that those agreed facts are more consistent with your client's explanation of the matters than the explanation put forward by the other side. Another valid method of argument at this stage is to ask the judge to prefer the oral evidence which has been supported by the documents rather than the evidence which is either unsupported or indeed contradicted by what has been contained in the documentation.

The advocate should tell the judge what facts he asks him to find. It is important at this stage to use to the judge the correct language of advocacy; the advocate will 'submit' to the judge. It is unprofessional to tell the judge what you 'think' or what you 'believe'.

Above all, it is important both in your final speech and throughout the conduct of the case to be yourself; inexperienced advocates sometimes imagine that they should put on some completely different personality in order to impress the court; nothing could be more silly. The advocate who is attractive is the advocate who is sincere and unaffected. By sincerity we do not mean that the advocate has to believe what his client has told him; but what he must do is to suspend any disbelief that he has once he has clear instructions about the way a case should proceed, and he must present his client's case in a manner which makes it clear that it is a version of events sincerely put forward to the court.

Finally, at this stage, it is important to point out that every advocate requires a high degree of courage if he is to succeed. It takes courage to appear at all in a public forum; most tribunals are aware of the difficulties of advocacy, and the typical judge today behaves with courtesy and consideration, particularly to the young advocates who are appearing before him. But every advocate on occasion has the misfortune to come before a judge who, for one reason or another, is bad tempered or is acting in a boorish manner; in these very trying circumstances the good advocate has to keep his end up and must, while remaining courteous to the tribunal, insist on behalf of his client that his case is properly heard. This requires a very high degree of courage and is one of the reasons why advocacy properly commands a high degree of respect from the public.

Further reading

Richard Du Cann, *The Art of the Advocate*, revised ed. (London: Penguin, 1993); Keith Evans, *The Golden Rules of Advocacy* (London: Blackstone, 1993), Michael Hyam, *Advocacy Skills*, 3rd ed. (London: Blackstone, 1995).

Note

1. The complete text of David Paul Brown's rules is to be found in Sir Frederic Wrottesley, *The Examination of Witnesses in Court*, 3rd ed. (London, 1961). The book is unfortunately now out of print but copies appear from time to time in bookshops and are well worth purchasing.

Thirteen

Preparing and Presenting a Criminal Case

Introduction

Even if you never intend to set foot in a civil court, and regard yourself as a confirmed criminal practitioner, we recommend that if you have not already done so, you read Chapter 12 of this book before proceeding further with this chapter. While there are certainly important differences of approach to advocacy as between civil and criminal cases, there is also a sense in which advocacy is a single art, and much that was said in Chapter 12 concerning general principles of good advocacy in civil cases is applicable equally to criminal cases in the magistrates' court. Good advocacy always takes account of the nature of the tribunal before which it is conducted, and you will naturally adapt any principle of advocacy to the extent necessary to conform to the requirements of the court in which you are appearing. However, it is surprising how much the successful advocate relies upon well-tried techniques, whatever the tribunal.

It is important in criminal cases no less than in civil cases to prepare well in advance of trial, and to prepare as thoroughly as you possibly can by arranging your papers, documents and exhibits in a logical sequence and by achieving a mastery of the facts and chronology of the case. It is also just as important to arrive at court in ample time, to spend time in court before your case is called on, so as to allow yourself time to assess the bench or the mood of the bench, and to conduct yourself in court in a professional and becoming manner. These are fundamental principles of good advocacy applicable to any case, and need not be repeated here.

A word must be said about two subjects — manner of dress and manner of addressing the court — on which, although the principles of good advocacy are the same, the detail must vary as between the county court and the magistrates' court.

Despite the apparently wide divergence of dress seen in magistrates' courts up and down the country, I recommend a conservative appearance for the advocate. Since robes are not worn in the magistrates' court, the anonymity of the uniform of gown, bands and wing collar (and wig, if applicable) cannot be relied upon to achieve the desired result. Your dress will, therefore, convey far more about you than would a mere disposition towards neatness in terms of a clean gown and starched bands. The safe rule for men is to wear a dark (i.e., black, grey or very dark blue) three-piece suit, in which definition I would include the traditional black jacket and waistcoat with pin-stripe trousers. For women, I would recommend a formal suit or dress with high neck and long sleeves, in the same colours. The object, of course, is not to distract the court from your advocacy by offering it any excuse for preoccupation with your appearance.

In the county court, the judge is addressed as 'your honour'. Would that such simplicity were recognised in the magistrates' court, for it should be. The correct mode of address to a bench of magistrates is not to the bench at all, but to the chairman or chairwoman, who is addressed as 'sir' or 'madam', as the case may be. The remaining magistrates need not be addressed directly, although it is good advocacy to refer to them occasionally as the 'colleagues' of the chairman or chairwoman, to show that you have not forgotten them. The appellation, 'your worships', so beloved of police officers, is inappropriate when used by professional advocates and sometimes irritates benches in London and other cities. It is particularly tactless to use it on a stipendiary magistrate sitting in the singular rather than the plural. One really undesirable appellation is that which describes the magistrates as 'learned'. This is a term of art for referring to members of the Bar or judges, and its abuse is, strangely, often resented by magistrates. It is permissible and courteous, although not strictly necessary, to use the word 'learned' when referring to the clerk. As with dress, the object of using correct forms of address is to avoid distracting the bench from your advocacy by focusing their attention on peripheral matters.

Always go armed with a text to which you can refer for points of law, evidence or procedure which may arise unexpectedly. The most convenient book for all normal purposes is the current edition of *Blackstone's Criminal Practice*.

The concept of the ideal closing speech

I recommend an approach to preparing criminal cases which may, at
first sight, appear eccentric. It is based on the concept of the ideal
closing speech, that is to say the closing speech which you, as an
advocate, would ideally like to make, if the evidence given in your case
were actually to justify it. The concept can be applied to an opening
speech, but is at its clearest when applied to a closing speech. Since
the prosecution have no right to a closing speech in the magistrates'
court, except for the limited purpose of responding to points of law,
we shall, for the purposes of illustration, concentrate on the defence
closing speech.

The concept is apparently eccentric because it seems premature to
sit down before trial, before any evidence is given, to write a closing
speech. This, however, is where the word 'ideal' comes into play. The
point is that to compose the strongest possible closing speech, the most
persuasive argument to the court that you can imagine on the basis of
your client's instructions, serves to focus your mind on the evidence
which would be required to put you in a position to make it. This does
not mean, of course, that you will be able to obtain the required
evidence, or that, even if you can obtain it, it will necessarily
underwrite every point you would ideally wish to make. But it does
provide you with a useful summary of the direction in which your trial
preparation should go — what witnesses must be interviewed, whether
character witnesses should be sought, how you will approach the
prosecution witnesses and any co-defendants in cross-examination,
whether a plan or photographs or other similar visual aids would be
useful, and a myriad of other matters. By preparing your ideal closing
speech, you have forced yourself to think about what you need in terms
of evidence for the effective presentation of your case. You have also,
incidentally, created an invaluable note to take to court, which will,
when amended to take account of the evidence actually given, provide
an excellent framework for the speech you will in fact make.

Gathering the evidence

One thing which should emerge with some clarity from your ideal
closing speech is a picture of the witnesses you will need to call at trial.
If you are prosecuting, you will have been provided with statements
from the available witnesses, and can usually assume that no others are

known. As a defender, you have to be more resourceful. At the outset of your involvement with the case, you may know of no witnesses apart from the defendant. Your first task will be to ascertain whether the defendant knows of any witnesses who might help. Having read Chapter 8, you will appreciate that, in addition to any factual witnesses, you should always consider whether expert or character witnesses might be desirable. Make sure that you locate and take a proof of evidence from all likely witnesses in good time. It is a serious error to leave this until the day before trial. For one thing, you do not know whether you may have to issue a witness summons to compel attendance. For another, what they have to tell you may suggest the need for further investigation. You may need to take further instructions from the defendant for use in conjunction with the evidence of the witnesses. Make sure that you have access to any useful documents or exhibits that the witnesses may have. Expert and character witnesses can often be difficult to find, since the quality of both is particularly important, and the need for prompt action is acute in their cases.

There is no property in a witness. In some cases, you will feel that a proposed witness for the prosecution should be interviewed. There is no reason why this should not be done, but there are guidelines. A Law Society ruling requires that you notify the police of your intention, and afford them the opportunity to be present. I also recommend that, whenever possible, you arrange for an independent solicitor to be present.

Gaining access to the prosecution evidence in other respects prior to trial is more problematic. One vexing and continually recurring question is whether or not you will be given a sight of the prosecution statements prior to trial. As long ago as the Criminal Law Act 1977 the Lord Chancellor was given power to make rules requiring the prosecution to furnish the defence with information concerning the proposed prosecution evidence. It was not until the Magistrates' Courts (Advance Information) Rules 1985 came into force on 20 May 1985, that the defence acquired any such right, and that right is very far from complete.

The rules apply only to cases involving offences triable either way, and not to purely summary offences. In the case of an offence triable either way, if, before the court considers whether the offence appears to be more suitable for summary trial or trial on indictment, the accused requests the prosecution to furnish him with advance information, the prosecution shall furnish him as soon as practicable with either:

(a)   a copy of those parts of every written statement which contain information as to the facts and matters of which the prosecutor proposes to adduce evidence in the proceedings; or

(b)   a summary of the facts and matters of which the prosecutor proposes to adduce evidence in the proceedings (rule 4).

The prosecution may decline to do this only where, in their opinion, disclosure would lead to intimidation or attempted intimidation of a witness. Where the prosecution fail to comply with the rules without sufficient cause, the court shall adjourn the proceedings pending compliance unless satisfied that the case for the accused will not be substantially prejudiced by non-compliance with the requirement.

Although these rules represent a welcome improvement when contrasted with the previous law, there are many cases in which the defence still have no right to see the prosecution statements. In these cases, the only course is to request information, and to point out to the prosecutor that much time would be saved if you did not have to stop to take instructions at frequent intervals because of surprise. This sometimes works, but ultimately depends on the goodwill of the prosecutor.

There is a general duty on the prosecution to inform the defence of the known previous convictions of a prosecution witness, and it is always proper for a defender to enquire about them before the trial begins. There are further duties on the prosecution to make available as a witness for the defence any person from whom they have taken a statement, and know to be capable of giving material evidence, but do not propose to call as a prosecution witness, and to advise the defence of any material inconsistency between the evidence given by a prosecution witness and a previous statement made by the witness to the prosecution. Neither duty obliges the prosecution actually to supply the defence with a copy of the witness's statement.

You are entitled to see the original of any exhibit which the prosecution intend to produce as evidence at trial, including any statement under caution made by your client. For the reasons discussed in Chapter 5, you should always avail yourself of this opportunity. You are also entitled to see the charge sheet, which surprisingly often proves to be a mine of useful information about times and places, and your client's possessions at the time of his arrest. The police will often, on request, allow you or your expert witness to inspect under supervision such exhibits as photographs, tapes and material objects. One object of this, quite apart from affording you and your expert witness access to the exhibits, is to check their originality and authenticity. There should be an unbroken chain of possession of exhibits which ensures that they can be positively identified as being what they purport to be, and that they have not been altered or tampered with. Unless the party producing an exhibit can demonstrate at least a *prima facie* case that this is so, the court should refuse to admit the exhibit into evidence. This is often of great significance when dealing with tapes, photographs, video-tapes and the like, but is often ignored when cross-examination of the custodians of the evidence would yield promising results. A pre-trial view of the exhibits, with your expert if appropriate, often opens up lines of inquiry. You should also consider visiting the *locus in quo*. Actually seeing the place where crucial events took place can greatly help your understanding of the case.

You should give some thought to preparing exhibits of your own. The use of photographs, plans, models and the like appears, for some reason, to be almost a prosecution prerogative. To ignore the possibilities of such demonstrative evidence is to ignore a potent forensic weapon, since it often conveys relevant facts to a court far more vividly than argument or oral evidence. When confronted with some illustrative device of this kind, the bench feel, understandably, more closely involved with the presentation of the case. They may also feel that a case which has been prepared with such care and forethought must command some credibility. It is surprising how little effort is really involved in the preparation of good photographs and other similar exhibits. As items of real evidence, they are admissible subject only to authentication, that is to say calling evidence from the maker of each exhibit to establish its originality and freedom from tampering and falsification.

Lastly, remember to comply with any requirements for disclosure of your evidence which may have been rendered necessary by your voluntary disclosure of the defence case under s. 6 of the Criminal Procedure and Investigations Act 1996. You will have done this to gain access to the prosecution's secondary disclosure material. We discussed this in detail in Chapter 6. Now, you must make sure that you have served your defence statement in a timely manner, and that there is no concern that the nature of the defence may have changed. If it has, for example, you have to call a different alibi witness, or you have simply reconsidered the nature of the defence, it would be advisable to notify the prosecution and the court, to prevent what would otherwise be the consequences of offering a defence inconsistent with that originally disclosed. The prosecution may also wish to inspect any items of evidence which you may intend to adduce.

Preparation of cross-examination

It is a trite saying, but a true one, that cross-examination is one of the most difficult arts that can confront the advocate in any court. Whole treatises have been written on the supposed techniques of cross-examination. Much of what has been written, while perfectly valid, relates to the colourful and theatrical style of cross-examination which is popularly supposed to be effective in front of a jury. In this day and age, it is doubtful whether such flamboyance of style is effective before any tribunal, and before a county court judge, a stipendiary magistrate or even an experienced lay bench, it may justly be compared to playing the second house at the Barnsley music-hall on a wet Monday evening.

We shall, therefore, confine ourselves to some very simple, but effective rules which govern good cross-examination under any circumstances. These rules will not make you into another Marshall Hall, for it is very difficult to say what makes the difference between a competent technician and a true artist in the field of cross-examination, but they should prevent you from making at any rate the most obvious and dire errors. They are four in number:

(a) Decide what kind of witness you have to cross-examine. Like all advocacy, cross-examination depends first and foremost upon good preparation. This is easier if you have access to the prosecution statements before trial, but in any case a certain degree of preparation is possible on the basis of your instructions. The most fundamental decision you must make, based on your instructions, the statement if you have it, and the demeanour of the witness while giving evidence in chief, is whether the witness is (i) dishonest, (ii) unreliable or (iii) mistaken, or whether the witness perhaps falls into some other category of your own invention. The importance of this decision, which must often be made very quickly, cannot be overstated. Firstly, on it depends whether your client may lose his shield because you have, in cross-examination, made an imputation on the character of the witness within the meaning of s. 1(f)(ii) of the Criminal Evidence Act 1898. In many cases you will have no choice. If your instructions are that 15 minutes' worth of alleged verbal admissions were never said at all, it is no good trying to suggest to the officer that he is mistaken about it. The allegation is one of perjury or fabrication of evidence, which is always an imputation on character. But more often, your instructions are consistent with unreliability or mistake, and these can be asserted without loss of the shield. Secondly, your classification of the witness is bound to govern the style of your cross-examination, and you must have clear in your mind, before you begin to cross-examine, what it is you hope to achieve. If the witness can be cross-examined satisfactorily as a category (ii) or category (iii) witness, why risk alienating the bench by setting out to prove that he is a liar falling squarely within category (i)? Benches, quite naturally, much prefer to avoid finding somebody to be a liar if it is possible that he is simply unreliable or mistaken.

(b) Keep aggression to a minimum. This rule follows from the first. Aggression is rarely commendable in a cross-examiner, and even when called for, requires great skill to execute properly. It is unforgivable for an advocate to harass, intimidate or argue with a witness, or to appear to do any of these things. Firmness is acceptable, as is persistence, but these qualities may be demonstrated without aggression. Unless you have committed yourself to a classification of the witness as falling within category (i), a reasonable, enquiring style is invariably more effective, and reduces the risk both of alienating the bench and of accidentally losing your client's shield. You only have to spend a little time watching the best cross-examiners at the Bar to appreciate how much more effective is a quiet, methodical approach than an all-out assault.

(c) Deal first with non-contentious matters. This rule stems from the fact that cross-examination has two purposes, and not just one. These were described in Chapter 11. Many advocates concentrate on the purpose of challenging the evidence in chief, to the exclusion of the purpose of eliciting facts favourable to the case of the cross-examiner, which have not emerged or which were insufficiently emphasised in chief. If you know that you will have to challenge certain evidence given by the witness, you may wish to divide your cross-examination into two phases. The first phase should be non-contentious. In this phase, you will be gathering facts about which the witness will not object to telling you. Only later will you move into phase two, the challenging phase, at the moment when you feel that the witness has given you all the voluntary assistance he is likely to give you. The consequence of reversing the order of these phases is, of course, that the witness will already feel hostile by the time you tone down your cross-examination to the non-contentious level, and is unlikely to give you much assistance.

(d)   Never ask an unnecessary question. The object of all examination of witnesses is to elicit sufficient evidence to build the foundation of your closing speech. One of the advantages of having prepared your ideal closing speech is that you should know what evidence you need in order to make the desired submissions. When you have gathered this evidence, stop. It is rightly said that one of the most difficult things for an advocate to learn is to shut up and sit down. Certainly, it can be a real exercise in self-discipline when the client is sitting behind you willing you to take the other side's witnesses on, and expecting to get his, or the Legal Aid Fund's money's worth in terms of forensic action. But the lesson is also one of the most important of all to learn, because many are the cases that are ruined by that one question too many. This is particularly critical in cross-examination, when it must be assumed that the witnesses on the other side are hostile. If a witness has not harmed your case, it is best not to cross-examine at all, unless you wish to bring out non-contentious facts. If you have to go further, it is a good working rule to confine cross-examination to the minimum necessary to put your case properly. Avoid the temptation to 'hammer home' some point which the witness may have made which is favourable to you; given a second chance, the witness may withdraw or qualify his answer and take away your advantage. The proper time to hammer a point home is in your closing speech, when the danger from witnesses has passed.

Never ask a witness to probe your client's state of mind; 'You have no reason to believe my client was dishonest, have you?' and the like gives the witness a standing invitation to sink you without trace. It is an unnecessary, and strictly inadmissible question (though your opponent is unlikely to object) since the witness does not know what your client's state of mind was, and his speculation on the subject is unlikely to help you.

Do not ask a witness to explain his reason for doing something, unless it is unavoidable, and it rarely is. The classic here is, 'Officer, why were you following my client?' The officer will eventually overcome his professional inhibitions and tell you, and since you asked him, it will sound pretty lame when you object that the answer is inadmissible. In summary, ask yourself constantly: have I now enough to make the points which I want to make in my closing speech, based on this witness's evidence? At the first moment when the answer to that question is in the affirmative, sit down and wait for the opportunity to make those points. Do not try to score additional points off the witness. You are much more likely to lose those you already have.

Preparing the defendant's evidence-in-chief

Chapter 12 has dealt already with a number of important matters concerning the technique of conducting an examination-in-chief. These are applicable to criminal trials just as much as to civil, and repay constant study and application. They can be applied to the evidence of the defendant and of any other witness, whether factual, expert or character, whom you may determine to call as a result of preparing your ideal closing speech. To that extent, we need not consider the evidence of the defendant as a separate subject. However, the evidence of the defendant sometimes calls for additional exercises in judgment, the theoretical basis for which has already been explored in previous chapters.

The first point on which the advocate's judgment is required derives from the fact that the defendant is not obliged to give evidence in his defence at all. Although competent, the defendant is not a compellable witness. Moreover, because of the burden and standard of proof in criminal cases, the defendant may simply remain silent and say to the prosecution, in effect, 'You have not proved your case; there is nothing for me to answer.' While this is all very well in theory, and sometimes works well in front of a jury, it is rarely a practical proposition in the magistrates' court, where the bench, as a broad matter of common sense, will inevitably find it suspicious if the defendant does not tell them his side of the story from the witness-box. As we saw in Chapter 6, the decision is also influenced by the possibility of an adverse inference being drawn against the defendant, if he does not give evidence. The choice is that of the defendant, not his advocate, but the defendant will almost always accept his advocate's advice on this matter, and in the magistrates' court, that advice should be to give evidence except in the rarest of cases. Such a case would probably only arise when the bench have agonised over a submission of no case to answer, and clearly regard the prosecution case as extremely weak. In this rare type of case, a decision not to call the defendant sometimes pushes the bench over the edge after your closing speech, and also avoids the possibility that the defendant may supply a case against himself which the prosecution have been unable to supply — a by no means unusual event in criminal trials.

The other major factor in planning the defendant's evidence in chief relates to his previous character. If the defendant is of good character, this fact should be brought out in cross-examination of the officer in charge of the case, by calling the defendant to say so and by calling a reputable and credible character witness, if one is available. As was said in Chapter 7, evidence of good character not only assists the credit of the defendant as a witness, but is actually some evidence tending to show that he is innocent.

Representing a client of previous bad character presents some difficult choices. Naturally, magistrates need little experience to realise the significance of a discreet silence about previous character during a trial. Nonetheless, it is a sound rule which should be followed in almost every case, that the defendant's bad character should be withheld from the bench whenever possible. Magistrates are quite used to suppressing the urge to speculate about the defendant's character, as it is in most cases a very difficult area in which to speculate, and they habitually decide cases without giving the subject a thought.

There are, however, some cases in which the voluntary revelation of the defendant's character may be advantageous, at least when compared to the alternatives. For example, where your client has undoubtedly lost his shield, the prosecutor will not agree to withhold cross-examination about character and you have no real argument for discretion, the best course is probably to introduce your client's character in chief. Unpalatable as this may be, it is generally better than waiting for it to be dragged out in cross-examination. This is designed to, and often does, take the wind out of the prosecutor's sails.

Another example is found in what we shall call in this book — it is not a known technical term — the doctrine of relative good character. The doctrine of relative good character comes into play when the client's previous character, though from a technical standpoint bad, is in some way sympathetic. The former rogue who has gone straight for many years offers one illustration, since his abstention from crime for a substantial time suggests an honest nature. The doctrine trades the defendant's right to withhold his character for the credit gained for frankness with the court. It may be applied where the defendant's bad character is concerned with offences of a radically different nature from that charged. A defendant charged with indecent assault on a child who volunteers his total criminal record consisting of a few convictions for theft may not only be gaining credit for frankness, but also asserting his lack of propensity to commit sexual offences. Sometimes a defendant with a record for similar offences may be well advised to reveal his character, where he has always readily admitted his guilt in the past by a plea of guilty.

The doctrine of relative good character is not an everyday weapon, but is to be used sparingly and with good judgment. There are also two essential steps to take before using it. The first is to check the defendant's record in meticulous detail. Nothing is worse than finding out too late that the defendant's record is far worse, or of a different nature than the defendant told you, and defendants do forget the details from time to time. The second is to explain to the defendant what you propose to do, and obtain his informed consent to the surrender of an important right. A sudden and unexpected allusion to bad character from one's own advocate in court tends to injure the always fragile relationship of trust between advocate and client.

Lastly, always consider the likely effect of the defendant's evidence on any co-defendants. Remember that if the defendant gives evidence against a co-defendant, he loses his shield with even more certainty than he does by making imputations on the character of prosecution witnesses. If the case inevitably involves a 'cut-throat' defence, fate leaves you no real choice but to ask the defendant questions which implicate the co-defendant, and this is quite enough to lose you your shield. But in cases where your defence does not depend upon implicating the co-defendant, make sure that your client does not launch a gratuitous attack on the co-defendant. It is bad enough to lose the shield in a good cause; to lose it unnecessarily is terrible.

All these considerations regarding the defendant's evidence require you to spend time with the defendant before the trial, explaining to him the principles involved and winning his confidence in the decisions you propose to take which will call for his cooperation as a witness. It is by no means a bad thing to give the defendant a 'dry run' through his evidence in chief in your office, before trial. Not only will it boost your client's confidence and hopefully improve his performance in the witness-box, but because of its immediacy, it is also a first-rate way of getting further instructions and warning yourself about the answers you are likely to receive in court. You would not be the first advocate to scrap and remodel in its entirety a proposed examination-in-chief after conducting a session of this kind.

Preparing and delivering your speech

The ability to make a good speech is the key to persuasion in advocacy. The word advocacy derives from the Latin *'ad vocare'*, meaning literally 'to call towards'. Advocacy is, then, the art of winning the listener over to the advocate's cause by persuasive speaking. Although every aspect of the advocate's presence in court, including the presentation of evidence, should be directed to this end, it is generally accepted that the art comes into its own most strongly in the making of a speech to the bench, judge or jury. We shall consider briefly three kinds of speech relevant to criminal trials, namely the opening speech, the submission of no case to answer and the closing speech. But it is appropriate to preface this discussion by one or two observations concerning style.

The best style to adopt in making any speech is your own. While there is nothing wrong with picking up useful techniques and phrases from other experienced advocates, an attempt to imitate the style of another is doomed to failure. The techniques you will learn by experience and by listening to others can be built into your style; no good advocate ever stops learning new techniques of speech or developing new ideas. Because the object is to persuade the court before which you are appearing, you will mould the content of the speech to be as pleasing to the court as possible. Your speech to a stipendiary magistrate should be very different from your speech to a lay bench on the same facts. Your speech to a bench known to you from long association with the court should be different from your speech to an unfamiliar bench on the same facts. In the same way, of course, in your local county court, your speech to Judge A who sits on Mondays should be different from your speech to Judge B who sits on Tuesdays. If, one Monday, Judge A is indisposed and you come before Judge B unexpectedly, you should make some swift revisions to your planned speech.

Of course, a primary reason for the recommendation that you spend time in court before your case is called on, is that it is important to find out as much as you can in that limited time about the bench, its attitudes, forensic taste and even its mood. The opportunity for such observation may be limited, but any information is better than none. The advantage of the local advocate appearing before a familiar local bench is considerable in this respect, and having such an advocate as your opponent in a strange court can put you at a disadvantage which should not be underestimated. In any court, it is a sound rule to be as brief as is consistent with a full presentation of your arguments. Not only does brevity always commend itself to a busy court, but it also reduces the risk that the impact of what you say, your persuasiveness, may be eroded by overstretching the attention span of the tribunal.

The purpose of an opening speech, whether made for the prosecution or, in very rare cases for the defence, is simply to give the court an overview of the evidence which is to follow, together with a short statement of the applicable law. It is almost always a mistake to make an opening speech for the defence. The nature of most defences appears quite clearly from the path taken in cross-examination, and only in a complex case involving a number of witnesses or very difficult evidence should an opening speech be contemplated. In all other cases, a defence opening speech is no more than an unnecessary risk that your right to make a closing speech, your real chance to be persuasive, will be lost. For the prosecution, conversely, the opening speech is the best opportunity to be persuasive. Some prosecutors forbear from making an opening speech in simple cases, but the best course would seem to make a speech of a brevity proportionate to the simplicity of the case. Brevity is always desirable in an opening. Unlike juries, magistrates do not need an exhaustive explanation of all the facts. Try to develop an outline of the salient facts and law, leaving the detail to emerge during the evidence. It gives an impression of disorganisation to seem to be reading the anticipated evidence directly from the statements, particularly if this involves a recitation of lengthy interviews. It is always far better not to read from any statement, and to make a concise summary of the anticipated evidence in your own words. An orderly presentation of the salient points will be clear and persuasive in itself. Omit from an opening speech any evidence which you are told by your opponent is alleged to be inadmissible. The procedure for dealing with this is described in Chapter 1.

A submission of no case to answer is made at the close of the prosecution case, and before any presentation of the defence case. Such a submission must be based either on the fact that there is no evidence to prove an essential element of the offence charged, or on a submission that the prosecution evidence has been so discredited by cross-examination, or is so manifestly unreliable that no reasonable tribunal could safely convict on it. What you say must, therefore, be directed to explaining to the bench why the case falls under one or both of those heads.

It is always a good beginning to remind the bench of the object of your submission, and to emphasise that because of the burden and standard of proof in criminal cases, they not only may, but should dismiss the charge without calling on the defence in a proper case. The great rule about submissions of no case is to make them only in cases where there is a reasonable prospect of success. Remember that if you fail, the case goes on, and you would much prefer not to have to go on with a bench profoundly irritated by having to sit through a hopeless submission. If the case presents a submission which, though not of the strongest, should be made, make it with truly exemplary brevity. A well made submission, based on plausible grounds, will not antagonise the bench and, even if unsuccessful, will have some value in preparing the bench for your closing speech. Even if they are not prepared to stop the case at the close of the prosecution case, the bench may be receptive to similar arguments at a later stage. Always be prepared to address the bench on any point of law necessary to sustain your submission, and when dealing with the law, allude to the clerk, inviting the bench to take his or her advice. Proper deference to the clerk is no less desirable in advocacy in the magistrates' court than to the bench itself.

The defence closing speech is the most potent of forensic weapons in a summary trial. If well prepared, it can have tremendous effect, yet very often, it appears that advocates do no more than say the first things that come into their heads immediately after the flurry of evidence has died down. It is true that time for reflection is short in a summary trial, and that you have to move from one phase of the trial to another with great rapidity. Nonetheless, proper preparation can compensate for much of this. If you have your note of your ideal closing speech, you will add and delete points in the briefest note form, as the evidence emerges. Since you should never write out any speech verbatim, you should have a more than sufficient note of the general order and content of your speech. Taking a note of the evidence is in itself difficult enough, especially when you are on your feet. But again, this can be solved to the extent necessary by leaving a space for the briefest note of the answer opposite your note of your proposed questions.

The content of a closing speech obviously varies widely from case to case, but here again, some guidelines can be established. It is always appropriate to refer briefly to the burden and standard of proof. The bench know perfectly well the principles of law involved, and you should couch your remarks in terms of 'reminding' the court of them. You should also deal with this subject in a few sentences. But it should not be omitted. It makes a good standard opening, during which you can compose and collect yourself a little after the heat of battle. The most recent battleground before your closing speech will often have been your client's evidence, and listening to this can be traumatic for any advocate. Moreover, the burden and standard of proof are vital elements of any criminal trial, and their inclusion at the outset should ensure that everything that follows is seen in that light. Some advocates make a second (extremely brief) mention of it as a concluding observation, and this is often worthwhile in a close case. If the bench are unsure and undecided, the burden and standard of proof are often determinative of the case.

Deal with the law applicable to the case if necessary, bearing in mind that the bench will permit the prosecution to reply on a point of law. Bear in mind the strictures set out in Chapter 12 against reading law reports to those who have no text to follow. In the magistrates' court, reading from law reports is never satisfactory. It is far better to summarise the law for the bench, refer by name to the authorities, and hand them to the clerk for his or her perusal.

When dealing with the facts, it is essential to avoid misstatements of the evidence, and exaggerated statements of the effect of the evidence. With the very best of intentions, this tendency can be difficult to avoid for any enthusiastic advocate. A closing speech sometimes carries its maker away, with the result that his or her memory of the evidence becomes increasingly rose-tinted as time goes on. Any misstatement of the evidence is likely to be picked up by the bench, who have listened to the evidence throughout without the distraction of papers and the conduct of the case. If you catch yourself misstating or exaggerating the evidence, apologise, refer to your notes and get it right. Realism is an essential component of good advocacy in every phase. It can be fatal to say that there is no evidence of something, when your true (and just as cogent) argument is that there is some evidence of it, but that the evidence is plainly insufficient, when judged by reference to the standard of proof. You should always admit the existence of whatever case there may be against you, and then argue against it to the maximum extent possible, rather than trying to bulldoze your way through with specious statements that there is no case against your client. The bench know better. Naked statements that there is no case or no evidence are never as cogent as a balanced, reasoned argument of why the prosecution have failed to discharge the heavy onus of proof which lies upon them in a criminal case.

For the reasons suggested in Chapter 12 in relation to addressing a county court judge, it is always preferable to put a case to a magistrates' court, whether consisting of a lay bench or a stipendiary magistrate, on the basis that the prosecution witnesses are unreliable or mistaken, than on the basis that they have committed perjury or fabricated evidence. This is particularly true when the witnesses concerned are police officers. There is nothing sinister in this. All courts prefer to believe that people are disposed to tell the truth, and it is comforting to all of us to hear that no allegation of improper conduct is being made against the police. The process of persuasion is made easier whenever the tribunal can be reassured on that point. In some cases, you will have no choice but to allege firmly that certain witnesses have been dishonest, but do not assume such a position without good reason.

Finally, bear in mind David Paul Brown's injunction cited in Chapter 12, that the advocate should act as though he is awake, and engaged in a matter of interest to him. Whether or not you believe your client's case is irrelevant; what counts is whether the court find that it has been disproved beyond reasonable doubt. Never even hint that you are a disbeliever. Suspend your disbelief, and be as persuasive as the nature of the case permits.

Further reading

See recommendations at the end of Chapter 12.

Appendix

Extracts from Statutes, Codes of Practice and Rules of Court

Criminal Evidence Act 1898, section 1, as amended

Competency of witnesses in criminal cases
1.   Every person charged with an offence shall be a competent witness for the defence at every stage of the proceedings, whether the person so charged is charged solely or jointly with any other person. Provided as follows:—

(a)   A person so charged shall not be called as a witness in pursuance of this Act except upon his own application:

(b)   [repealed]

(c)   [repealed]

(d)   [repealed]

(e)   A person charged and being a witness in pursuance of this Act may be asked any question in cross-examination notwithstanding that it would tend to criminate him as to the offence charged:

(f)   A person charged and called as a witness in pursuance of this Act shall not be asked, and if asked shall not be required to answer, any question tending to show that he has committed or been convicted of or been charged with any offence other than that wherewith he is then charged, or is of bad character, unless—

(i)   the proof that he has committed or been convicted of such other offence is admissible evidence to show that he is guilty of the offence wherewith he is then charged; or

(ii)   he has personally or by his advocate asked questions of the witnesses for the prosecution with a view to establish his own good character, or has given evidence of his good character, or the nature or conduct of the defence is such as to involve imputations on the character of the prosecutor or the witnesses for the prosecution; or the deceased victim of the alleged crime; or

(iii)   he has given evidence against any other person charged in the same proceedings:

(g)   Every person called as a witness in pursuance of this Act shall, unless otherwise ordered by the court, give his evidence from the witness-box or other place from which the other witnesses give their evidence:

(h)   [repealed].

Police and Criminal Evidence Act 1984, sections 58 and 76–80

Access to legal advice
58.—(1)   A person arrested and held in custody in a police station or other premises shall be entitled, if he so requests, to consult a solicitor privately at any time.

(2)   Subject to subsection (3) below, a request under subsection (1) above and the time at which it was made shall be recorded in the custody record.

(3)   Such a request need not be recorded in the custody record of a person who makes it at a time while he is at a court after being charged with an offence.

(4)   If a person makes such a request, he must be permitted to consult a solicitor as soon as is practicable except to the extent that delay is permitted by this section.

(5)   In any case he must be permitted to consult a solicitor within 36 hours from the relevant time, as defined in section 41(2) above.

(6)   Delay in compliance with a request is only permitted—

(a)   in the case of a person who is in police detention for a serious arrestable offence; and

(b)   if an officer of at least the rank of superintendent authorises it.

(7)   An officer may give an authorisation under subsection (6) above orally or in writing but, if he gives it orally, he shall confirm it in writing as soon as is practicable.

(8)   Subject to subsection (8A) below an officer may only authorise delay where he has reasonable grounds for believing that the exercise of the right conferred by subsection (1) above at the time when the person detained desires to exercise it—

(a)   will lead to interference with or harm to evidence connected with a serious arrestable offence or interference with or physical injury to other persons; or

(b)   will lead to the alerting of other persons suspected of having committed such an offence but not yet arrested for it; or

(c)   will hinder the recovery of any property obtained as a result of such an offence.

(8A)   An officer may also authorise delay where the serious arrestable offence is a drug trafficking offence or an offence to which Part VI of the Criminal Justice Act 1988 applies and the officer has reasonable grounds for believing—

(a)   where the offence is a drug trafficking offence, that the detained person has benefited from drug trafficking and that the recovery of the value of that person's proceeds of drug trafficking will be hindered by the exercise of the right conferred by subsection (1) above; and

(b)   where the offence is one to which Part VI of the Criminal Justice Act 1988 applies, that the detained person has benefited from the offence and that the recovery of the value of the property obtained by that person from or in connection with the offence or of the pecuniary advantage derived by him from or in connection with it will be hindered by the exercise of the right conferred by subsection (1) above.

(9)   If delay is authorised—

(a)   the detained person shall be told the reason for it; and

(b)   the reason shall be noted on his custody record.

(10)   The duties imposed by subsection (9) above shall be performed as soon as is practicable.

(11)   There may be no further delay in permitting the exercise of the right conferred by subsection (1) above once the reason for authorising delay ceases to subsist.

(12)   The reference in subsection (1) above to a person arrested includes a reference to a person who has been detained under the terrorism provisions.

(13)   In the application of this section to a person who has been arrested or detained under the terrorism provisions—

(a)   subsection (5) above shall have effect as if for the words from 'within' onwards there were substituted the words 'before the end of the period beyond which he may no longer be detained without the authority of the Secretary of State';

(b)   subsection (6)(a) above shall have effect as if for the words 'for a serious arrestable offence' there were substituted the words 'under the terrorism provisions'; and

(c)   subsection (8) above shall have effect as if at the end there were added

'or

(d)   will lead to interference with the gathering of information about the commission, preparation or instigation of acts of terrorism; or

(e)   by alerting any person, will make it more difficult—

(i)   to prevent an act of terrorism; or

(ii)   to secure the apprehension, prosecution or conviction of any person in connection with the commission, preparation or instigation of an act of terrorism.'

(14)   If an officer of appropriate rank has reasonable grounds for believing that, unless he gives a direction under subsection (15) below, the exercise by a person arrested or detained under the terrorism provisions of the right conferred by subsection (1) above will have any of the consequences specified in subsection (8) above (as it has effect by virtue of subsection (13) above), he may give a direction under that subsection.

(15)   A direction under this subsection is a direction that a person desiring to exercise the right conferred by subsection (1) above may only consult a solicitor in the sight and hearing of a qualified officer of the uniformed branch of the force of which the officer giving the direction is a member.

(16)   An officer is qualified for the purpose of subsection (15) above if—

(a)   he is of at least the rank of inspector; and

(b)   in the opinion of the officer giving the direction he has no connection with the case.

(17)   An officer is of appropriate rank to give a direction under subsection (15) above if he is of at least the rank of Commander or Assistant Chief Constable.

(18)   A direction under subsection (15) above shall cease to have effect once the reason for giving it ceases to subsist.

Confessions

76.—(1)   In any proceedings a confession made by an accused person may be given in evidence against him in so far as it is relevant to any matter in issue in the proceedings and is not excluded by the court in pursuance of this section.

(2) If, in any proceedings where the prosecution proposes to give in evidence a confession made by an accused person, it is represented to the court that the confession was or may have been obtained—

(a) by oppression of the person who made it; or

(b) in consequence of anything said or done which was likely, in the circumstances existing at the time, to render unreliable any confession which might be made by him in consequence thereof, the court shall not allow the confession to be given in evidence against him except in so far as the prosecution proves to the court beyond reasonable doubt that the confession (notwithstanding that it may be true) was not obtained as aforesaid.

(3) In any proceedings where the prosecution proposes to give in evidence a confession made by an accused person, the court may of its own motion require the prosecution, as a condition of allowing it to do so, to prove that the confession was not obtained as mentioned in subsection (2) above.

(4) The fact that a confession is wholly or partly excluded in pursuance of this section shall not affect the admissibility in evidence—

(a) of any facts discovered as a result of the confession; or

(b) where the confession is relevant as showing that the accused speaks, writes or expresses himself in a particular way, of so much of the confession as is necessary to show that he does so.

(5) Evidence that a fact to which this subsection applies was discovered as a result of a statement made by an accused person shall not be admissible unless evidence of how it was discovered is given by him or on his behalf.

(6) Subsection (5) above applies—

(a) to any fact discovered as a result of a confession which is wholly excluded in pursuance of this section; and

(b) to any fact discovered as a result of a confession which is partly so excluded, if the fact is discovered as a result of the excluded part of the confession.

(7) Nothing in Part VII of this Act shall prejudice the admissibility of a confession made by an accused person.

(8) In this section 'oppression' includes torture, inhuman or degrading treatment, and the use or threat of violence (whether or not amounting to torture).

Confessions by mentally handicapped persons

77.—(1) Without prejudice to the general duty of the court at a trial on indictment to direct the jury on any matter on which it appears to the court appropriate to do so, where at such a trial—

(a) the case against the accused depends wholly or substantially on a confession by him; and

(b) the court is satisfied—

(i) that he is mentally handicapped; and

(ii) that the confession was not made in the presence of an independent person,

the court shall warn the jury that there is special need for caution before convicting the accused in reliance on the confession, and shall explain that the need arises because of the circumstances mentioned in paragraphs (a) and (b) above.

(2) In any case where at the summary trial of a person for an offence it appears to the court that a warning under subsection (1) above would be required if the trial were on indictment, the court shall treat the case as one in which there is a special need for caution before convicting the accused on his confession.

(3) In this section—

'independent person' does not include a police officer or a person employed for, or engaged on, police purposes;

'mentally handicapped', in relation to a person, means that he is in a state of arrested or incomplete development of mind which includes significant impairment of intelligence and social functioning; and

'police purposes' has the meaning assigned to it by section 101(2) of the Police Act 1996.

Exclusion of unfair evidence

78.—(1) In any proceedings the court may refuse to allow evidence on which the prosecution proposes to rely to be given if it appears to the court that, having regard to all the circumstances, including the circumstances in which the evidence was obtained, the admission of the evidence would have such an adverse effect on the fairness of the proceedings that the court ought not to admit it.

(2) Nothing in this section shall prejudice any rule of law requiring a court to exclude evidence.

Time for taking accused's evidence

79.—If at the trial of any person for an offence—

(a)   the defence intends to call two or more witnesses to the facts of the case; and

(b)   those witnesses include the accused,

the accused shall be called before the other witness or witnesses unless the court in its discretion otherwise directs.

Competence and compellability of accused's spouse

80.—(1)   In any proceedings the wife or husband of the accused shall be competent to give evidence—

(a)   subject to subsection (4) below, for the prosecution; and

(b)   on behalf of the accused or any person jointly charged with the accused.

(2)   In any proceedings the wife or husband of the accused shall, subject to subsection (4) below, be compellable to give evidence on behalf of the accused.

(3)   In any proceedings the wife or husband of the accused shall, subject to subsection (4) below, be compellable to give evidence for the prosecution or on behalf of any person jointly charged with the accused if and only if—

(a)   the offence charged involves an assault on, or injury or a threat of injury to, the wife or husband of the accused or a person who was at the material time under the age of 16; or

(b)   the offence charged is a sexual offence alleged to have been committed in respect of a person who was at the material time under that age; or

(c)   the offence charged consists of attempting or conspiring to commit, or of aiding, abetting, counselling, procuring or inciting the commission of, an offence falling within paragraph (a) or (b) above.

(4)   Where a husband and wife are jointly charged with an offence neither spouse shall at the trial be competent or compellable by virtue of subsection (1)(a), (2) or (3) above to give evidence in respect of that offence unless that spouse is not, or is no longer, liable to be convicted of that offence at the trial as a result of pleading guilty or for any other reason.

(5)   In any proceedings a person who has been but is no longer married to the accused shall be competent and compellable to give evidence as if that person and the accused had never been married.

(6)   Where in any proceedings the age of any person at any time is material for the purposes of subsection (3) above, his age at the material time shall for the purposes of that provision be deemed to be

or to have been that which appears to the court to be or to have been his age at that time.

(7)   In subsection (3)(b) above 'sexual offence' means an offence under the Sexual Offences Act 1956, the Indecency with Children Act 1960, the Sexual Offences Act 1967, section 54 of the Criminal Law Act 1977 or the Protection of Children Act 1978.

(8)   The failure of the wife or husband of the accused to give evidence shall not be made the subject of any comment by the prosecution.

(9)   Section 1(d) of the Criminal Evidence Act 1898 (communications between husband and wife) and section 43(1) of the Matrimonial Causes Act 1965 (evidence as to marital intercourse) shall cease to have effect.

Code of Practice (C) for the Detention, Treatment and Questioning of Persons by Police Officers

1.   General

1.1   All persons in custody must be dealt with expeditiously, and released as soon as the need for detention has ceased to apply.

1.1A   A custody officer is required to perform the functions specified in this code as soon as is practicable. A custody officer shall not be in breach of this code in the event of delay provided that the delay is justifiable and that every reasonable step is taken to prevent unnecessary delay. The custody record shall indicate where a delay has occurred and the reason why. [See Note 1H]

1.2   This code of practice must be readily available at all police stations for consultation by police officers, detained persons and members of the public.

1.3   The notes for guidance included are not provisions of this code, but are guidance to police officers and others about its application and interpretation. Provisions in the annexes to this code are provisions of this code.

1.4   If an officer has any suspicion, or is told in good faith, that a person of any age may be mentally disordered or mentally handicapped, or mentally incapable of understanding the significance of questions put to him or his replies, then that person shall be treated as a mentally disordered or mentally handicapped person for the purposes of this code. [See Note 1G]

1.5   If anyone appears to be under the age of 17 then he shall be treated as a juvenile for the purposes of this code in the absence of clear evidence to show that he is older.

1.6   If a person appears to be blind or seriously visually handicapped, deaf, unable to read, unable to speak or has difficulty orally because of a speech impediment, he should be treated as such for the purposes of this code in the absence of clear evidence to the contrary.

1.7   In this code 'the appropriate adult' means:

(a)   in the case of a juvenile:

(i)   his parent or guardian (or, if he is in care, the care authority or voluntary organisation. The term 'in care' is used in this code to cover all cases in which a juvenile is 'looked after' by a local authority under the terms of the Children Act 1989);

(ii)   a social worker;

(iii)   failing either of the above, another responsible adult aged 18 or over who is not a police officer or employed by the police.

(b)   in the case of a person who is mentally disordered or mentally handicapped:

(i)   a relative, guardian or other person responsible for his care or custody;

(ii)   someone who has experience of dealing with mentally disordered or mentally handicapped people but is not a police officer or employed by the police (such as an approved social worker as defined by the Mental Health Act 1983 or a specialist social worker); or

(iii)   failing either of the above, some other responsible adult aged 18 or over who is not a police officer or employed by the police. [See Note 1E]

1.8   Whenever this code requires a person to be given certain information he does not have to be given it if he is incapable at the time of understanding what is said to him or is violent or likely to become violent or is in urgent need of medical attention, but he must be given it as soon as practicable.

1.9   Any reference to a custody officer in this code includes an officer who is performing the functions of a custody officer.

1.10   Subject to paragraph 1.12, this code applies to people who are in custody at police stations in England and Wales whether or not they have been arrested for an offence and to those who have been removed to a police station as a place of safety under sections 135 and 136 of the Mental Health Act 1983. Section 15 (reviews and extensions of detention) however applies solely to people in police detention, for example those who have been brought to a police station under arrest for an offence or have been arrested at a police station for an offence after attending there voluntarily.

1.11   People in police detention include anyone taken to a police station after being arrested under section 14 of the Prevention of Terrorism (Temporary Provisions) Act 1989 or under paragraph 6 of schedule 5 to that Act by an examining officer who is a constable.

1.12   This code does not apply to the following groups of people in custody:

(i)   people who have been arrested by officers from a police force in Scotland exercising their powers of detention under section 137(2) of the Criminal Justice and Public Order Act 1994 (cross border powers of arrest etc.);

(ii)   people arrested under section 3(5) of the Asylum and Immigration Appeals Act 1993 for the purpose of having their fingerprints taken;

(iii)   people who have been served a notice advising them of their detention under powers contained in the Immigration Act 1971;

(iv)   convicted or remanded prisoners held in police cells on behalf of the Prison Service under the Imprisonment (Temporary Provisions) Act 1980);

but the provisions on conditions of detention and treatment in sections 8 and 9 of this code must be considered as the minimum standards of treatment for such detainees.

Notes for Guidance

1A   Although certain sections of this code (e.g. section 9 – treatment of detained persons) apply specifically to people in custody at police stations, those there voluntarily to assist with an investigation should be treated with no less consideration (e.g. offered refreshments at appropriate times) and enjoy an absolute right to obtain legal advice or communicate with anyone outside the police station.

1B   This code does not affect the principle that all citizens have a duty to help police officers to prevent crime and discover offenders. This is a civic rather than a legal duty; but when a police officer is trying to discover whether, or by whom, an offence has been committed he is entitled to question any person from whom he thinks useful information can be obtained, subject to the restrictions imposed by this code. A person's declaration that he is unwilling to reply does not alter this entitlement.

1C   A person, including a parent or guardian, should not be an appropriate adult if he is suspected of involvement in the offence in question, is the victim, is a witness, is involved in the investigation or has received admissions prior to attending to act as the appropriate adult. If the parent of a juvenile is estranged from the juvenile, he should not be asked to act as the appropriate adult if the juvenile expressly and specifically objects to his presence.

1D   If a juvenile admits an offence to or in the presence of a social worker other than during the time that the social worker is acting as the appropriate adult for that juvenile, another social worker should be the appropriate adult in the interest of fairness.

1E   In the case of people who are mentally disordered or mentally handicapped, it may in certain circumstances be more satisfactory for all concerned if the appropriate adult is someone who has experience or training in their care rather than a relative lacking such qualifications. But if the person himself prefers a relative to a better qualified stranger or objects to a particular person as the appropriate adult, his wishes should if practicable be respected.

1EE A person should always be given an opportunity, when an appropriate adult is called to the police station, to consult privately with a solicitor in the absence of the appropriate adult if they wish to do so.

1F   A solicitor or lay visitor who is present at the police station in that capacity may not act as the appropriate adult.

1G   The generic term 'mental disorder' is used throughout this code. 'Mental disorder' is defined in section 1(2) of the Mental Health Act 1983 as 'mental illness, arrested or incomplete development of mind, psychopathic disorder and any other disorder or disability of mind'. It should be noted that 'mental disorder' is different from 'mental handicap' although the two are dealt with similarly throughout this code. Where the custody officer has any doubt as to the mental state or capacity of a person detained an appropriate adult should be called.

1H   Paragraph 1.1A is intended to cover the kinds of delays which may occur in the processing of detained persons because, for example, a large number of suspects are brought into the police station simultaneously to be placed in custody, or interview rooms are all being used, or where there are difficulties in contacting an appropriate adult, solicitor or interpreter.

1I   It is important that the custody officer reminds the appropriate adult and the detained person of the right to legal advice and records any reasons for waiving it in accordance with section 6 of this code.

2.   Custody records

2.1   A separate custody record must be opened as soon as practicable for each person who is brought to a police station under arrest or is arrested at the police station having attended there voluntarily. All information which has to be recorded under this code must be recorded as soon as practicable in the custody record unless otherwise specified. Any audio or video recording made in the custody area is not part of the custody record.

2.2 In the case of any action requiring the authority of an officer of a specified rank, his name and rank must be noted in the custody record. The recording of names does not apply to officers dealing with people detained under the Prevention of Terrorism (Temporary Provisions) Act 1989. Instead the record shall state the warrant or other identification number and duty station of such officers.

2.3 The custody officer is responsible for the accuracy and completeness of the custody record and for ensuring that the record or a copy of the record accompanies a detained person if he is transferred to another police station. The record shall show the time of and reason for transfer and the time a person is released from detention.

2.4 A solicitor or appropriate adult must be permitted to consult the custody record of a person detained as soon as practicable after their arrival at the police station. When a person leaves police detention or is taken before a court, he or his legal representative or his appropriate adult shall be supplied on request with a copy of the custody record as soon as practicable. This entitlement lasts for 12 months after his release.

2.5 The person who has been detained, the appropriate adult, or the legal representative shall be permitted to inspect the original custody record after the person has left police detention provided they give reasonable notice of their request. A note of any such inspection shall be made in the custody record.

2.6 All entries in custody records must be timed and signed by the maker. In the case of a record entered on a computer this shall be timed and contain the operator's identification. Warrant or other identification numbers shall be used rather than names in the case of detention under the Prevention of Terrorism (Temporary Provisions) Act 1989.

2.7 The fact and time of any refusal by a person to sign a custody record when asked to do so in accordance with the provisions of this code must itself be recorded.

3. Initial action

(a) Detained persons: normal procedure

3.1 When a person is brought to a police station under arrest or is arrested at the police station having attended there voluntarily, the custody officer must tell him clearly of the following rights and of the fact that they are continuing rights which may be exercised at any stage during the period in custody.

(i)   the right to have someone informed of his arrest in accordance with section 5 below;

(ii)   the right to consult privately with a solicitor and the fact that independent legal advice is available free of charge; and

(iii)   the right to consult these codes of practice.

[See Note 3E]

3.2   In addition the custody officer must give the person a written notice setting out the above three rights, the right to a copy of the custody record in accordance with paragraph 2.4 above and the caution in the terms prescribed in section 10 below. The notice must also explain the arrangements for obtaining legal advice. The custody officer must also give the person an additional written notice briefly setting out his entitlements while in custody. [See Notes 3A and 3B] The custody officer shall ask the person to sign the custody record to acknowledge receipt of these notices and any refusal to sign must be recorded on the custody record.

3.3   A citizen of an independent Commonwealth country or a national of a foreign country (including the Republic of Ireland) must be informed as soon as practicable of his rights of communication with his High Commission, Embassy or Consulate. [See Section 7]

3.4   The custody officer shall note on the custody record any comment the person may make in relation to the arresting officer's account but shall not invite comment. If the custody officer authorises a person's detention he must inform him of the grounds as soon as practicable and in any case before that person is then questioned about any offence. The custody officer shall note any comment the person may make in respect of the decision to detain him but, again, shall not invite comment. The custody officer shall not put specific questions to the person regarding his involvement in any offence, nor in respect of any comments he may make in response to the arresting officer's account or the decision to place him in detention. Such an exchange is likely to constitute an interview as defined by paragraph 11.1A and would require the associated safeguards included in section 11. [See also paragraph 11.13 in respect of unsolicited comments.]

3.5   The custody officer shall ask the detained person whether at this time he would like legal advice (see paragraph 6.5). The person shall be asked to sign the custody record to confirm his decision. The custody officer is responsible for ensuring that in confirming any decision the person signs in the correct place.

3.5A   If video cameras are installed in the custody area, notices which indicate that cameras are in use shall be prominently displayed. Any request by a detained person or other person to have video cameras switched off shall be refused.

(b)   Detained persons: special groups

3.6   If the person appears to be deaf or there is doubt about his hearing or speaking ability or ability to understand English, and the custody officer cannot establish effective communication, the custody officer must as soon as practicable call an interpreter and ask him to provide the information required above. [See Section 13]

3.7   If the person is a juvenile, the custody officer must, if it is practicable, ascertain the identity of a person responsible for his welfare. That person may be his parent or guardian (or, if he is in care, the care authority or voluntary organisation) or any other person who has, for the time being, assumed responsibility for his welfare. That person must be informed as soon as practicable that the juvenile has been arrested, why he has been arrested and where he is detained. This right is in addition to the juvenile's right in section 5 of the code not to be held incommunicado. [See Note 3C]

3.8   In the case of a juvenile who is known to be subject to a supervision order, reasonable steps must also be taken to notify the person supervising him.

3.9   If the person is a juvenile, is mentally handicapped or appears to be suffering from a mental disorder, then the custody officer must, as soon as practicable, inform the appropriate adult (who in the case of a juvenile may or may not be a person responsible for his welfare, in accordance with paragraph 3.7 above) of the grounds for his detention and his whereabouts, and ask the adult to come to the police station to see the person.

3.10   It is imperative that a mentally disordered or mentally handicapped person who has been detained under section 136 of the Mental Health Act 1983 shall be assessed as soon as possible. If that assessment is to take place at the police station, an approved social worker and a registered medical practitioner shall be called to the police station as soon as possible in order to interview and examine the person. Once the person has been interviewed and examined and suitable arrangements have been made for his treatment or care, he can no longer be detained under section 136. The person should not be released until he has been seen by both the approved social worker and the registered medical practitioner.

3.11   If the appropriate adult is already at the police station, then the provisions of paragraphs 3.1 to 3.5 above must be complied with in his presence. If the appropriate adult is not at the police station when the provisions of paragraphs 3.1 to 3.5 above are complied with, then these provisions must be complied with again in the presence of the appropriate adult once that person arrives.

3.12   The person shall be advised by the custody officer that the appropriate adult (where applicable) is there to assist and advise him and that he can consult privately with the appropriate adult at any time.

3.13   If, having been informed of the right to legal advice under paragraph 3.11 above, either the appropriate adult or the person detained wishes legal advice to be taken, then the provisions of section 6 of this code apply. [See Note 3G]

3.14   If the person is blind or seriously visually handicapped or is unable to read, the custody officer should ensure that his solicitor, relative, the appropriate adult or some other person likely to take an interest in him (and not involved in the investigation) is available to help in checking any documentation. Where this code requires written consent or signification then the person who is assisting may be asked to sign instead if the detained person so wishes. [See Note 3F]

(c)   Persons attending a police station voluntarily

3.15   Any person attending a police station voluntarily for the purpose of assisting with an investigation may leave at will unless placed under arrest. If it is decided that he should not be allowed to leave then he must be informed at once that he is under arrest and brought before the custody officer, who is responsible for ensuring that he is notified of his rights in the same way as other detained persons. If he is not placed under arrest but is cautioned in accordance with section 10 below, the officer who gives the caution must at the same time inform him that he is not under arrest, that he is not obliged to remain at the police station but that if he remains at the police station he may obtain free and independent legal advice if he wishes. The officer shall point out that the right to legal advice includes the right to speak with a solicitor on the telephone and ask him if he wishes to do so.

3.16   If a person who is attending the police station voluntarily (in accordance with paragraph 3.15) asks about his entitlement to legal advice, he shall be given a copy of the notice explaining the arrangements for obtaining legal advice. [See paragraph 3.2]

(d) Documentation

3.17 The grounds for a person's detention shall be recorded, in his presence if practicable.

3.18 Action taken under paragraphs 3.6 to 3.14 shall be recorded.

Notes for Guidance

3A The notice of entitlements is intended to provide detained persons with brief details of their entitlements over and above the statutory rights which are set out in the notice of rights. The notice of entitlements should list the entitlements contained in this code, including visits and contact with outside parties (including special provisions for Commonwealth citizens and foreign nationals), reasonable standards of physical comfort, adequate food and drink, access to toilets and washing facilities, clothing, medical attention, and exercise where practicable. It should also mention the provisions relating to the conduct of interviews, the circumstances in which an appropriate adult should be available to assist the detained person and his statutory rights to make representation whenever the period of his detention is reviewed.

3B In addition to the notices in English, translations should be available in Welsh, the main ethnic minority languages and the principal European languages whenever they are likely to be helpful.

3C If the juvenile is in the care of a local authority or voluntary organisation but is living with his parents or other adults responsible for his welfare then, although there is no legal obligation on the police to inform them, they as well as the authority or organisation should normally be contacted unless suspected of involvement in the offence concerned. Even if a juvenile in care is not living with his parents, consideration should be given to informing them as well.

3D Most local authority Social Services Departments can supply a list of interpreters who have the necessary skills and experience to interpret for the deaf at police interviews. The local Community Relations Council may be able to provide similar information in cases where the person concerned does not understand English. [See Section 13]

3E The right to consult the codes of practice under paragraph 3.1 above does not entitle the person concerned to delay unreasonably any necessary investigative or administrative action while he does so. Procedures requiring the provision of breath, blood or urine specimens under the terms of the Road Traffic Act 1988 need not be delayed.

3F   Blind or seriously visually handicapped persons may be unwilling to sign police documents. The alternative of their representative signing on their behalf seeks to protect the interests of both police and detained people.

3G   The purpose of paragraph 3.13 is to protect the rights of a juvenile, mentally disordered or mentally handicapped person who may not understand the significance of what is being said to him. If such a person wishes to exercise the right to legal advice the appropriate action should be taken straightaway and not delayed until the appropriate adult arrives.

4. Detained persons' property

(a) Action

4.1   The custody officer is responsible for:

   (a)   ascertaining:

      (i)   what property a detained person has with him when he comes to the police station (whether on arrest, re-detention on answering to bail, commitment to prison custody on the order or sentence of a court, lodgement at the police station with a view to his production in court from such custody, arrival at a police station on transfer from detention at another police station or from hospital or on detention under section 135 or 136 of the Mental Health Act 1983);

      (ii)   what property he might have acquired for an unlawful or harmful purpose while in custody;

   (b)   the safekeeping of any property which is taken from him and which remains at the police station.

To these ends the custody officer may search him or authorise his being searched to the extent that he considers necessary (provided that a search of intimate parts of the body or involving the removal of more than outer clothing may only be made in accordance with Annex A to this code). A search may only be carried out by an officer of the same sex as the person searched. [See Note 4A]

4.2   A detained person may retain clothing and personal effects at his own risk unless the custody officer considers that he may use them to cause harm to himself or others, interfere with evidence, damage property or effect an escape or they are needed as evidence. In this event the custody officer may withhold such articles as he considers necessary. If he does so he must tell the person why.

4.3   Personal effects are those items which a person may lawfully need or use or refer to while in detention but do not include cash and other items of value.

(b)   Documentation
4.4   The custody officer is responsible for recording all property brought to the police station which a detained person had with him, or had taken from him on arrest. The detained person shall be allowed to check and sign the record of property as correct. Any refusal to sign should be recorded.
4.5   If a detained person is not allowed to keep any article of clothing or personal effects the reason must be recorded.

Notes for Guidance
4A   Section 54(1) of PACE and paragraph 4.1 require a detained person to be searched where it is clear that the custody officer will have continuing duties in relation to that person or where that person's behaviour or offence makes an inventory appropriate. They do not require *every* detained person to be searched. Where, for example, it is clear that a person will only be detained for a short period and is not to be placed in a cell, the custody officer may decide not to search him. In such a case the custody record will be endorsed 'not searched', paragraph 4.4 will not apply, and the person will be invited to sign the entry. Where the person detained refuses to sign, the custody officer will be obliged to ascertain what property he has on him in accordance with paragraph 4.1.
4B   Paragraph 4.4 does not require the custody officer to record on the custody record property in the possession of the person on arrest, if by virtue of its nature, quantity or size, it is not practicable to remove it to the police station.
4C   Paragraph 4.4 above is not to be taken as requiring that items of clothing worn by the person be recorded unless withheld by the custody officer in accordance with paragraph 4.2.

5.   Right not to be held incommunicado
(a)   Action
5.1   Any person arrested and held in custody at a police station or other premises may on request have one person known to him or who is likely to take an interest in his welfare informed at public expense of his whereabouts as soon as practicable. If the person cannot be contacted the person who has made the request may choose up to two alternatives. If they too cannot be contacted the person in charge of detention or of the investigation has discretion to allow further attempts until the information has been conveyed. [See Notes 5C and 5D]

5.2   The exercise of the above right in respect of each of the persons nominated may be delayed only in accordance with Annex B to this code.

5.3   The above right may be exercised on each occasion that a person is taken to another police station.

5.4   The person may receive visits at the custody officer's discretion. [See Note 5B]

5.5   Where an enquiry as to the whereabouts of the person is made by a friend, relative or person with an interest in his welfare, this information shall be given, if he agrees and if Annex B does not apply. [See Note 5D]

5.6   Subject to the following condition, the person shall be supplied with writing materials on request and allowed to speak on the telephone for a reasonable time to one person [See Notes 5A and 5E]. Where an officer of the rank of inspector or above considers that the sending of a letter or the making of a telephone call may result in:

(a)   any of the consequences set out in the first and second paragraphs of Annex B and the person is detained in connection with an arrestable or a serious arrestable offence, for which purpose, any reference to a serious arrestable offence in Annex B includes an arrestable offence; or

(b)   either of the consequences set out in paragraph 8 of Annex B and the person is detained under the Prevention of Terrorism (Temporary Provisions) Act 1989;

that officer can deny or delay the exercise of either or both these privileges. However, nothing in this section permits the restriction or denial of the rights set out in paragraphs 5.1 and 6.1.

5.7   Before any letter or message is sent, or telephone call made, the person shall be informed that what he says in any letter, call or message (other than in the case of a communication to a solicitor) may be read or listened to as appropriate and may be given in evidence. A telephone call may be terminated if it is being abused. The costs can be at public expense at the discretion of the custody officer.

(b)   Documentation

5.8   A record must be kept of:

(a)   any request made under this section and the action taken on it;

(b)   any letters, messages or telephone calls made or received or visits received; and

(c)   any refusal on the part of the person to have information about himself or his whereabouts given to an outside enquirer. The person must be asked to countersign the record accordingly and any refusal to sign shall be recorded.

Notes for Guidance

5A   An interpreter may make a telephone call or write a letter on a person's behalf.

5B   In the exercise of his discretion the custody officer should allow visits where possible in the light of the availability of sufficient manpower to supervise a visit and any possible hindrance to the investigation.

5C   If the person does not know of anyone to contact for advice or support or cannot contact a friend or relative, the custody officer should bear in mind any local voluntary bodies or other organisations who might be able to offer help in such cases. But if it is specifically legal advice that is wanted, then paragraph 6.1 below will apply.

5D   In some circumstances it may not be appropriate to use the telephone to disclose information under paragraphs 5.1 and 5.5 above.

5E   The telephone call at paragraph 5.6 is in addition to any communication under paragraphs 5.1 and 6.1.

6.   Right to legal advice

(a)   Action

6.1   Subject to the provisos in Annex B all people in police detention must be informed that they may at any time consult and communicate privately, whether in person, in writing or by telephone with a solicitor, and that independent legal advice is available free of charge from the duty solicitor. [See paragraph 3.1 and Note 6B and Note 6J]

6.2   [Not Used]

6.3   A poster advertising the right to have legal advice must be prominently displayed in the charging area of every police station. [See Note 6H]

6.4   No police officer shall at any time do or say anything with the intention of dissuading a person in detention from obtaining legal advice.

6.5   The exercise of the right of access to legal advice may be delayed only in accordance with Annex B to this code. Whenever legal advice is requested (and unless Annex B applies) the custody officer must act without delay to secure the provision of such advice to the person concerned. If, on being informed or reminded of the right to legal advice, the person declines to speak to a solicitor in person, the officer shall point out that the right to legal advice includes the right to speak with a solicitor on the telephone and ask him if he wishes to do so. If the person continues to waive his right to legal advice the officer shall ask him the reasons for doing so, and any reasons shall be recorded on the custody record or the interview record as appropriate. Reminders of the right to legal advice must be given in accordance with paragraphs 3.5, 11.2, 15.3, 16.4 and 16.5 of this code and paragraphs 2.15(ii) and 5.2 of Code D. Once it is clear that a person neither wishes to speak to a solicitor in person nor by telephone he should cease to be asked his reasons. [See Note 6K]

6.6   A person who wants legal advice may not be interviewed or continue to be interviewed until he has received it unless:

(a)   Annex B applies; or

(b)   an officer of the rank of superintendent or above has reasonable grounds for believing that:

(i)   delay will involve an immediate risk of harm to persons or serious loss of, or damage to, property; or

(ii)   where a solicitor, including a duty solicitor, has been contacted and has agreed to attend, awaiting his arrival would cause unreasonable delay to the process of investigation; or

(c)   the solicitor nominated by the person, or selected by him from a list:

(i)   cannot be contacted; or

(ii)   has previously indicated that he does not wish to be contacted; or

(iii)   having been contacted, has declined to attend;

and the person has been advised of the Duty Solicitor Scheme but has declined to ask for the duty solicitor, or the duty solicitor is unavailable. (In these circumstances the interview may be started or continued without further delay provided that an officer of the rank of Inspector or above has given agreement for the interview to proceed in those circumstances – See Note 6B).

(d)   the person who wanted legal advice changes his mind.

In these circumstances the interview may be started or continued without further delay provided that the person has given his agreement in writing or on tape to being interviewed without receiving legal advice and that an officer of the rank of inspector or above, having inquired into the person's reasons for his change of mind, has given authority for the interview to proceed. Confirmation of the person's agreement, his change of mind, his reasons where given and the name of the authorising officer shall be recorded in the taped or written interview record at the beginning or re-commencement of interview. [See Note 6I]

6.7   Where 6.6(b)(i) applies, once sufficient information to avert the risk has been obtained, questioning must cease until the person has received legal advice unless 6.6(a), (b)(ii), (c) or (d) apply.

6.8   Where a person has been permitted to consult a solicitor and the solicitor is available (i.e. present at the station or on his way to the station or easily contactable by telephone) at the time the interview begins or is in progress, the solicitor must be allowed to be present while he is interviewed.

6.9   The solicitor may only be required to leave the interview if his conduct is such that the investigating officer is unable properly to put questions to the suspect. [See Notes 6D and 6E]

6.10   If the investigating officer considers that a solicitor is acting in such a way, he will stop the interview and consult an officer not below the rank of superintendent, if one is readily available, and otherwise an officer not below the rank of inspector who is not connected with the investigation. After speaking to the solicitor, the officer who has been consulted will decide whether or not the interview should continue in the presence of that solicitor. If he decides that it should not, the suspect will be given the opportunity to consult another solicitor before the interview continues and that solicitor will be given an opportunity to be present at the interview.

6.11   The removal of a solicitor from an interview is a serious step and, if it occurs, the officer of superintendent rank or above who took the decision will consider whether the incident should be reported to the Law Society. If the decision to remove the solicitor has been taken by an officer below the rank of superintendent, the facts must be reported to an officer of superintendent rank or above who will similarly consider whether a report to the Law Society would be appropriate. Where the solicitor concerned is a duty solicitor, the report should be both to the Law Society and to the Legal Aid Board.

6.12   In Codes of Practice issued under the Police and Criminal Evidence Act 1984, 'solicitor' means a solicitor who holds a current practising certificate, a trainee solicitor, a duty solicitor representative or an accredited representative included on the register of representatives maintained by the Legal Aid Board. If a solicitor wishes to send a non-accredited or probationary representative to provide advice on his behalf, then that person shall be admitted to the police station for this purpose unless an officer of the rank of inspector or above considers that such a visit will hinder the investigation of crime and directs otherwise. (Hindering the investigation of a crime does not include giving proper legal advice to a detained person in accordance with Note 6D.) Once admitted to the police station, the provisions of paragraphs 6.6 to 6.10 apply.

6.13 In exercising his discretion under paragraph 6.12, the officer should take into account in particular whether the identity and status of the non-accredited or probationary representative have been [satis-factorily] established; whether he is of suitable character to provide legal advice (a person with a criminal record is unlikely to be suitable unless the conviction was for a minor offence and is not of recent date); and any other matters in any written letter of authorisation provided by the solicitor on whose behalf the clerk or legal executive is attending the police station. [See Note 6F]

6.14 If the inspector refuses access to a non-accredited or probationary representative or a decision is taken that such a person should not be permitted to remain at an interview, he must forthwith notify a solicitor on whose behalf the non-accredited or probationary representative was to have acted or was acting, and give him an opportunity to make alternative arrangements. The detained person must also be informed and the custody record noted.

6.15 If a solicitor arrives at the station to see a particular person, that person must (unless Annex B applies) be informed of the solicitor's arrival whether or not he is being interviewed and asked whether he would like to see him. This applies even if the person concerned has already declined legal advice or having requested it, subsequently agreed to be interviewed without having received advice. The solicitor's attendance and the detained person's decision must be noted in the custody record.

(b) Documentation

6.16 Any request for legal advice and the action taken on it shall be recorded.

6.17 If a person has asked for legal advice and an interview is begun in the absence of a solicitor or his representative (or the solicitor or his representative has been required to leave an interview), a record shall be made in the interview record.

Notes for Guidance

6A In considering whether paragraph 6.6(b) applies, the officer should where practicable ask the solicitor for an estimate of the time that he is likely to take in coming to the station, and relate this information to the time for which detention is permitted, the time of day (i.e. whether the period of rest required by paragraph 12.2 is imminent) and the requirements of other investigations in progress. If the solicitor says that he is on his way to the station or that he will set off immediately, it will not normally be appropriate to begin an interview before he arrives. If it appears that it will be necessary to begin an interview before the solicitor's arrival he should be given an indication of how long the police would be able to wait before paragraph 6.6(b) applies so that he has an opportunity to make arrangements for legal advice to be provided by someone else.

6B   A person who asks for legal advice should be given an opportunity to consult a specific solicitor or another solicitor from that solicitor's firm or the duty solicitor. If advice is not available by these means, or he does not wish to consult the duty solicitor, the person should be given an opportunity to choose a solicitor from a list of those willing to provide legal advice. If this solicitor is unavailable, he may choose up [to] two alternatives. If these attempts to secure legal advice are unsuccessful, the custody officer has discretion to allow further attempts until a solicitor has been contacted and agrees to provide legal advice. Apart from carrying out his duties under Note 6B, a police officer must not advise the suspect about any particular firm of solicitors.

6C   [Not Used]

6D   A detained person has a right to free legal advice and to be represented by a solicitor. The solicitor's only role in the police station is to protect and advance the legal rights of his client. On occasions this may require the solicitor to give advice which has the effect of his client avoiding giving evidence which strengthens a prosecution case. The solicitor may intervene in order to seek clarification or to challenge an improper question to his client or the manner in which it is put, or to advise his client not to reply to particular questions, or if he wishes to give his client further legal advice. Paragraph 6.9 will only apply if the solicitor's approach or conduct prevents or unreasonably obstructs proper questions being put to the suspect or his response being recorded. Examples of unacceptable conduct include answering questions on a suspect's behalf or providing written replies for him to quote.

6E   In a case where an officer takes the decision to exclude a solicitor, he must be in a position to satisfy the court that the decision was properly made. In order to do this he may need to witness what is happening himself.

6F   If an officer of at least the rank of inspector considers that a particular solicitor or firm of solicitors is persistently sending non-accredited or probationary representatives who are unsuited to provide legal advice, he should inform an officer of at least the rank of superintendent, who may wish to take the matter up with the Law Society.

6G   Subject to the constraints of Annex B, a solicitor may advise more than one client in an investigation if he wishes. Any question of a conflict of interest is for the solicitor under his professional code of conduct. If, however, waiting for a solicitor to give advice to one client may lead to unreasonable delay to the interview with another, the provisions of paragraph 6.6(b) may apply.

6H   In addition to the poster in English advertising the right to legal advice, a poster or posters containing translations into Welsh, the main ethnic minority languages and the principal European languages should be displayed wherever they are likely to be helpful and it is practicable to do so.

6I   Paragraph 6.6(d) requires the authorisation of an officer of the rank of inspector or above, to the continuation of an interview, where a person who wanted legal advice changes his mind. It is permissible for such authorisation to be given over the telephone, if the authorising officer is able to satisfy himself as to the reason for the person's change of mind and is satisfied that it is proper to continue the interview in those circumstances.

6J   Where a person chooses to speak to a solicitor on the telephone, he should be allowed to do so in private unless this is impractical because of the design and layout of the custody area or the location of telephones.

6K   A person is not obliged to give reasons for declining legal advice and should not be pressed if he does not wish to do so.

7.   Citizens of Independent Commonwealth countries or foreign nationals

(a)   Action

7.1   Any citizen of an independent Commonwealth country or a national of a foreign country (including the Republic of Ireland) may communicate at any time with his High Commission, Embassy or Consulate. He must be informed of this right as soon as practicable.

He must also be informed as soon as practicable of his right, upon request to have his High Commission, Embassy or Consulate told of his whereabouts and the grounds for his detention. Such a request should be acted upon as soon as practicable.

7.2   If a person is detained who is a citizen of an independent Commonwealth or foreign country with which a bilateral consular convention or agreement is in force requiring notification of arrest, the appropriate High Commission, Embassy or Consulate shall be informed as soon as practicable, subject to paragraph 7.4 below. The countries to which this applies as at 1 January 1995 are listed in Annex F.

7.3   Consular officers may visit one of their nationals who is in police detention to talk to him and, if required, to arrange for legal advice. Such visits shall take place out of the hearing of a police officer.

7.4   Notwithstanding the provisions of consular conventions, where the person is a political refugee (whether for reasons of race, nationality, political opinion or religion) or is seeking political asylum, a consular officer shall not be informed of the arrest of one of his nationals or given access or information about him except at the person's express request.

(b)   Documentation

7.5   A record shall be made when a person is informed of his rights under this section and of any communications with a High Commission, Embassy or Consulate.

Note for Guidance

7A   The exercise of the rights in this section may not be interfered with even though Annex B applies.

8.   Conditions of Detention

(a)   Action

8.1   So far as is practicable, not more than one person shall be detained in each cell.

8.2   Cells in use must be adequately heated, cleaned and ventilated. They must be adequately lit, subject to such dimming as is compatible with safety and security to allow people detained overnight to sleep. No additional restraints shall be used within a locked cell unless absolutely necessary, and then only suitable handcuffs. In the case of a mentally handicapped or mentally disordered person, particular care must be taken when deciding whether to use handcuffs. [See Annex E paragraph 13]

8.3   Blankets, mattresses, pillows and other bedding supplied shall be of a reasonable standard and in a clean and sanitary condition. [See Note 8B]

8.4   Access to toilet and washing facilities must be provided.

8.5   If it is necessary to remove a person's clothes for the purposes of investigation, for hygiene or health reasons or for cleaning, replacement clothing of a reasonable standard of comfort and cleanliness shall be provided. A person may not be interviewed unless adequate clothing has been offered to him.

8.6   At least two light meals and one main meal shall be offered in any period of 24 hours. [See Note 8C] Drinks should be provided at meal times and upon reasonable request between meal times. Whenever necessary, advice shall be sought from the police surgeon on medical or dietary matters. As far as practicable, meals provided shall offer a varied diet and meet any special dietary needs or religious beliefs that the person may have; he may also have meals supplied by his family or friends at his or their own expense. [See Note 8B]

8.7   Brief outdoor exercise shall be offered daily if practicable.

8.8   A juvenile shall not be placed in a police cell unless no other secure accommodation is available and the custody officer considers that it is not practicable to supervise him if he is not placed in a cell or the custody officer considers that a cell provides more comfortable accommodation than other secure accommodation in the police station. He may not be placed in a cell with a detained adult.

8.9   Reasonable force may be used if necessary for the following purposes:

   (i)   to secure compliance with reasonable instructions, including instructions given in pursuance of the provisions of a code of practice; or

   (ii)   to prevent escape, injury, damage to property or the destruction of evidence.

8.10   People detained shall be visited every hour, and those who are drunk, at least every half hour. A person who is drunk shall be roused and spoken to on each visit. [See Note 8A] Should the custody officer feel in any way concerned about the person's condition, for example because he fails to respond adequately when roused, then the officer shall arrange for medical treatment in accordance with paragraph 9.2 of this code.

(b)   Documentation

8.11   A record must be kept of replacement clothing and meals offered.

8.12   If a juvenile is placed in a cell, the reason must be recorded.

Notes for Guidance
8A   Whenever possible juveniles and other persons at risk should be visited more frequently.
8B   The provisions in paragraphs 8.3 and 8.6 respectively regarding bedding and a varied diet are of particular importance in the case of a person detained under the Prevention of Terrorism (Temporary Provisions) Act 1989, immigration detainees and others who are likely to be detained for an extended period.
8C   Meals should so far as practicable be offered at recognised meal times.

9.   Treatment of Detained Persons
(a)   General
9.1   If a complaint is made by or on behalf of a detained person about his treatment since his arrest, or it comes to the notice of any officer that he may have been treated improperly, a report must be made as soon as practicable to an officer of the rank of inspector or above who is not connected with the investigation. If the matter concerns a possible assault or the possibility of the unnecessary or unreasonable use of force then the police surgeon must also be called as soon as practicable.
(b)   Medical Treatment
9.2   The custody officer must immediately call the police surgeon (or, in urgent cases, – for example, where a person does not show signs of sensibility or awareness, – must send the person to hospital or call the nearest available medical practitioner) if a person brought to a police station or already detained there:

    (a)   appears to be suffering from physical illness or a mental disorder; or

    (b)   is injured; or

    (c)   [Not Used]

    (d)   fails to respond normally to questions or conversation (other than through drunkenness alone); or

    (e)   otherwise appears to need medical attention.

This applies even if the person makes no request for medical attention and whether or not he has already had medical treatment elsewhere (unless brought to the police station direct from hospital). It is not intended that the contents of this paragraph should delay the transfer of a person to a place of safety under section 136 of the Mental Health

Act 1983 where that is applicable. Where an assessment under that Act is to take place at the police station, the custody officer has discretion not to call the police surgeon so long as he believes that the assessment by a registered medical practitioner can be undertaken without undue delay. [See Note 9A]

9.3   If it appears to the custody officer, or he is told, that a person brought to the police station under arrest may be suffering from an infectious disease of any significance he must take steps to isolate the person and his property until he has obtained medical directions as to where the person should be taken, whether fumigation should take place and what precautions should be taken by officers who have been or will be in contact with him.

9.4   If a detained person requests a medical examination the police surgeon must be called as soon as practicable. He may in addition be examined by a medical practitioner of his own choice at his own expense.

9.5   If a person is required to take or apply any medication in compliance with medical directions, but prescribed before the person's detention, the custody officer should consult the police surgeon prior to the use of the medication. The custody officer is responsible for the safekeeping of any medication and for ensuring that the person is given the opportunity to take or apply medication which the police surgeon has approved. However no police officer may administer medicines which are also controlled drugs subject to the Misuse of Drugs Act 1971 for this purpose. A person may administer a controlled drug to himself only under the personal supervision of the police surgeon. The requirement for personal supervision will have been satisfied if the custody officer consults the police surgeon (this may be done by telephone) and both the police surgeon and the custody officer are satisfied that, in all the circumstances, self administration of the controlled drug will not expose the detained person, police officers or anyone to the risk of harm or injury. If so satisfied, the police surgeon may authorise the custody officer to permit the detained person to administer the controlled drug. If the custody officer is in any doubt, the police surgeon should be asked to attend. Such consultation should be noted in the custody record.

9.6   If a detained person has in his possession or claims to need medication relating to a heart condition, diabetes, epilepsy or a condition of comparable potential seriousness then, even though paragraph 9.2 may not apply, the advice of the police surgeon must be obtained.

(c)   Documentation

9.7   A record must be made of any arrangements made for an examination by a police surgeon under paragraph 9.1 above and of any complaint reported under that paragraph together with any relevant remarks by the custody officer.

9.8   A record must be kept of any request for a medical examination under paragraph 9.4, of the arrangements for any examination made, and of any medical directions to the police.

9.9   Subject to the requirements of section 4 above the custody record shall include not only a record of all medication that a detained person has in his possession on arrival at the police station but also a note of any such medication he claims he needs but does not have with him.

Notes for Guidance

9A   The need to call a police surgeon need not apply to minor ailments or injuries which do not need attention. However, all such ailments or injuries must be recorded in the custody record and any doubt must be resolved in favour of calling the police surgeon.

9B   It is important to remember that a person who appears to be drunk or behaving abnormally may be suffering from illness or the effects of drugs or may have sustained injury (particularly head injury) which is not apparent, and that someone needing or addicted to certain drugs may experience harmful effects within a short time of being deprived of their supply. Police should therefore always call the police surgeon when in any doubt, and act with all due speed.

9C   If a medical practitioner does not record his clinical findings in the custody record, the record must show where they are recorded.

10.   Cautions

(a)   When a caution must be given

10.1   A person whom there are grounds to suspect of an offence must be cautioned before any questions about it (or further questions if it is his answers to previous questions which provide the grounds for suspicion) are put to him regarding his involvement or suspected involvement in that offence if his answers or his silence (i.e. failure or refusal to answer a question or to answer satisfactorily) may be given in evidence to a court in a prosecution. He therefore need not be cautioned if questions are put for other purposes, for example, solely to establish his identity or his ownership of any vehicle or to obtain information in accordance with any relevant statutory requirement (see paragraph 10.5C) or in furtherance of the proper and effective conduct of a search (for example to determine the need to search in the exercise of powers of stop and search or to seek cooperation while carrying out a search), or to seek verification of a written record in accordance with paragraph 11.13.

10.2   Whenever a person who is not under arrest is initially cautioned or is reminded that he is under caution (see paragraph 10.5) he must at the same time be told that he is not under arrest and is not obliged to remain with the officer (see paragraph 3.15).

10.3   A person must be cautioned upon arrest for an offence unless:

(a)   it is impracticable to do so by reason of his condition or behaviour at the time; or

(b)   he has already been cautioned immediately prior to arrest in accordance with paragraph 10.1 above.

(b)   Action: general

10.4   The caution shall be in the following terms:

'You do not have to say anything. But it may harm your defence if you do not mention when questioned something which you later rely on in court. Anything you do say may be given in evidence.'

Minor deviations do not constitute a breach of this requirement provided that the sense of the caution is preserved. [See Note 10C]

10.5   When there is a break in questioning under caution the interviewing officer must ensure that the person being questioned is aware that he remains under caution. If there is any doubt the caution should be given again in full when the interview resumes. [See Note 10A]

Special warnings under sections 36 and 37 of the Criminal Justice and Public Order Act 1994

10.5A   When a suspect who is interviewed after arrest fails or refuses to answer certain questions, or to answer them satisfactorily, after due warning, a court or jury may draw such inferences as appear proper under sections 36 and 37 of the Criminal Justice and Public Order Act 1994. This applies when:

(a)   a suspect is arrested by a constable and there is found on his person, or in or on his clothing or footwear, or otherwise in his possession, or in the place where he was arrested, any objects, marks or substances, or marks on such objects, and the person fails or refuses to account for the objects, marks or substances found; or

(b)   an arrested person was found by a constable at a place at or about the time the offence for which he was arrested, is alleged to have been committed, and the person fails or refuses to account for his presence at that place.

10.5B   For an inference to be drawn from a suspect's failure or refusal to answer a question about one of these matters or to answer it satisfactorily, the interviewing officer must first tell him in ordinary language:

(a)   what offence he is investigating;

(b)   what fact he is asking the suspect to account for;

(c)   that he believes this fact may be due to the suspect's taking part in the commission of the offence in question;

(d)   that a court may draw a proper inference if he fails or refuses to account for the fact about which he is being questioned;

(e)   that a record is being made of the interview and that it may be given in evidence if he is brought to trial.

10.5C   Where, despite the fact that a person has been cautioned, failure to cooperate may have an effect on his immediate treatment, he should be informed of any relevant consequences and that they are not affected by the caution. Examples are when his refusal to provide his name and address when charged may render him liable to detention, or when his refusal to provide particulars and information in accordance with a statutory requirement, for example, under the Road Traffic Act 1988, may amount to an offence or may make him liable to arrest.

(c)   Juveniles, the mentally disordered and the mentally handicapped

10.6   If a juvenile or a person who is mentally disordered or mentally handicapped is cautioned in the absence of the appropriate adult, the caution must be repeated in the adult's presence.

(d)   Documentation

10.7   A record shall be made when a caution is given under this section, either in the officer's pocket book or in the inteview record as appropriate.

Notes for Guidance

10A   In considering whether or not to caution again after a break, the officer should bear in mind that he may have to satisfy a court that the person understood that he was still under caution when the interview resumed.

10B   [Not Used]

10C   If it appears that a person does not understand what the caution means, the officer who has given it should go on to explain it in his own words.

10D   [Not Used]

11. Interviews: general

(a) Action

11.1A   An interview is the questioning of a person regarding his involvement or suspected involvement in a criminal offence or offences which, by virtue of paragraph 10.1 of Code C, is required to be carried out under caution. Procedures undertaken under section 7 of the Road Traffic Act 1988 do not constitute interviewing for the purpose of this code.

11.1   Following a decision to arrest a suspect he must not be interviewed about the relevant offence except at a police station or other authorised place of detention unless the consequent delay would be likely:

(a)   to lead to interference with or harm to evidence connected with an offence or interference with or physical harm to other people; or

(b)   to lead to the alerting of other people suspected of having committed an offence but not yet arrested for it; or

(c)   to hinder the recovery of property obtained in consequence of the commission of an offence.

Interviewing in any of these circumstances shall cease once the relevant risk has been averted or the necessary questions have been put in order to attempt to avert that risk.

11.2   Immediately prior to the commencement or re-commencement of any interview at a police station or other authorised place of detention, the interviewing officer shall remind the suspect of his entitlement to free legal advice and that the interview can be delayed for him to obtain legal advice (unless the exceptions in paragraph 6.6 or Annex C apply). It is the responsibility of the interviewing officer to ensure that all such reminders are noted in the record of interview.

11.2A   At the beginning of an interview carried out in a police station, the interviewing officer, after cautioning the suspect, shall put to him any significant statement or silence which occurred before his arrival at the police station, and shall ask him whether he confirms or denies that earlier statement or silence and whether he wishes to add anything. A 'significant' statement or silence is one which appears capable of being used in evidence against the suspect, in particular a direct admission of guilt, or failure or refusal to answer a question or to answer it satisfactorily, which might give rise to an inference under part III of the Criminal Justice and Public Order Act 1994.

11.3   No police officer may try to obtain answers to questions or to elicit a statement by the use of oppression. Except as provided for in paragraph 10.5C, no police officer shall indicate, except in answer to a direct question, what action will be taken on the part of the police if the person being interviewed answers questions, makes a statement or refuses to do either. If the person asks the officer directly what action will be taken in the event of his answering questions, making a statement or refusing to do either, then the officer may inform the person what action the police propose to take in that event provided that action is itself proper and warranted.

11.4   As soon as a police officer who is making enquiries of any person about an offence believes that a prosecution should be brought against him and that there is sufficient evidence for it to succeed, he should ask the person if he has anything further to say. If the person indicates that he has nothing more to say the officer shall without delay cease to question him about that offence. This should not, however, be taken to prevent officers in revenue cases or acting under the confiscation provisions of the Criminal Justice Act 1988 or the Drug Trafficking [Act 1994] from inviting suspects to complete a formal question and answer record after the interview is concluded.

(b)   Interview records

11.5   (a)   An accurate record must be made of each interview with a person suspected of an offence, whether or not the interview takes place at a police station.

(b)   The record must state the place of the interview, the time it begins and ends, the time the record is made (if different), any breaks in the interview and the names of all those present; and must be made on the forms provided for this purpose or in the officer's pocket-book or in accordance with the code of practice for the tape-recording of police interviews with suspects (Code E).

(c)   The record must be made during the course of the interview, unless in the investigating officer's view this would not be practicable or would interfere with the conduct of the interview, and must constitute either a verbatim record of what has been said or, failing this, an account of the interview which adequately and accurately summarises it.

11.6   The requirement to record the names of all those present at an interview does not apply to police officers interviewing people detained under the Prevention of Terrorism (Temporary Provisions) Act 1989. Instead the record shall state the warrant or other identification number and duty station of such officers.

11.7   If an interview record is not made during the course of the interview it must be made as soon as practicable after its completion.

11.8   Written interview records must be timed and signed by the maker.

11.9   If an interview record is not completed in the course of the interview the reason must be recorded in the officer's pocket book.

11.10   Unless it is impracticable the person interviewed shall be given the opportunity to read the interview record and to sign it as correct or to indicate the respects in which he considers it inaccurate. If the interview is tape-recorded the arrangements set out in Code E apply. If the person concerned cannot read or refuses to read the record or to sign it, the senior police officer present shall read it over to him and ask him whether he would like to sign it as correct (or make his mark) or to indicate the respects in which he considers it inaccurate. The police officer shall then certify on the interview record itself what has occurred. [See Note 11D]

11.11   If the appropriate adult or the person's solicitor is present during the interview, he shall also be given an opportunity to read and sign the interview record (or any written statement taken down by a police officer).

11.12   Any refusal by a person to sign an interview record when asked to do so in accordance with the provisions of the code must itself be recorded.

11.13   A written record shall also be made of any comments made by a suspected person, including unsolicited comments, which are outside the context of an interview but which might be relevant to the offence. Any such record must be timed and signed by the maker. Where practicable the person shall be given the opportunity to read that record and to sign it as correct or to indicate the respects in which he considers it inaccurate. Any refusal to sign shall be recorded. [See Note 11D]

(c)   Juveniles, mentally disordered people and mentally handicapped people

11.14   A juvenile or a person who is mentally disordered or mentally handicapped, whether suspected or not, must not be interviewed or asked to provide or sign a written statement in the absence of the appropriate adult unless paragraph 11.1 or Annex C applies.

11.15   Juveniles may only be interviewed at their places of education in exceptional circumstances and then only where the principal or his nominee agrees. Every effort should be made to notify both the parent(s) or other person responsible for the juvenile's welfare and the appropriate adult (if this is a different person) that the police want to interview the juvenile and reasonable time should be allowed to enable the appropriate adult to be present at the interview. Where awaiting the appropriate adult would cause unreasonable delay and unless the interviewee is suspected of an offence against the educational establishment, the principal or his nominee can act as the appropriate adult for the purposes of the interview.

11.16 Where the appropriate adult is present at an interview, he should be informed that he is not expected to act simply as an observer; and also that the purposes of his presence are, first, to advise the person being questioned and to observe whether or not the interview is being conducted properly and fairly, and secondly, to facilitate communication with the person being interviewed.

Notes for Guidance

11A   [Not Used]

11B   It is important to bear in mind that, although juveniles or people who are mentally disordered or mentally handicapped are often capable of providing reliable evidence, they may, without knowing or wishing to do so, be particularly prone in certain circumstances to provide information which is unreliable, misleading or self-incriminating. Special care should therefore always be exercised in questioning such a person, and the appropriate adult should be involved, if there is any doubt about a person's age, mental state or capacity. Because of the risk of unreliable evidence it is also important to obtain corroboration of any facts admitted whenever possible.

11C   It is preferable that a juvenile is not arrested at his place of education unless this is unavoidable. Where a juvenile is arrested at his place of education, the principal or his nominee must be informed.

11D   When a suspect agrees to read records of interviews and of other comments and to sign them as correct, he should be asked to endorse the record with words such as 'I agree that this is a correct record of what was said' and add his signature. Where the suspect does not agree with the record, the officer should record the details of any disagreement and then ask the suspect to read these details and then sign them to the effect that they accurately reflect his disagreement. Any refusal to sign when asked to do so shall be recorded.

12. Interviews in police stations

(a) Action

12.1   If a police officer wishes to interview, or conduct enquiries which require the presence of a detained person, the custody officer is responsible for deciding whether to deliver him into his custody.

12.2   In any period of 24 hours a detained person must be allowed a continuous period of at least 8 hours for rest, free from questioning, travel or any interruption by police officers in connection with the investigation concerned. This period should normally be at night. The period of rest may not be interrupted or delayed, except at the request of the person, his appropriate adult or his legal representative, unless there are reasonable grounds for believing that it would:

(i)   involve a risk of harm to persons or serious loss of, or damage to, property; or

(ii)   delay unnecessarily the person's release from custody; or

(iii)   otherwise prejudice the outcome of the investigation.

If a person is arrested at a police station after going there voluntarily, the period of 24 hours runs from the time of his arrest and not the time of arrival at the police station. Any action which is required to be taken in accordance with section 8 of this code, or in accordance with medical advice or at the request of the detained person, his appropriate adult or his legal representative, does not constitute an interruption to the rest period such that a fresh period must be allowed.

12.3   A detained person may not be supplied with intoxicating liquor except on medical directions. No person, who is unfit through drink or drugs to the extent that he is unable to appreciate the significance of questions put to him and his answers, may be questioned about an alleged offence in that condition except in accordance with Annex C. [See Note 12B]

12.4   As far as practicable interviews shall take place in interview rooms which must be adequately heated, lit and ventilated.

12.5   People being questioned or making statements shall not be required to stand.

12.6   Before the commencement of an interview each interviewing officer shall identify himself and any other officers present by name and rank to the person being interviewed, except in the case of persons detained under the Prevention of Terrorism (Temporary Provisions) Act 1989 when each officer shall identify himself by his warrant or other identification number and rank rather than his name.

12.7   Breaks from interviewing shall be made at recognised meal times. Short breaks for refreshment shall also be provided at intervals of approximately two hours, subject to the interviewing officer's discretion to delay a break if there are reasonable grounds for believing that it would:

(i)   involve a risk of harm to people or serious loss of, or damage to, property;

(ii)   delay unnecessarily the person's release from custody; or

(iii)   otherwise prejudice the outcome of the investigation.
[See Note 12C]

12.8   If in the course of the interview a complaint is made by the person being questioned or on his behalf concerning the provisions of this code then the interviewing officer shall:

(i)   record it in the interview record; and

(ii)   inform the custody officer, who is then responsible for dealing with it in accordance with section 9 of this code.

(b)   Documentation

12.9   A record must be made of the time at which a detained person is not in the custody of the custody officer, and why; and of the reason for any refusal to deliver him out of that custody.

12.10   A record must be made of any intoxicating liquor supplied to a detained person, in accordance with paragraph 12.3 above.

12.11   Any decision to delay a break in an interview must be recorded, with grounds, in the interview record.

12.12   All written statements made at police stations under caution shall be written on the forms provided for the purpose.

12.13   All written statements made under caution shall be taken in accordance with Annex D to this code.

Notes for Guidance

12A   If the interview has been contemporaneously recorded and the record signed by the person interviewed in accordance with paragraph 11.10 above, or has been tape recorded, it is normally unnecessary to ask for a written statement. Statements under caution should normally be taken in these circumstances only at the person's express wish. An officer may, however, ask him whether or not he wants to make such a statement.

12B   The police surgeon can give advice about whether or not a person is fit to be interviewed in accordance with paragraph 12.3 above.

12C   Meal breaks should normally last at least 45 minutes and shorter breaks after two hours should last at least 15 minutes. If the interviewing officer delays a break in accordance with paragraph 12.7 of this code and prolongs the interview, a longer break should then be provided. If there is a short interview, and a subsequent short interview is contemplated, the length of the break may be reduced if there are reasonable grounds to believe that this is necessary to avoid any of the consequences in paragraph 12.7(i) to (iii).

13. Interpreters

(a) General

13.1 Information on obtaining the services of a suitably qualified interpreter for the deaf or for people who do not understand English is given in Note for Guidance 3D.

(b) Foreign languages

13.2 Except in accordance with paragraph 11.1 or unless Annex C applies, a person must not be interviewed in the absence of a person capable of acting as interpreter if:

    (a) he has difficulty in understanding English;

    (b) the interviewing officer cannot himself speak the person's own language; and

    (c) the person wishes an interpreter to be present.

13.3 The interviewing officer shall ensure that the interpreter makes a note of the interview at the time in the language of the person being interviewed for use in the event of his being called to give evidence, and certifies its accuracy. He shall allow sufficient time for the interpreter to make a note of each question and answer after each has been put or given and interpreted. The person shall be given an opportunity to read it or have it read to him and sign it as correct or to indicate the respects in which he considers it inaccurate. If the interview is tape-recorded the arrangements set out in Code E apply.

13.4 In the case of a person making a statement in a language other than English:

    (a) the interpreter shall take down the statement in the language in which it is made;

    (b) the person making the statement shall be invited to sign it; and

    (c) an official English translation shall be made in due course.

(c) Deaf people and people with a speech handicap

13.5 If a person appears to be deaf or there is doubt about his hearing or speaking ability, he must not be interviewed in the absence of an interpreter unless he agrees in writing to be interviewed without one or paragraph 11.1 or Annex C applies.

13.6 An interpreter shall also be called if a juvenile is interviewed and the parent or guardian present as the appropriate adult appears to be deaf or there is doubt about his hearing or speaking ability, unless he agrees in writing that the interview should proceed without one or paragraph 11.1 or Annex C applies.

13.7   The interviewing officer shall ensure that the interpreter is given an opportunity to read the record of the interview and to certify its accuracy in the event of his being called to give evidence.

(d)   Additional rules for detained persons

13.8   All reasonable attempts should be made to make clear to the detained person that interpreters will be provided at public expense.

13.9   Where paragraph 6.1 applies and the person concerned cannot communicate with the solicitor, whether because of language, hearing or speech difficulties, an interpreter must be called. The interpreter may not be a police officer when interpretation is needed for the purposes of obtaining legal advice. In all other cases a police officer may only interpret if he first obtains the detained person's (or the appropriate adult's) agreement in writing or if the interview is tape-recorded in accordance with Code E.

13.10   When a person is charged with an offence who appears to be deaf or there is doubt about his hearing or speaking ability or ability to understand English, and the custody officer cannot establish effective communication, arrangements must be made for an interpreter to explain as soon as practicable the offence concerned and any other information given by the custody officer.

(e)   Documentation

13.11   Action taken to call an interpreter under this section and any agreement to be interviewed in the absence of an interpreter must be recorded.

Note for Guidance

13A   If the interpreter is needed as a prosecution witness at the person's trial, a second interpreter must act as the court interpreter.

14.   Questioning: special restrictions

14.1   If a person has been arrested by one police force on behalf of another and the lawful period of detention in respect of that offence has not yet commenced in accordance with section 41 of the Police and Criminal Evidence Act 1984 no questions may be put to him about the offence while he is in transit between the forces except in order to clarify any voluntary statement made by him.

14.2   If a person is in police detention at a hospital he may not be questioned without the agreement of a responsible doctor. [See Note 14A]

Note for Guidance

14A   If questioning takes place at a hospital under paragraph 14.2 (or on the way to or from a hospital) the period concerned counts towards the total period of detention permitted.

15.   Reviews and extensions of detention

(a)   Action

15.1   The review officer is responsible under section 40 of the Police and Criminal Evidence Act 1984 (or, in terrorist cases, under Schedule 3 to the Prevention of Terrorism (Temporary Provisions) Act 1989) for determining whether or not a person's detention continues to be necessary. In reaching a decision he shall provide an opportunity to the detained person himself to make representations (unless he is unfit to do so because of his condition or behaviour) or to his solicitor or the appropriate adult if available at the time. Other people having an interest in the person's welfare may make representations at the review officer's discretion.

15.2   The same people may make representations to the officer determining whether further detention should be authorised under section 42 of the Act or under Schedule 3 to the 1989 Act. [See Note 15A]

15.2A   After hearing any representations, the review officer or officer determining whether further detention should be authorised shall note any comment the person may make if the decision is to keep him in detention. The officer shall not put specific questions to the suspect regarding his involvement in any offence, nor in respect of any comments he may make in response to the decision to keep him in detention. Such an exchange is likely to constitute an interview as defined by paragraph 11.1A and would require the associated safe-guards included in section 11. [See also paragraph 11.13]

(b)   Documentation

15.3   Before conducting a review the review officer must ensure that the detained person is reminded of his entitlement to free legal advice (see paragraph 6.5). It is the responsibility of the review officer to ensure that all such reminders are noted in the custody record.

15.4   The grounds for and extent of any delay in conducting a review shall be recorded.

15.5   Any written representations shall be retained.

15.6   A record shall be made as soon as practicable of the outcome of each review and application for a warrant of further detention or its extension.

Notes for Guidance

15A   If the detained person is likely to be asleep at the latest time when a review of detention or an authorisation of continued detention may take place, the appropriate officer should bring it forward so that the detained person may make representations without being woken up.

15B   An application for a warrant of further detention or its extension should be made between 10am and 9pm, and if possible during normal court hours. It will not be practicable to arrange for a court to sit specially outside the hours of 10am to 9pm. If it appears possible that a special sitting may be needed (either at a weekend, Bank/Public Holiday or on a weekday outside normal court hours but between 10am and 9pm) then the clerk to the justices should be given notice and informed of this possibility, while the court is sitting if possible.

15C   If in the circumstances the only practicable way of conducting a review is over the telephone then this is permissible, provided that the requirements of section 40 of the Police and Criminal Evidence Act 1984 or of schedule 3 to the Prevention of Terrorism (Temporary Provisions) Act 1989 are observed. However, a review to decide whether to authorise a person's continued detention under section 42 of the 1984 Act must be done in person rather than over the telephone.

16.   Charging of detained persons

(a)   Action

16.1   When an officer considers that there is sufficient evidence to prosecute a detained person, and that there is sufficient evidence for a prosecution to succeed, and that the person has said all that he wishes to say about the offence, he shall without delay (and subject to the following qualification) bring him before the custody officer who shall then be responsible for considering whether or not he should be charged. When a person is detained in respect of more than one offence it is permissible to delay bringing him before the custody officer until the above conditions are satisfied in respect of all the offences (but see paragraph 11.4). Any resulting action should be taken in the presence of the appropriate adult if the person is a juvenile or mentally disordered or mentally handicapped.

16.2   When a detained person is charged with or informed that he may be prosecuted for an offence he shall be cautioned in the following terms:

'You do not have to say anything. But it may harm your defence if you do not mention now something which you later rely on in court. Anything you do say may be given in evidence.'

16.3 At the time a person is charged he shall be given a written notice showing particulars of the offence with which he is charged and including the name of the officer in the case (in terrorist cases, the officer's warrant or other identification number instead), his police station and the reference number for the case. So far as possible the particulars of the charge shall be stated in simple terms, but they shall also show the precise offence in law with which he is charged. The notice shall begin with the following words:

> 'You are charged with the offence(s) shown below. You do not have to say anything. But it may harm your defence if you do not mention now something which you later rely on in court. Anything you do say may be given in evidence.'

If the person is a juvenile or is mentally disordered or mentally handicapped the notice shall be given to the appropriate adult.

16.4 If at any time after a person has been charged with or informed that he may be prosecuted for an offence, a police officer wishes to bring to the notice of that person any written statement made by another person or the content of an interview with another person, he shall hand to that person a true copy of any such written statement or bring to his attention the content of the interview record, but shall say or do nothing to invite any reply or comment save to warn him that he does not have to say anything but that anything he does say may be given in evidence and to remind him of his right to legal advice in accordance with paragraph 6.5 above. If the person cannot read then the officer may read it to him. If the person is a juvenile or mentally disordered or mentally handicapped the copy shall also be given to, or the interview record brought to the attention of, the appropriate adult.

16.5 Questions relating to an offence may not be put to a person after he has been charged with that offence, or informed that he may be prosecuted for it, unless they are necessary for the purpose of preventing or minimising harm or loss to some other person or to the public or for clearing up an ambiguity in a previous answer or statement, or where it is in the interests of justice that the person should have put to him and have an opportunity to comment on information concerning the offence which has come to light since he was charged or informed that he might be prosecuted. Before any such questions are put to him, he shall be warned that he does not have to say anything but that anything he does say may be given in evidence and reminded of his right to legal advice in accordance with paragraph 6.5 above. [See Note 16A]

16.6   Where a juvenile is charged with an offence and the custody officer authorises his continued detention he must try to make arrangements for the juvenile to be taken into the care of a local authority to be detained pending appearance in court unless he certifies that it is impracticable to do so, or, in the case of a juvenile of at least 12 years of age, no secure accommodation is available and there is a risk to the public of serious harm from that juvenile, in accordance with section 38(6) of the Police and Criminal Evidence Act 1984, as amended by section 59 of the Criminal Justice Act 1991 and section 24 of the Criminal Justice and Public Order Act 1994. [See Note 16B]

(b)   Documentation

16.7   A record shall be made of anything a detained person says when charged.

16.8   Any questions put after charge and answers given relating to the offence shall be contemporaneously recorded in full on the forms provided and the record signed by that person or, if he refuses, by the interviewing officer and any third parties present. If the questions are tape-recorded the arrangements set out in Code E apply.

16.9   If it is not practicable to make arrangements for the transfer of a juvenile into local authority care in accordance with paragraph 16.6 above the custody officer must record the reasons and make out a certificate to be produced before the court together with the juvenile.

Notes for Guidance

16A   The service of the Notice of Intended Prosecution under sections 1 and 2 of the Road Traffic Offenders Act 1988 does not amount to informing a person that he may be prosecuted for an offence and so does not preclude further questioning in relation to that offence.

16B   Except as provided for in 16.6 above, neither a juvenile's behaviour nor the nature of the offence with which he is charged provides grounds for the custody officer to decide that it is impracticable to seek to arrange for his transfer to the care of the local authority. Similarly, the lack of secure local authority accommodation shall not make it impracticable for the custody officer to transfer him. The availability of secure accommodation is only a factor in relation to a juvenile aged 12 or over when the local authority accommodation would not be adequate to protect the public from serious harm from the juvenile. The obligation to transfer a juvenile to local authority accommodation applies as much to a juvenile charged during the daytime as it does to a juvenile to be held overnight, subject to a requirement to bring the juvenile before a court under section 46 of the Police and Criminal Evidence Act 1984.

ANNEX A
INTIMATE AND STRIP SEARCHES [SEE PARAGRAPH 4.1]

A. INTIMATE SEARCH

1. An 'intimate search' is a search which consists of the physical examination of a person's body orifices other than the mouth.

(a) Action

2. Body orifices other than the mouth may be searched only if an officer of the rank of superintendent or above has reasonable grounds for believing:

(a)   that an article which could cause physical injury to the detained person or others at the police station has been concealed; or

(b)   that the person has concealed a Class A drug which he intended to supply to another or to export; and

(c)   that in either case an intimate search is the only practicable means of removing it.

The reasons why an intimate search is considered necessary shall be explained to the person before the search takes place.

3. An intimate search may only be carried out by a registered medical practitioner or registered nurse, unless an officer of at least the rank of superintendent considers that this is not practicable and the search is to take place under sub-paragraph 2(a) above.

4. An intimate search under sub-paragraph 2(a) above may take place only at a hospital, surgery, other medical premises or police station. A search under sub-paragraph 1(b) may take place only at a hospital, surgery or other medical premises.

5. An intimate search at a police station of a juvenile or a mentally disordered or mentally handicapped person may take place only in the presence of an appropriate adult of the same sex (unless the person specifically requests the presence of a particular adult of the opposite sex who is readily available). In the case of a juvenile the search may take place in the absence of the appropriate adult only if the juvenile signifies in the presence of the appropriate adult that he prefers the search to be done in his absence and the appropriate adult agrees. A record shall be made of the juvenile's decision and signed by the appropriate adult.

6. Where an intimate search under sub-paragraph 2(a) above is carried out by a police officer, the officer must be of the same sex as the person searched. Subject to paragraph 5 above, no person of the opposite sex who is not a medical practitioner or nurse shall be present,

nor shall anyone whose presence is unnecessary but a minimum of two
people, other than the person searched, must be present during the
search. The search shall be conducted with proper regard to the
sensitivity and vulnerability of the person in these circumstances.

(b)   Documentation

7.   In the case of an intimate search the custody officer shall as soon
as practicable record which parts of the person's body were searched,
who carried out the search, who was present, the reasons for the search
and its result.

8.   If an intimate search is carried out by a police officer, the reason
why it was impracticable for a suitably qualified person to conduct it
must be recorded.

B.   STRIP SEARCH

9.   A strip search is a search involving the removal of more than outer
clothing.

(a)   Action

10.   A strip search may take place only if it is considered necessary
to remove an article which a person would not be allowed to keep, and
the officer reasonably considers that the person might have concealed
such an article. Strip searches shall not be routinely carried out where
there is no reason to consider that articles have been concealed.

The conduct of strip searches

11.   The following procedures shall be observed when strip searches
are conducted:

(a)   a police officer carrying out a strip search must be of the
same sex as the person searched;

(b)   the search shall take place in an area where the person being
searched cannot be seen by anyone who does not need to be present,
nor by a member of the opposite sex (except an appropriate adult who
has been specifically requested by the person being searched);

(c)   except in cases of urgency, where there is a risk of serious
harm to the person detained or to others, whenever a strip search
involves exposure of intimate parts of the body, there must be at
least two people present other than the person searched, and if the
search is of a juvenile or a mentally disordered or mentally
handicapped person, one of the people must be the appropriate adult.
Except in urgent cases as above, a search of a juvenile may take
place in the absence of the appropriate adult only if the juvenile
signifies in the presence of the appropriate adult that he prefers the

search to be done in his absence and the appropriate adult agrees. A record shall be made of the juvenile's decision and signed by the appropriate adult. The presence of more than two people, other than an appropriate adult, shall be permitted only in the most exceptional circumstances;

(d) the search shall be conducted with proper regard to the sensitivity and vulnerability of the person in these circumstances and every reasonable effort shall be made to secure the person's co-operation and minimise embarrassment. People who are searched should not normally be required to have all their clothes removed at the same time, for example, a man shall be allowed to put on his shirt before removing his trousers, and a woman shall be allowed to put on her blouse and upper garments before further clothing is removed;

(e) where necessary to assist the search, the person may be required to hold his or her arms in the air or to stand with his or her legs apart and to bend forward so that a visual examination may be made of the genital and anal areas provided that no physical contact is made with any body orifice;

(f) if, during a search, articles are found, the person shall be asked to hand them over. If articles are found within any body orifice other than the mouth, and the person refuses to hand them over, their removal would constitute an intimate search, which must be carried out in accordance with the provisions of part A of this Annex;

(g) a strip search shall be conducted as quickly as possible, and the person searched allowed to dress as soon as the procedure is complete.

(b)   Documentation

12.   A record shall be made on the custody record of a strip search including the reason it was considered necessary to undertake it, those present and any result.

ANNEX B
DELAY IN NOTIFYING ARREST OR ALLOWING ACCESS TO LEGAL ADVICE

A.   Persons detained under the Police and Criminal Evidence Act 1984

(a)   Action

1.   The rights set out in sections 5 or 6 of the code or both may be delayed if the person is in police detention in connection with a serious

arrestable offence, has not yet been charged with an offence and an officer of the rank of superintendent or above has reasonable grounds for believing that the exercise of either right:

(i)   will lead to interference with or harm to evidence connected with a serious arrestable offence or interference with or physical injury to other people; or

(ii)   will lead to the alerting of other people suspected of having committed such an offence but not yet arrested for it; or

(iii)   will hinder the recovery of property obtained as a result of such an offence.

[See Note B3]

2.   These rights may also be delayed where the serious arrestable offence is either:

(i)   a drug trafficking offence and the officer has reasonable grounds for believing that the detained person has benefited from drug trafficking, and that the recovery of the value of that person's proceeds of drug trafficking will be hindered by the exercise of either right or;

(ii)   an offence to which part VI of the Criminal Justice Act 1988 (covering confiscation orders) applies and the officer has reasonable grounds for believing that the detained person has benefited from the offence, and that the recovery of the value of the property obtained by that person from or in connection with the offence, or if the pecuniary advantage derived by him from or in connection with it, will be hindered by the exercise of either right.

3.   Access to a solicitor may not be delayed on the grounds that he might advise the person not to answer any questions or that the solicitor was initially asked to attend the police station by someone else, provided that the person himself then wishes to see the solicitor. In the latter case the detained person must be told that the solicitor has come to the police station at another person's request, and must be asked to sign the custody record to signify whether or not he wishes to see the solicitor.

4.   These rights may be delayed only for as long as is necessary and, subject to paragraph 9 below, in no case beyond 36 hours after the relevant time as defined in section 41 of the Police and Criminal Evidence Act 1984. If the above grounds cease to apply within this time, the person must as soon as practicable be asked if he wishes to exercise either right, the custody record must be noted accordingly, and action must be taken in accordance with the relevant section of the code.

5. A detained person must be permitted to consult a solicitor for a reasonable time before any court hearing.

(b) Documentation

6. The grounds for action under this Annex shall be recorded and the person informed of them as soon as practicable.

7. Any reply given by a person under paragraphs 4 or 9 must be recorded and the person asked to endorse the record in relation to whether he wishes to receive legal advice at this point.

B. Persons detained under the Prevention of Terrorism (Temporary Provisions) Act 1989

(a) Action

8. The rights set out in sections 5 or 6 of this code or both may be delayed if paragraph 1 above applies or if an officer of the rank of superintendent or above has reasonable grounds for believing that the exercise of either right:

(a) will lead to interference with the gathering of information about the commission, preparation or instigation of acts of terrorism; or

(b) by alerting any person, will make it more difficult to prevent an act of terrorism or to secure the apprehension, prosecution or conviction of any person in connection with the commission, preparation or instigation of an act of terrorism.

9. These rights may be delayed only for as long as is necessary and in no case beyond 48 hours from the time of arrest. If the above grounds cease to apply within this time, the person must as soon as practicable be asked if he wishes to exercise either right, the custody record must be noted accordingly, and action must be taken in accordance with the relevant section of this code.

10. Paragraphs 3 and 5 above apply.

(b) Documentation

11. Paragraphs 6 and 7 above apply.

Notes for Guidance

B1 Even if Annex B applies in the case of a juvenile, or a person who is mentally disordered or mentally handicapped, action to inform the appropriate adult (and the person responsible for a juvenile's welfare, if that is a different person) must nevertheless be taken in accordance with paragraph 3.7 and 3.9 of this code.

B2 In the case of Commonwealth citizens and foreign nationals see Note 7A.

B3   Police detention is defined in section 118(2) of the Police and Criminal Evidence Act 1984.

B4   The effect of paragraph 1 above is that the officer may authorise delaying access to a specific solicitor only if he has reasonable grounds to believe that that specific solicitor will, inadvertently or otherwise, pass on a message from the detained person or act in some other way which will lead to any of the three results in paragraph 1 coming about. In these circumstances the officer should offer the detained person access to a solicitor (who is not the specific solicitor referred to above) on the Duty Solicitor Scheme.

B5   The fact that the grounds for delaying notification of arrest under paragraph 1 above may be satisfied does not automatically mean that the grounds for delaying access to legal advice will also be satisfied.

ANNEX C
VULNERABLE SUSPECTS: URGENT INTERVIEWS AT POLICE STATIONS

1.   When an interview is to take place in a police station or other authorised place of detention if, and only if, an officer of the rank of superintendent or above considers that delay will lead to the consequences set out in paragraph 11.1(a) to (c) of this Code:

(a)   a person heavily under the influence of drink or drugs may be interviewed in that state; or

(b)   a juvenile or a person who is mentally disordered or mentally handicapped may be interviewed in the absence of the appropriate adult; or

(c)   a person who has difficulty in understanding English or who has a hearing disability may be interviewed in the absence of an interpreter.

2.   Questioning in these circumstances may not continue once sufficient information to avert the immediate risk has been obtained.

3.   A record shall be made of the grounds for any decision to interview a person under paragraph 1 above.

Note for Guidance

C1   The special groups referred to in this Annex are all particularly vulnerable. The provisions of the Annex, which override safeguards designed to protect them and to minimise the risk of interviews producing unreliable evidence, should be applied only in exceptional cases of need.

ANNEX D
WRITTEN STATEMENTS UNDER CAUTION
[SEE PARAGRAPH 12.13]

(a) Written by a person under caution

1.   A person shall always be invited to write down himself what he wants to say.

2.   Where the person wishes to write it himself, he shall be asked to write out and sign, before writing what he wants to say, the following:

I make this statement of my own free will. I understand that I do not have to say anything but that it may harm my defence if I do not mention when questioned something which I later rely on in court. This statement may be given in evidence.

3.   Any person writing his own statement shall be allowed to do so without any prompting except that a police officer may indicate to him which matters are material or question any ambiguity in the statement.

(b) Written by a police officer

4.   If a person says that he would like someone to write it for him, a police officer shall write the statement, but, before starting, he must ask him to sign, or make his mark, to the following:

'I, ..., wish to make a statement. I want someone to write down what I say. I understand that I need not say anything but that it may harm my defence if I do not mention when questioned something which I later rely on in court. This statement may be given in evidence.'

5.   Where a police officer writes the statement, he must take down the exact words spoken by the person making it and he must not edit or paraphrase it. Any questions that are necessary (e.g. to make it more intelligible) and the answers given must be recorded contemporaneously on the statement form.

6.   When the writing of a statement by a police officer is finished the person making it shall be asked to read it and to make any corrections, alterations or additions he wishes. When he has finished reading it he shall be asked to write and sign or make his mark on the following certificate at the end of the statement:

'I have read the above statement, and I have been able to correct, alter or add anything I wish. This statement is true. I have made it of my own free will.'

7.   If the person making the statement cannot read, or refuses to read it, or to write the above mentioned certificate at the end of it or to sign it, the senior police officer present shall read it to him and ask him

whether he would like to correct, alter or add anything and to put his signature or make his mark at the end. The police officer shall then certify on the statement itself what has occurred.

ANNEX E
SUMMARY OF PROVISIONS RELATING TO MENTALLY DISORDERED AND MENTALLY HANDICAPPED PEOPLE

1. If an officer has any suspicion, or is told in good faith, that a person of any age may be mentally disordered or mentally handicapped, or mentally incapable of understanding the significance of questions put to him or his replies, then that person shall be treated as mentally disordered or mentally handicapped for the purposes of this code. [See paragraph 1.4]

2. In the case of a person who is mentally disordered or mentally handicapped, 'the appropriate adult' means:

    (a) a relative, guardian or some other person responsible for his care or custody;

    (b) someone who has experience of dealing with mentally disordered or mentally handicapped people but is not a police officer or employed by the police; or

    (c) failing either of the above, some other responsible adult aged 18 or over who is not a police officer or employed by the police. [See paragraph 1.7(b)]

3. If the custody officer authorises the detention of a person who is mentally handicapped or appears to be suffering from a mental disorder he must as soon as practicable inform the appropriate adult of the grounds for the person's detention and his whereabouts, and ask the adult to come to the police station to see the person. If the appropriate adult is already at the police station when information is given as required in paragraphs 3.1 to 3.5 the information must be given to the detained person in the appropriate adult's presence. If the appropriate adult is not at the police station when the provisions of 3.1 to 3.5 are complied with then these provisions must be complied with again in the presence of the appropriate adult once that person arrives. [See paragraphs 3.9 and 3.11]

4. If the appropriate adult, having been informed of the right to legal advice, considers that legal advice should be taken, the provisions of section 6 of the code apply as if the mentally disordered or mentally handicapped person had requested access to legal advice. [See paragraph 3.13 and Note E2]

5. If a person brought to a police station appears to be suffering from mental disorder or is incoherent other than through drunkenness alone,

or if a detained person subsequently appears to be mentally disordered, the custody officer must immediately call the police surgeon or, in urgent cases, send the person to hospital or call the nearest available medical practitioner. It is not intended that these provisions should delay the transfer of a person to a place of safety under section 136 of the Mental Health Act 1983 where that is applicable. Where an assessment under that Act is to take place at the police station, the custody officer has discretion not to call the police surgeon so long as he believes that the assessment by a registered medical practitioner can be undertaken without undue delay. [See paragraph 9.2]

6.   It is imperative that a mentally disordered or mentally handicapped person who has been detained under section 136 of the Mental Health Act 1983 should be assessed as soon as possible. If that assessment is to take place at the police station, an approved social worker and a registered medical practitioner should be called to the police station as soon as possible in order to interview and examine the person. Once the person has been interviewed and examined and suitable arrangements have been made for his treatment or care, he can no longer be detained under section 136. The person shall not be released until he has been seen by both the approved social worker and the registered medical practitioner. [See paragraph 3.10]

7.   If a mentally disordered or mentally handicapped person is cautioned in the absence of the appropriate adult, the caution must be repeated in the appropriate adult's presence. [See paragraph 10.6]

8.   A mentally disordered or mentally handicapped person must not be interviewed or asked to provide or sign a written statement in the absence of the appropriate adult unless the provisions of paragraph 11.1 or Annex C of this code apply. Questioning in these circumstances may not continue in the absence of the appropriate adult once sufficient information to avert the risk has been obtained. A record shall be made of the grounds for any decision to begin an interview in these circumstances. [See paragraphs 11.1 and 11.14 and Annex C]

9.   Where the appropriate adult is present at an interview, he should be informed that he is not expected to act simply as an observer; and also that the purposes of his presence are, first, to advise the person being interviewed and to observe whether or not the interview is being conducted properly and fairly, and, secondly to facilitate communication with the person being interviewed. [See paragraph 11.16]

10.   If the detention of a mentally disordered or mentally handicapped person is reviewed by a review officer or a superintendent, the

appropriate adult must, if available at the time, be given an opportunity to make representations to the officer about the need for continuing detention. [See paragraphs 15.1 and 15.2]

11. If the custody officer charges a mentally disordered or mentally handicapped person with an offence or takes such other action as is appropriate when there is sufficient evidence for a prosecution this must be done in the presence of the appropriate adult. The written notice embodying any charge must be given to the appropriate adult. [See paragraphs 16.1 to 16.3]

12. An intimate or strip search of a mentally disordered or mentally handicapped person may take place only in the presence of the appropriate adult of the same sex, unless the person specifically requests the presence of a particular adult of the opposite sex. A strip search may take place in the absence of an appropriate adult only in cases of urgency where there is a risk of serious harm to the person detained or to others. [See Annex A, paragraphs 5 and 11(c)]

13. Particular care must be taken when deciding whether to use handcuffs to restrain a mentally disordered or mentally handicapped person in a locked cell. [See paragraph 8.2]

Notes for Guidance

E1 In the case of mentally disordered or mentally handicapped people, it may in certain circumstances be more satisfactory for all concerned if the appropriate adult is someone who has experience or training in their care rather than a relative lacking such qualifications. But if the person himself prefers a relative to a better qualified stranger or objects to a particular person as the appropriate adult, his wishes should if practicable be respected. [See Note 1E]

E2 The purpose of the provision at paragraph 3.13 is to protect the rights of a mentally disordered or mentally handicapped person who does not understand the significance of what is being said to him. If the person wishes to exercise the right to legal advice, the appropriate action should be taken and not delayed until the appropriate adult arrives. [See Note 3G] A mentally disordered or mentally handicapped person should always be given an opportunity, when an appropriate adult is called to the police station, to consult privately with a solicitor in the absence of the appropriate adult if he wishes to do so. [See Note 1EE].

E3 It is important to bear in mind that although mentally disordered or mentally handicapped [people are] often capable of providing reliable evidence, they may, without knowing or wishing to do so, be particularly prone in certain circumstances to provide information which is unreliable, misleading or self-incriminating. Special care should therefore always be exercised in questioning such a person, and the appropriate adult involved, if there is any doubt about a person's mental state or capacity. Because of the risk of unreliable evidence, it is important to obtain corroboration of any facts admitted whenever possible. [See Note 11B]

E4 Because of the risks referred to in Note E3, which the presence of the appropriate adult is intended to minimise, officers of superintendent rank or above should exercise their discretion to authorise the commencement of an interview in the adult's absence only in exceptional cases, where it is necessary to avert an immediate risk of serious harm. [See paragraph 11.1 and Annex C and Note C1]

ANNEX F
COUNTRIES WITH WHICH BILATERAL CONSULAR CONVENTIONS OR AGREEMENTS REQUIRING NOTIFICATION OF THE ARREST AND DETENTION OF THEIR NATIONALS ARE IN FORCE AS AT 1 JANUARY 1995

Armenia	Kyrgyzstan
Austria	Macedonia
Azerbaijan	Mexico
Belarus	Moldova
Belgium	Mongolia
Bosnia-Herzegovina	Norway
Bulgaria	Poland
China*	Romania
Croatia	Russia
Cuba	Slovak Republic
Czech Republic	Slovenia
Denmark	Spain
Egypt	Sweden
France	Tajikistan
Georgia	Turkmenistan
German Federal Republic	Ukraine
Greece	USA
Hungary	Uzbekistan
Kazakhstan	Yugoslavia

*Police are required to inform Chinese officials of arrest/detention in the Manchester consular district only. This comprises Derbyshire, Durham, Greater Manchester, Lancashire, Merseyside, North, South and West Yorkshire, and Tyne and Wear.

CODE OF PRACTICE (E) ON TAPE RECORDING OF INTERVIEWS WITH SUSPECTS

1. General

1.1 This code of practice must be readily available for consultation by police officers, detained persons and members of the public at every police station to which an order made under section 60(1)(b) of the Police and Criminal Evidence Act 1984 applies.

1.2 The notes for guidance included are not provisions of this code. They form guidance to police officers and others about its application and interpretation.

1.3 Nothing in this code shall be taken as detracting in any way from the requirements of the Code of Practice for the Detention, Treatment and Questioning of Persons by Police Officers (Code C). [See Note 1A]

1.4 This code does not apply to those groups of people listed in paragraph 1.12 of Code C.

1.5 In this code the term 'appropriate adult' has the same meaning as in paragraph 1.7 of Code C; and the term 'solicitor' has the same meaning as in paragraph 6.12 of Code C.

Notes for Guidance

1A As in Code C, references to custody officers include those carrying out the functions of a custody officer.

2. Recording and the sealing of master tapes

2.1 Tape recording of interviews shall be carried out openly to instil confidence in its reliability as an impartial and accurate record of the interview. [See Note 2A]

2.2 One tape, referred to in this code as the master tape, will be sealed before it leaves the presence of the suspect. A second tape will be used as a working copy. The master tape is either one of the two tapes used in a twin deck machine or the only tape used in a single deck machine. The working copy is either the second tape used in a twin deck machine or a copy of the master tape made by a single deck machine. [See Notes 2B and 2C]

Notes for Guidance
2A   Police Officers will wish to arrange that, as far as possible, tape recording arrangements are unobtrusive. It must be clear to the suspect, however, that there is no opportunity to interfere with the tape recording equipment or the tapes.
2B   The purpose of sealing the master tape before it leaves the presence of the suspect is to establish his confidence that the integrity of the tape is preserved. Where a single deck machine is used the working copy of the master tape must be made in the presence of the suspect and without the master tape having left his sight. The working copy shall be used for making further copies where the need arises. The recorder will normally be capable of recording voices and have a time coding or other security device.
2C   Throughout this code any reference to 'tapes' shall be construed as 'tape', as appropriate, where a single deck machine is used.

3.   Interviews to be tape recorded
3.1   Subject to paragraph 3.2 below, tape recording shall be used at police stations for any interview:
     (a)   with a person who has been cautioned in accordance with section 10 of Code C in respect of an indictable offence (including an offence triable either way) [see Notes 3A and 3B];
     (b)   which takes place as a result of a police officer exceptionally putting further questions to a suspect about an offence described in sub-paragraph (a) above after he has been charged with, or informed he may be prosecuted for, that offence [see Note 3C]; or
     (c)   in which a police officer wishes to bring to the notice of a person, after he has been charged with, or informed he may be prosecuted for an offence described in sub-paragraph (a) above, any written statement made by another person, or the content of an interview with another person [see Note 3D].
3.2   Tape recording is not required in respect of the following:
     (a)   an interview with a person arrested under section 14(1)(a) or schedule 5 paragraph 6 of the Prevention of Terrorism (Temporary Provisions) Act 1989 or an interview with a person being questioned in respect of an offence where there are reasonable grounds for suspecting that it is connected to terrorism or was committed in furtherance of the objectives of an organisation engaged in terrorism. This sub-paragraph applies only where the terrorism is connected with the affairs of Northern Ireland or is terrorism of any other description

except terrorism connected solely with the affairs of the United Kingdom or any part of the United Kingdom other than Northern Ireland. 'Terrorism' has the meaning given by section 20(1) of the Prevention of Terrorism (Temporary Provisions) Act 1989 [see Notes 3E, 3F, 3G and 3H];

(b) an interview with a person suspected on reasonable grounds of an offence under section 1 of the Official Secrets Act 1911 [see Note 3H].

3.3 The custody officer may authorise the interviewing officer not to tape record the interview:

(a) where it is not reasonably practicable to do so because of failure of the equipment or the non-availability of a suitable interview room or recorder and the authorising officer considers on reasonable grounds that the interview should not be delayed until the failure has been rectified or a suitable room or recorder becomes available [see Note 3J]; or

(b) where it is clear from the outset that no prosecution will ensue. In such cases the interview shall be recorded in writing and in accordance with section 11 of Code C. In all cases the custody officer shall make a note in specified terms of the reasons for not tape recording. [See Note 3K]

3.4 Where an interview takes place with a person voluntarily attending the police station and the police officer has grounds to believe that person has become a suspect (i.e. the point at which he should be cautioned in accordance with paragraph 10.1 of Code C) the continuation of the interview shall be tape recorded, unless the custody officer gives authority in accordance with the provisions of paragraph 3.3 above for the continuation of the interview not to be recorded.

3.5 The whole of each interview shall be tape recorded, including the taking and reading back of any statement.

Notes for Guidance

3A Nothing in this code is intended to preclude tape recording at police discretion of interviews at police stations with persons cautioned in respect of offences not covered by paragraph 3.1, or responses made by interviewees after they have been charged with, or informed they may be prosecuted for, an offence, provided that this code is complied with.

3B Attention is drawn to the restrictions in paragraph 12.3 of Code C on the questioning of persons unfit through drink or drugs to the extent that they are unable to appreciate the significance of questions put to them or of their answers.

3C Circumstances in which a suspect may be questioned about an offence after being charged with it are set out in paragraph 16.5 of Code C.

3D Procedures to be followed when a person's attention is drawn after charge to a statement made by another person are set out in paragraph 16.4 of Code C. One method of bringing the content of an interview with another person to the notice of a suspect may be to play him a tape recording of that interview.

3E Section 14(1)(a) of the Prevention of Terrorism (Temporary Provisions) Act 1989, permits the arrest without warrant of a person reasonably suspected to be guilty of an offence under section 2, 8, 10 or 11 of the Act.

3F Section 20(1) of the Prevention of Terrorism (Temporary Provisions) Act 1989 says 'terrorism means the use of violence for political ends, and includes any use of violence for the purpose of putting the public or any section of the public in fear'.

3G It should be noted that the provisions of paragraph 3.2 apply only to those suspected of offences connected with terrorism connected with Northern Ireland, or with terrorism of any other description other than terrorism connected solely with the affairs of the United Kingdom or any part of the United Kingdom other than Northern Ireland, or offences committed in furtherance of such terrorism. Any interviews with those suspected of offences connected with terrorism of any other description or in furtherance of the objectives of an organisation engaged in such terrorism should be carried out in compliance with the rest of this code.

3H When it only becomes clear during the course of an interview which is being tape recorded that the interviewee may have committed an offence to which paragraph 3.2 applies the interviewing officer should turn off the tape recorder.

3J Where practicable, priority should be given to tape recording interviews with persons who are suspected of more serious offences.

3K A decision not to tape record an interview for any reason may be the subject of comment in court. The authorising officer should therefore be prepared to justify his decision in each case.

4. The interview

(a) Commencement of interviews

4.1 When the suspect is brought into the interview room the police officer shall without delay, but in the sight of the suspect, load the tape recorder with clean tapes and set it to record. The tapes must be unwrapped or otherwise opened in the presence of the suspect. [See Note 4A]

4.2   The police officer shall then tell the suspect formally about the tape recording. He shall say:

    (a)   that the interview is being tape recorded;

    (b)   his name and rank and the name and rank of any other police officer present except in the case of enquiries linked to the investigation of terrorism where warrant or other identification numbers shall be stated rather than names;

    (c)   the name of the suspect and any other party present (e.g. a solicitor);

    (d)   the date, time of commencement and place of the interview; and

    (e)   that the suspect will be given a notice about what will happen to the tapes.

[See Note 4B]

4.3   The police officer shall then caution the suspect in the following terms:

> You do not have to say anything. But it may harm your defence if you do not mention when questioned something which you later rely on in court. Anything you do say may be given in evidence.

Minor deviations do not constitute a breach of this requirement provided that the sense of the caution is preserved. [See Note 4C].

4.3A   The police officer shall remind the suspect of his right to free and independent legal advice and that he can speak to a solicitor on the telephone in accordance with paragraph 6.5 of Code C.

4.3B   The police officer shall then put to the suspect any significant statement or silence (i.e. failure or refusal to answer a question or to answer it satisfactorily) which occurred before the start of the tape-recorded interview, and shall ask him whether he confirms or denies that earlier statement or silence or whether he wishes to add anything. A 'significant' statement or silence means one which appears capable of being used in evidence against the suspect, in particular a direct admission of guilt, or failure or refusal to answer a question or to answer it satisfactorily, which might give rise to an inference under Part III of the Criminal Justice and Public Order Act 1994.

Special warnings under Sections 36 and 37 of the Criminal Justice and Public Order Act 1994

4.3C   When a suspect who is interviewed after arrest fails or refuses to answer certain questions, or to answer them satisfactorily, after due warning, a court or jury may draw a proper inference from this silence under sections 36 and 37 of the Criminal Justice and Public Order Act 1994. This applies when:

(a)   a suspect is arrested by a constable and there is found on his person, or in or on his clothing or footwear, or otherwise in his possession, or in the place where he was arrested, any objects, marks or substances, or marks on such objects, and the person fails or refuses to account for the objects, marks or substances found; or

(b)   an arrested person was found by a constable at a place at or about the time the offence for which he was arrested, is alleged to have been committed, and the person fails or refuses to account for his presence at that place.

4.3D   For an inference to be drawn from a suspect's failure or refusal to answer a question about one of these matters or to answer it satisfactorily, the interviewing officer must first tell him in ordinary language:

(a)   what offence he is investigating;

(b)   what fact he is asking the suspect to account for;

(c)   that he believes this fact may be due to the suspect's taking part in the commission of the offence in question;

(d)   that a court may draw a proper inference from his silence if he fails or refuses to account for the fact about which he is being questioned;

(e)   that a record is being made of the interview and may be given in evidence if he is brought to trial.

4.3E   Where, despite the fact that a person has been cautioned, failure to co-operate may have an effect on his immediate treatment, he should be informed of any relevant consequences and that they are not affected by the caution. Examples are when his refusal to provide his name and address when charged may render him liable to detention, or when his refusal to provide particulars and information in accordance with a statutory requirement, for example, under the Road Traffic Act 1988, may amount to an offence or may make him liable to arrest.

(b)   Interviews with the deaf

4.4   If the suspect is deaf or there is doubt about his hearing ability, the police officer shall take a contemporaneous note of the interview in accordance with the requirements of Code C, as well as tape record it in accordance with the provisions of this code. [See Notes 4E and 4F]

(c)   Objections and complaints by the suspect

4.5   If the suspect raises objections to the interview being tape recorded either at the outset or during the interview or during a break in the interview, the police officer shall explain the fact that the interview is being tape recorded and that the provisions of this code require that the suspect's objections should be recorded on tape. When any objections have been recorded on tape or the suspect has refused to have his objections recorded, the police officer may turn off the recorder. In this eventuality he shall say that he is turning off the recorder and give his reasons for doing so and then turn it off. The police officer shall then make a written record of the interview in accordance with section 11 of Code C. If, however, the police officer reasonably considers that he may proceed to put questions to the suspect with the tape recorder still on, he may do so. [See Note 4G]

4.6   If in the course of an interview a complaint is made by the person being questioned, or on his behalf, concerning the provisions of this code or of Code C, then the officer shall act in accordance with paragraph 12.8 of Code C. [See Notes 4H and 4J]

4.7   If the suspect indicates that he wishes to tell the police officer about matters not directly connected with the offence of which he is suspected and that he is unwilling for these matters to be recorded on tape, he shall be given the opportunity to tell the police officer about these matters after the conclusion of the formal interview.

(d)   Changing tapes

4.8   When the recorder indicates that the tapes have only a short time left to run, the police officer shall tell the suspect that the tapes are coming to an end and round off that part of the interview. If the police officer wishes to continue the interview but does not already have a second set of tapes, he shall obtain a set. The suspect shall not be left unattended in the interview room. The police officer will remove the tapes from the tape recorder and insert the new tapes which shall be unwrapped or otherwise opened in the suspect's presence. The tape recorder shall then be set to record on the new tapes. Care must be taken, particularly when a number of sets of tapes have been used, to ensure that there is no confusion between the tapes. This may be done by marking the tapes with an identification number immediately they are removed from the tape recorder.

(e)   Taking a break during interview

4.9   When a break is to be taken during the course of an interview and the interview room is to be vacated by the suspect, the fact that a break is to be taken, the reason for it and the time shall be recorded on tape. The tapes shall then be removed from the tape recorder and the procedures for the conclusion of an interview set out in paragraph 4.14 below followed.

4.10 When a break is to be a short one and both the suspect and a police officer are to remain in the interview room the fact that a break is to be taken, the reasons for it and the time shall be recorded on tape. The tape recorder may be turned off; there is, however, no need to remove the tapes and when the interview is recommenced the tape recording shall be continued on the same tapes. The time at which the interview recommences shall be recorded on tape.

4.11 When there is a break in questioning under caution the interviewing officer must ensure that the person being questioned is aware that he remains under caution and of his right to legal advice. If there is any doubt the caution must be given again in full when the interview resumes. [See Notes 4K and 4L]

(f) Failure of recording equipment

4.12 If there is a failure of equipment which can be rectified quickly, for example by inserting new tapes, the appropriate procedures set out in paragraph 4.8 shall be followed, and when the recording is resumed the officer shall explain what has happened and record the time the interview recommences. If, however, it will not be possible to continue recording on that particular tape recorder and no replacement recorder or recorder in another interview room is readily available, the interview may continue without being tape recorded. In such circumstances the procedures in paragraphs 3.3 above for seeking the authority of the custody officer will be followed. [See Note 4M]

(g) Removing tapes from the recorder

4.13 Where tapes are removed from the recorder in the course of an interview, they shall be retained and the procedures set out in paragraph 4.15 below followed.

(h) Conclusion of interview

4.14 At the conclusion of the interview, the suspect shall be offered the opportunity to clarify anything he has said and to add anything he may wish.

4.15 At the conclusion of the interview, including the taking and reading back of any written statement, the time shall be recorded and the tape recorder switched off. The master tape shall be sealed with a master tape label and treated as an exhibit in accordance with the force standing orders. The police officer shall sign the label and ask the suspect and any third party present to sign it also. If the suspect or third party refuses to sign the label, an officer of at least the rank of inspector, or if one is not available the custody officer, shall be called into the interview room and asked to sign it. In the case of enquiries linked to the investigation of terrorism, an officer who signs the label shall use his warrant or other identification number.

4.16   The suspect shall be handed a notice which explains the use which will be made of the tape recording and the arrangements for access to it and that a copy of the tape shall be supplied as soon as practicable if the person is charged or informed that he will be prosecuted.

Notes for Guidance

4A   The police officer should attempt to estimate the likely length of the interview and ensure that the appropriate number of clean tapes and labels with which to seal the master copies are available in the interview room.

4B   It will be helpful for the purpose of voice identification if the officer asks the suspect and any other people present to identify themselves.

4C   If it appears that a person does not understand what the caution means, the officer who has given it should go on to explain it in his own words.

4D   [Not Used]

4E   This provision is intended to give the deaf equivalent rights of first hand access to the full interview record as other suspects.

4F   The provisions of paragraphs 13.2, 13.5 and 13.9 of Code C on interpreters for the deaf or for interviews with suspects who have difficulty in understanding English continue to apply. In a tape recorded interview there is no requirement on the interviewing officer to ensure that the interpreter makes a separate note of interview as prescribed in section 13 of Code C.

4G   The officer should bear in mind that a decision to continue recording against the wishes of the suspect may be the subject of comment in court.

4H   Where the custody officer is called immediately to deal with the complaint, wherever possible the tape recorder should be left to run until the custody officer has entered the interview room and spoken to the person being interviewed. Continuation or termination of the interview should be at the discretion of the interviewing officer pending action by an inspector under paragraph 9.1 of Code C.

4I   [Not Used]

4J   Where the complaint is about a matter not connected with this code of practice or Code C, the decision to continue with the interview is at the discretion of the interviewing officer. Where the interviewing officer decides to continue with the interview the person being interviewed shall be told that the complaint will be brought to the attention of the custody officer at the conclusion of the interview. When the interview is concluded the interviewing officer must, as soon as practicable, inform the custody officer of the existence and nature of the complaint made.

4K   In considering whether to caution again after a break, the officer should bear in mind that he may have to satisfy a court that the person understood that he was still under caution when the interview resumed.

4L   The officer should bear in mind that it may be necessary to show to the court that nothing occurred during a break in an interview or between interviews which influenced the suspect's recorded evidence. The officer should consider, therefore, after a break in an interview or at the beginning of a subsequent interview summarising on tape the reason for the break and confirming this with the suspect.

4M   If one of the tapes breaks during the interview it should be sealed as a master tape in the presence of the suspect and the interview resumed where it left off. The unbroken tape should be copied and the original sealed as a master tape in the suspect's presence, if necessary after the interview. If equipment for copying the unbroken tape is not readily available, both tapes should be sealed in the suspect's presence and the interview begun again. If the tape breaks when a single deck machine is being used and the machine is one where a broken tape cannot be copied on available equipment, the tape should be sealed as a master tape in the suspect's presence and the interview begun again.

5.   After the interview

5.1   The police officer shall make a note in his notebook of the fact that the interview has taken place and has been recorded on tape, its time, duration and date and the identification number of the master tape.

5.2   Where no proceedings follow in respect of the person whose interview was recorded the tapes must nevertheless be kept securely in accordance with paragraph 6.1 and Note 6A.

Note for Guidance

5A   Any written record of a tape recorded interview shall be made in accordance with national guidelines approved by the Secretary of State.

6. Tape security

6.1   The officer in charge of each police station at which interviews with suspects are recorded shall make arrangements for master tapes to be kept securely and their movements accounted for on the same basis as other material which may be used for evidential purposes, in accordance with force standing orders. [See Note 6A]

6.2   A police officer has no authority to break the seal on a master tape which is required for criminal proceedings. If it is necessary to gain access to the master tape, the police officer shall arrange for its seal to be broken in the presence of a representative of the Crown Prosecution Service. The defendant or his legal adviser shall be informed and given a reasonable opportunity to be present. If the defendant or his legal representative is present he shall be invited to reseal and sign the master tape. If either refuses or neither is present this shall be done by the representative of the Crown Prosecution Service. [See Notes 6B and 6C]

6.3   Where no criminal proceedings result it is the responsibility of the chief officer of police to establish arrangements for the breaking of the seal on the master tape, where this becomes necessary.

Notes for Guidance

6A   This section is concerned with the security of the master tape which will have been sealed at the conclusion of the interview. Care should, however, be taken of working copies of tapes since their loss or destruction may lead unnecessarily to the need to have access to master tapes.

6B   If the tape has been delivered to the Crown Court for their keeping after committal for trial the crown prosecutor will apply to the chief clerk of the Crown Court centre for the release of the tape for unsealing by the crown prosecutor.

6C   Reference to the Crown Prosecution Service or to the crown prosecutor in this part of the code shall be taken to include any other body or person with a statutory responsibility for prosecution for whom the police conduct any tape recorded interviews.

Criminal Justice Act 1988, sections 23 to 26, 32 and 32A

First-hand hearsay

23.—(1)   Subject—
    (a)   to subsection (4) below;

(b)   to paragraph 1A of Schedule 2 to the Criminal Appeal Act 1968 (evidence given orally at original trial to be given orally at retrial); and

(c)   to section 69 of the Police and Criminal Evidence Act 1984 (evidence from computer records),

a statement made by a person in a document shall be admissible in criminal proceedings as evidence of any fact of which direct oral evidence by him would be admissible if—

(i)   the requirements of one of the paragraphs of subsection (2) below are satisfied; or

(ii)   the requirements of subsection (3) below are satisfied.

(2)   The requirements mentioned in subsection (1)(i) above are—

(a)   that the person who made the statement is dead or by reason of his bodily or mental condition unfit to attend as a witness;

(b)   that—

(i)   the person who made the statement is outside the United Kingdom; and

(ii)   it is not reasonably practicable to secure his attendance; or

(c)   that all reasonable steps have been taken to find the person who made the statement, but that he cannot be found.

(3)   The requirements mentioned in subsection (1)(ii) above are—

(a)   that the statement was made to a police officer or some other person charged with the duty of investigating offences or charging offenders; and

(b)   that the person who made it does not give oral evidence through fear or because he is kept out of the way.

(4)   Subsection 1 above does not render admissible a confession made by an accused person that would not be admissible under section 76 of the Police and Criminal Evidence Act 1984.

(5)   This section shall not apply to proceedings before a magistrates' court inquiring into an offence as examining justices.

Business etc. documents
24.—(1)   Subject—

(a)   to subsections (3) and (4) below;

(b)   to paragraph 1A of Schedule 2 to the Criminal Appeal Act 1968, and

(c)   to section 69 of the Police and Criminal Evidence Act 1984.

a statement in a document shall be admissible in criminal proceedings as evidence of any fact of which direct oral evidence would be admissible, if the following conditions are satisfied—

(i)   the document was created or received by a person in the course of a trade, business, profession or other occupation, or as the holder of a paid or unpaid office; and

(ii)   the information contained in the document was supplied by a person (whether or not the maker of the statement) who had, or may reasonably be supposed to have had, personal knowledge of the matters dealt with.

(2)   Subsection (1) above applies whether the information contained in the document was supplied directly or indirectly but, if it was supplied indirectly, only if each person through whom it was supplied received it—

(a)   in the course of a trade, business, profession or other occupation; or

(b)   as the holder of a paid or unpaid office.

(3)   Subsection (1) above does not render admissible a confession made by an accused person that would not be admissible under section 76 of the Police and Criminal Evidence Act 1984.

(4)   A statement prepared otherwise than in accordance with section 3 of the Criminal Justice (International Co-operation) Act 1990 below or an order under paragraph 6 of Schedule 13 to this Act or under section 30 or 31 below for the purposes—

(a)   of pending or contemplated criminal proceedings; or

(b)   of a criminal investigation,

shall not be admissible by virtue of subsection (1) above unless—

(i)   the requirements of one of the paragraphs of subsection (2) of section 23 above are satisfied; or

(ii)   the requirements of subsection (3) of that section are satisfied; or

(iii)   the person who made the statement cannot reasonably be expected (having regard to the time which has elapsed since he made the statement and to all the circumstances) to have any recollection of the matters dealt with in the statement.

(5)   This section shall not apply before a magistrates' court inquiring into an offence as examining justices.

Principles to be followed by court
25.—(1)   If, having regard to all the circumstances—

(a)   the Crown Court—

(i)   on a trial on indictment;

(ii)   on an appeal from a magistrates' court;

(iii)   on the hearing of an application under section 6 of the criminal Justice Act 1987 (applications for dismissal or charges of fraud transferred from magistrates' court or Crown Court);

(iv)   on the hearing of an application under paragraph 5 of Schedule 6 to the Criminal Justice Act 1991 (applications for dismissal of charges in certain cases involving children transferred from magistrates' courts to Crown Court); or

(b)   the criminal division of the Court of Appeal; or

(c)   a magistrates' court on a trial of an information,

is of the opinion that in the interests of justice a statement which is admissible by virtue of section 23 or 24 above nevertheless ought not to be admitted, it may direct that the statement shall not be admitted.

(2)   Without prejudice to the generality of subsection (1) above, it shall be the duty of the court to have regard—

(a)   to the nature and source of the document containing the statement and to whether or not, having regard to its nature and source and to any other circumstances that appear to the court to be relevant, it is likely that the document is authentic;

(b)   to the extent to which the statement appears to supply evidence which would otherwise not be readily available;

(c)   to the relevance of the evidence that it appears to supply to any issue which is likely to have to be determined in the proceedings; and

(d)   to any risk, having regard in particular to whether it is likely to be possible to controvert the statement if the person making it does not attend to give oral evidence in the proceedings, that its admission or exclusion will result in unfairness to the accused or, if there is more than one, to any of them.

Statements in documents that appear to have been prepared for purposes of criminal proceedings or investigations
26.   Where a statement which is admissible in criminal proceedings by virtue of section 23 or 24 above appears to the court to have been prepared, otherwise than in accordance with section 3 of the Criminal Justice (International Co-operation) Act 1990 below or an order under paragraph 6 of Schedule 13 to this Act or under section 30 or 31 below, for the purposes—

(a)   of pending or contemplated criminal proceedings; or

(b)   of a criminal investigation,

the statement shall not be given in evidence in any criminal proceedings without the leave of the court, and the court shall not give leave unless it is of the opinion that the statement ought to be admitted in the interests of justice; and in considering whether its admission would be in the interests of justice, it shall be the duty of the court to have regard—

    (i)   to the contents of the statement;

    (ii)   to any risk, having regard in particular to whether it is likely to be possible to controvert the statement if the person making it does not attend to give oral evidence in the proceedings, that its admission or exclusion will result in unfairness to the accused or, if there is more than one, to any of them; and

    (iii)   to any other circumstances that appear to the court to be relevant.

This section shall not apply to proceedings before a magistrates' court inquiring into an offence as examining justices.

Evidence through television links

32.—(1) A person other than the accused may give evidence through a live television link in proceedings to which subsection (1A) below applies if—

    (a)   the witness is outside the United Kingdom; or

    (b)   the witness is a child, or is to be cross-examined following the admission under section 32A below of a video recording of testimony from him, and the offence is one to which subsection (2) below applies,

but evidence may not be so given without the leave of the court.

    (1A)   This subsection applies—

    (a)   to trials on indictment, appeals to the criminal division of the Court of Appeal and hearings of references under section 9 of the Criminal Appeal Act 1995; and

    (b)   to proceedings in youth courts, appeals to the Crown Court arising out of such proceedings and hearings of references under section 11 of the Criminal Appeal Act 1995 so arising.

    (2)   This subsection applies:

    (a)   to an offence which involves an assault on, or injury or a threat of injury to, a person;

    (b)   to an offence under section 1 of the Children and Young Persons Act 1933 (cruelty to persons under 16);

    (c)   to an offence under the Sexual Offences Act 1956, the Indecency with Children Act 1960, the Sexual Offences Act 1967, section 54 of the Criminal Law Act 1977 or the Protection of Children Act 1978; and

(d)   to an offence which consists of attemping or conspiring to commit, or of aiding, abetting, counselling, procuring or inciting the commission of, an offence falling within paragraph (a), (b) or (c) above.

(3)   A statement made on oath by a witness outside the United Kingdom and given in evidence through a link by virtue of this section shall be treated for the purposes of section 1 of the Perjury Act 1911 as having been made in the proceedings in which it is given in evidence.

(3A)   Where, in the case of any proceedings before a youth court—

(a)   leave is given by virtue of subsection (1)(b) above for evidence to be given through a television link; and

(b)   suitable facilities for receiving such evidence are not available at any petty-sessional court-house in which the court can (apart from this subsection) lawfully sit,

the court may sit for the purposes of the whole or any part of those proceedings at any place at which such facilities are available and which has been appointed for the purposes of this subsection by the justices acting for the petty sessions area for which the court acts.

(3B)   A place appointed under subsection (3A) above may be outside the petty sessions area for which it is appointed; but it shall be deemed to be in that area for the purpose of the jurisdiction of the justices acting for that area.

(3C)   Where—

(a)   the court gives leave for a person to give evidence through a live television link, and

(b)   the leave is given by virtue of subsection (1)(b) above,

then, subject to subsection (3D) below, the person concerned may not give evidence otherwise than through a live television link.

(3D)   In a case falling within subsection (3C) above the court may give permission for the person to give evidence otherwise than through a live television link if it appears to the court to be in the interests of justice to give such permission.

(3E)   Permission may be given under subsection (3D) above—

(a)   on an application by a party to the case, or

(b)   of the court's own motion;

but no application may be made under paragraph (a) above unless there has been a material change of circumstances since the leave was given by virtue of subsection (1)(b) above.

(4)   Without prejudice to the generality of any enactment confer-ring power to make rules to which this subsection applies, such rules

may make such provision as appears to the authority making them to be necessary or expedient for the purposes of this section.

(5) The rules to which subsection (4) above applies are Magistrates' Courts Rules, Crown Court Rules and Criminal Appeal Rules.

(6) Subsection (7) of section 32A below shall apply for the purposes of this section as it applies for the purposes of that section, but with the omission of the references to a person being, in the cases there mentioned, under the age of fifteen years or under the age of eighteen years.

Note

Subsections (3C), (3D) and (3E) have effect where the leave concerned is given on or after a day appointed by the Secretary of State under the Criminal Procedure, and Investigations Act 1996, s. 62. No day had been appointed when this edition went to press.

Video recordings of testimony from child witnesses

32A.—(1) This section applies in relation to the following proceedings, namely—

(a) trials on indictment for any offence to which section 32(2) above applies;

(b) appeals to the criminal division of the Court of Appeal and hearings of references under section 9 of the Criminal Appeal Act 1995 in respect of any such offence; and

(c) proceedings in youth courts for any such offence, appeals to the Crown Court arising out of such proceedings and hearing of references under section 11 of the Criminal Appeal Act 1995 so arising.

(2) In any such proceedings a video recording of an interview which:

(a) is conducted between an adult and a child who is not the accused or one of the accused ('the child witness'); and

(b) relates to any matter in issue in the proceedings, may, with the leave of the court, be given in evidence in so far as it is not excluded by the court under subsection (3) below.

(3) Where a video recording is tendered in evidence under this section, the court shall (subject to the exercise of any power of the court to exclude evidence which is otherwise admissible) give leave under subsection (2) above unless—

(a) it appears that the child witness will not be available for cross-examination;

(b) any rules of court requiring disclosure of the circumstances in which the recording was made have not been complied with to the satisfaction of the court; or

(c) the court is of the opinion, having regard to all the circumstances of the case, that in the interests of justice the recording ought not to be admitted;

and where the court gives such leave it may, if it is of the opinion that in the interests of justice any part of the recording ought not to be admitted, direct that that part shall be excluded.

(4) In considering whether any part of a recording ought to be excluded under subsection (3) above, the court shall consider whether any prejudice to the accused, or one of the accused, which might result from the admission of that part is outweighed by the desirability of showing the whole, or substantially the whole, of the recorded interview.

(5) Where a video recording is admitted under this section—

(a) the child witness shall be called by the party who tendered it in evidence;

(b) that witness shall not be examined in chief on any matter which, in the opinion of the court, has been dealt with adequately in his recorded testimony.

(6) Where a video recording is given in evidence under this section, any statement made by the child witness which is disclosed by the recording shall be treated as if given by that witness in direct oral testimony; and accordingly—

(a) any such statement shall be admissible evidence of any fact of which such testimony from him would be admissible;

(b) no such statement shall be capable of corroborating any other evidence given by him;

and in estimating the weight, if any, to be attached to such a statement, regard shall be had to all the circumstances from which any inference can reasonably be drawn (as to its accuracy and otherwise).

(6A) Where the court gives leave under subsection (2) above the child witness shall not give relevant evidence (within the meaning given by subsection (6D) below) otherwise than by means of the video recording; but this is subject to subsection (6B) below.

(6B) In a case falling within subsection (6A) above the court may give permission for the child witness to give relevant evidence (within the meaning given by subsection (6D) below) otherwise than by means of the video recording if it appears to the court to be in the interests of justice to give such permission.

(6C)   Permission may be given under subsection (6B) above—
(a)   on an application by a party to the case, or
(b)   of the court's own motion;
but no application may be made under paragraph (a) above unless there has been a material change of circumstances since the leave was given under subsection (2) above.

(6D)   For the purposes of subsections (6A) and (6B) above evidence is relevant evidence if—
(a)   it is evidence in chief on behalf of the party who tendered the video recording, and
(b)   it relates to matter which, in the opinion of the court, is dealt with in the recording and which the court has not directed to be excluded under subsection (3) above.

(7)   In this section 'child' means a person who:
(a)   in the case of an offence failing within section 32(2)(a) or (b) above, is under fourteen years of age or, if he was under that age when the video recording was made, is under fifteen years of age; or
(b)   in the case of an offence falling within section 32(2)(c) above, is under seventeen years of age or, if he was under that age when the video recording was made, is under eighteen years of age.

(8)   Any reference in subsection (7) above to an offence falling within paragraph (a), (b) or (c) of section 32(2) above includes a reference to an offence which consists of attempting or conspiring to commit, or of aiding, abetting, counselling, procuring or inciting the commission of, an offence falling within that paragraph.

(9)   In this section—
'statement' includes any representation of fact, whether made in words or otherwise;
'video recording' means any recording, on any medium, from which a moving image may by any means be produced and includes the accompanying sound-track.

(10)   A magistrates' court inquiring into an offence as examining justices under section 6 of the Magistrates' Courts Act 1980 may consider any video recording as respects which leave under subsection (2) above is sought at the trial.

(11)   Without prejudice to the generality of any enactment conferring power to make rules of court, such rules may make such provision

as appears to the authority making them to be necessary or expedient for the purposes of this section.

(12)   Nothing in this section shall prejudice the admissibility of any video recording which would be admissible apart from this section.

Note

Subsections (6A) to (6D) have effect where the leave concerned is given on or after a day appointed by the Secretary of State under the Criminal Procedure and Investigations Act 1996, s. 62. No day had been appointed when this edition went to press. Provision is made in the Criminal Justice and Public Order Act 1994, s. 168(3) and sch. 11, for the repeal of subsection (10) but had not been brought into force when this edition went to press.

Schedule 2   Documentary Evidence — Supplementary

1.   Where a statement is admitted as evidence in criminal proceedings by virtue of Part II of this Act—

(a)   any evidence which, if the person making the statement had been called as a witness, would have ben admissible as relevant to his credibility as a witness shall be admissible for that purpose in those proceedings;

(b)   evidence may, with the leave of the court, be given of any matter which, if that person had been called as a witness, could have been put to him in cross-examination as relevant to his credibility as a witness but of which evidence could not have been adduced by the cross-examining party; and

(c)   evidence tending to prove that that person, whether before or after making the statement, made (whether orally or not) some other statement which is inconsistent with it shall be admissible for the purpose of showing that he has contradicted himself.

2.   A statement which is given in evidence by virtue of Part II of this Act shall not be capable of corroborating evidence given by the person making it.

3.   In estimating the weight, if any, to be attached to such a statement regard shall be had to all the circumstances from which any inference can reasonably be drawn as to its accuracy or otherwise.

4.   Without prejudice to the generality of any enactment conferring power to make them—

    (a)   Crown Court Rules;

    (b)   Criminal Appeal Rules; and

    (c)   rules under section 144 of the Magistrates' Courts Act 1980,

may make such provision as appears to the authority making any of them to be necessary or expedient for the purposes of Part II of this Act.

5.—(1) In Part II of this Act—

'document' means anything in which information of any description is recorded;

'copy', in relation to a document, means anything onto which information recorded in the document has been copied, by whatever means and whether directly or indirectly; and

'statement' means any representation of fact, however made.

(2) For the purposes of Part II of this Act evidence which, by reason of a defect of speech or hearing, a person called as a witness gives in writing or by signs shall be treated as given orally.

6. In Part II of this Act 'confession' has the meaning assigned to it by section 82 of the Police and Criminal Evidence Act 1984.

Civil Evidence Act 1995 (1995, c. 38)

Admissibility of hearsay evidence

1.—(1) In civil proceedings evidence shall not be excluded on the ground that it is hearsay.

    (2) In this Act—

    (a) 'hearsay' means a statement made otherwise than by a person while giving oral evidence in the proceedings which is tendered as evidence of the matters stated; and

    (b) references to hearsay include hearsay of whatever degree.

    (3) Nothing in this Act affects the admissibility of evidence admissible apart from this section.

    (4) The provisions of sections 2 to 6 (safeguards and supplementary provisions relating to hearsay evidence) do not apply in relation to hearsay evidence admissible apart from this section, notwithstanding that it may also be admissible by virtue of this section.

Notice of proposal to adduce hearsay evidence

2.—(1) A party proposing to adduce hearsay evidence in civil proceedings shall, subject to the following provisions of this section, give to the other party or parties to the proceedings—

   (a)   such notice (if any) of that fact, and

   (b)   on request, such particulars of or relating to the evidence,

as is reasonable and practicable in the circumstances for the purpose of enabling him or them to deal with any matters arising from its being hearsay.

   (2)   Provision may be made by rules of court—

   (a)   specifying classes of proceedings or evidence in relation to which subsection (1) does not apply, and

   (b)   as to the manner in which (including the time within which) the duties imposed by that subsection are to be complied with in the cases where it does apply.

   (3)   Subsection (1) may also be excluded by agreement of the parties; and compliance with the duty to give notice may in any case be waived by the person to whom notice is required to be given.

   (4)   A failure to comply with subsection (1), or with rules under subsection (2)(b), does not affect the admissibility of the evidence but may be taken into account by the court—

   (a)   in considering the exercise of its powers with respect to the course of proceedings and costs, and

   (b)   as a matter adversely affecting the weight to be given to the evidence in accordance with section 4.

Power to call witness for cross-examination on hearsay statement

3.   Rules of court may provide that where a party to civil proceedings adduces hearsay evidence of a statement made by a person and does not call that person as a witness, any other party to the proceedings may, with the leave of the court, call that person as a witness and cross-examine him on the statement as if he had been called by the first-mentioned party and as if the hearsay statement were his evidence in chief.

Considerations relevant to weighing of hearsay evidence

4.—(1)   In estimating the weight (if any) to be given to hearsay evidence in civil proceedings the court shall have regard to any circumstances from which any inference can reasonably be drawn as to the reliability or otherwise of the evidence.

   (2)   Regard may be had, in particular, to the following—

   (a)   whether it would have been reasonable and practicable for the party by whom the evidence was adduced to have produced the maker of the original statement as a witness;

(b)   whether the original statement was made contemporaneously with the occurrence or existence of the matters stated;

(c)   whether the evidence involves multiple hearsay;

(d)   whether any person involved had any motive to conceal or misrepresent matters;

(e)   whether the original statement was an edited account, or was made in collaboration with another or for a particular purpose;

(f)   whether the circumstances in which the evidence is adduced as hearsay are such as to suggest an attempt to prevent proper evaluation of its weight.

Competence and credibility

5.—(1)   Hearsay evidence shall not be admitted in civil proceedings if or to the extent that it is shown to consist of, or to be proved by means of, a statement made by a person who at the time he made the statement was not competent as a witness.

For this purpose 'not competent as a witness' means suffering from such mental or physical infirmity, or lack of understanding, as would render a person incompetent as a witness in civil proceedings; but a child shall be treated as competent as a witness if he satisfies the requirements of section 96(2)(a) and (b) of the Children Act 1989 (conditions for reception of unsworn evidence of child).

(2)   Where in civil proceedings hearsay evidence is adduced and the maker of the original statement, or of any statement relied upon to prove another statement, is not called as a witness—

(a)   evidence which if he had been so called would be admissible for the purpose of attacking or supporting his credibility as a witness is admissible for that purpose in the proceedings; and

(b)   evidence tending to prove that, whether before or after he made the statement, he made any other statement inconsistent with it is admissible for the purpose of showing that he had contradicted himself.

Provided that evidence may not be given of any matter of which, if he had been called as a witness and had denied that matter in cross-examination, evidence could not have been adduced by the cross-examining party.

Previous statements of witnesses

6.—(1)   Subject as follows, the provisions of this Act as to hearsay evidence in civil proceedings apply equally (but with any necessary modifications) in relation to a previous statement made by a person called as a witness in the proceedings.

(2)   A party who has called or intends to call a person as a witness in civil proceedings may not in those proceedings adduce evidence of a previous statement made by that person, except—

(a)   with the leave of the court, or

(b)   for the purpose of rebutting a suggestion that his evidence has been fabricated.

This shall not be construed as preventing a witness statement (that is, a written statement of oral evidence which a party to the proceedings intends to lead) from being adopted by a witness in giving evidence or treated as his evidence.

(3)   Where in the case of civil proceedings section 3, 4 or 5 of the Criminal Procedure Act 1865 applies, which make provision as to—

(a)   how far a witness may be discredited by the party producing him,

(b)   the proof of contradictory statements made by a witness, and

(c)   cross-examination as to previous statements in writing,

this Act does not authorise the adducing of evidence of a previous inconsistent or contradictory statement otherwise than in accordance with those sections.

This is without prejudice to any provision made by rules of court under section 3 above (power to call witness for cross-examination on hearsay statement).

(4)   Nothing in this Act affects any of the rules of law as to the circumstances in which, where a person called as a witness in civil proceedings is cross-examined on a document used by him to refresh his memory, that document may be made evidence in the proceedings.

(5)   Nothing in this section shall be construed as preventing a statement of any description referred to above from being admissible by virtue of section 1 as evidence of the matters stated.

Interpretation

13.   In this Act—

'civil proceedings' has the meaning given by section 11 and 'court' and 'rules of court' shall be construed in accordance with that section;

'document' means anything in which information of any description is recorded, and 'copy', in relation to a document, means anything onto which information recorded in the document has been copied, by whatever means and whether directly or indirectly;

'hearsay' shall be construed in accordance with section 1(2);

'oral evidence' includes evidence which, by reason of a defect of speech or hearing, a person called as a witness gives in writing or by signs;

'the original statement', in relation to hearsay evidence, means the underlying statement (if any) by—

(a)   in the case of evidence of fact, a person having personal knowledge of that fact, or

(b)   in the case of evidence of opinion, the person whose opinion it is; and

'statement' means any representation of fact or opinion, however made.

County Court Rules 1981, Order 20, rules 27 and 28

Restrictions on adducing expert evidence
27.—(1)   Except—

(a)   with the leave of the court,

(b)   in accordance with the provisions of Order 17, rule 11, or

(c)   where all parties agree,

no expert evidence may be adduced at the trial or hearing of an action or matter, unless the party seeking to adduce the evidence has applied to the court to determine whether a direction should be given under rule 37, 38 or 41 (whichever is appropriate) of RSC Order 38, as applied by rule 28 of this Order, and has complied with any direction given on the application.

(2)   Nothing in paragraph (1) shall apply to expert evidence which is permitted to be given by affidavit or which is to be adduced in an action or matter in which no defence or answer has been filed or in proceedings referred to arbitration under section 64 of the Act [1].

(3)   Nothing in paragraph (1) shall affect the enforcement under any other provision of these rules (except Order 29, rule 1) of a direction given under this Part of this Order.

Note

1.   That is, the County Courts Act 1984 (CCR, Ord. 1, r. 3).

Application of RSC
28.   RSC Order 38, rules 37 to 44, shall apply in relation to an application under rule 27 of this Order as they apply in relation to an application under rule 36(1) of the said Order 38.

Rules of the Supreme Court 1965, Order 38, rules 36 to 44

These rules were added by Rules of the Supreme Court (Amendment) 1974 (SI 1974/295). Rule 40 was revoked by Rules of the Supreme Court (Amendment No. 2) 1980 (SI 1980/1010); new r. 37 was substituted by Rules of the Supreme Court (Amendment No. 4) 1989 (SI 1989/2427), r. 15; and new r. 38 was substituted by Rules of the Supreme Court (Amendment) 1987 (SI 1987/1423), r. 41.

Restrictions on adducing expert evidence
36.—(1) Except with the leave of the court or where all parties agree, no expert evidence may be adduced at the trial or hearing of any cause or matter unless the party seeking to adduce the evidence—

(a) has applied to the court to determine whether a direction should be given under rule 37 or 41 (whichever is appropriate) and has complied with any direction given on the application, or

(b) has complied with automatic directions taking effect under Order 25, rule 8(1)(b).

(2) Nothing in paragraph (1) shall apply to evidence which is permitted to be given by affidavit or shall affect the enforcement under any other provision of these Rules (except Order 45, rule 5) of a direction given under this Part of this Order.

Note

As amended by Rules of the Supreme Court (Amendment No. 2) 1980 (SI 1980/1010), r. 10(1), and Rules of the Supreme Court (Amendment) 1987 (SI 1987/1423), r. 40.

Direction that expert report be disclosed
37.—(1) Subject to paragraph (2), where in any cause or matter an application is made under rule 36(1) in respect of oral expert evidence, then, unless the court considers that there are special reasons for not doing so, it shall direct that the substance of the evidence be disclosed in the form of a written report or reports to such other parties and within such period as the court may specify.

(2) Nothing in paragraph (1) shall require a party to disclose a further medical report if he proposes to rely at the trial only on the report provided pursuant to Order 18, rule 12(1A) or (1B) but, where a party claiming damages for personal injuries discloses a further

report, that report shall be accompanied by a statement of the special damages claimed and in this paragraph, 'statement of the special damages claimed has the same meaning as in Order 18, rule 12(1C).

Meeting of experts
38.   In any cause or matter the court may, if it thinks fit, direct that there be a meeting 'without prejudice' of such experts within such periods before or after the disclosure of their reports as the court may specify, for the purpose of identifying those parts of their evidence which are in issue. Where such a meeting takes place the experts may prepare a joint statement indicating those parts of their evidence on which they are, and those on which they are not, in agreement.

Disclosure of part of expert evidence
39.   Where the Court considers that any circumstances rendering it undesirable to give a direction under rule 37 . . . [1] relate to part only of the evidence sought to be adduced, the Court may, if it thinks fit, direct disclosure of the remainder.

Note

1.   Words deleted by Rules of the Supreme Court (Amendment) 1987 (SI 1987/1423), r. 42.

Expert evidence contained in statement
41.   Where an application is made under rule 36 in respect of expert evidence contained in a statement and the applicant alleges that the maker of the statement cannot or should not be called as a witness, the Court may direct that the provisions of rules 20 to 23 and 25 to 33 shall apply with such modifications as the Court thinks fit.

Putting in evidence expert report disclosed by another party
42.   A party to any cause or matter may put in evidence any expert report disclosed to him by any other party in accordance with this Part of this Order.

Time for putting expert report in evidence
43.   Where a party to any cause or matter calls as a witness the maker of a report which has been disclosed . . . [1] in accordance with a direction given under rule 37 . . . [2], the report may be put in evidence

at the commencement of its maker's examination-in-chief or at such other time as the Court may direct.

Notes

1. Words deleted by Rules of the Supreme Court (Amendment No. 2) 1982 (SI 1982/1111).
2. Words deleted by Rules of the Supreme Court (Amendment) 1987 (SI 1987/1423), r. 43.

Revocation and variation of directions
44. Any direction given under this Part of this Order may on sufficient cause being shown be revoked or varied by a subsequent direction given at or before the trial of the cause or matter.

Index

Accomplices
  corroboration 141
  see also Co-defendants
Admissibility 1, 2, 9, 10–12, 207
  conditional on secondary issues
      10, 13
  confessions 64–5
  court as final arbiter 11
  de bene esse 10, 11
  expert reports 152–3
  general approach to arguments
      14–17
  judicial discretion 17–19
  objections to 12–17
  obliterating inadmissible
      evidence 13
  rules governing 10–11, 16–17
Admissions 51–2
Adverse witnesses *see* Hostile
    witnesses
Advocates
  courage 211
  dress 202–3, 213
  manner in court 207–8, 228
  politeness 207–8
Agency, hearsay 52
Appropriate adult 238–9, 263, 264
Arrest of witnesses 138–9

Beyond reasonable doubt 8–9
Breach of contract, burden of proof
    6
Brown, David Paul 205, 211, 228
Brown's rules 205–8
Burden of proof 2, 3–7
  breach of contract 6
  confessions 70–1
  defence not required to bear 4,
      5–6

Burden of proof – *continued*
  evidential 4
  fundamental rule 3
  legal 4
  negligence 6
  reference in closing speech
      226–7
  in regulatory offence cases 6
Business records 50, 55–7, 295–6

Cautions 258–60
  statements written under
      279–80
Character 107–26
  areas for consideration 108
  bad 114–18
    confessions revealing 86–7
    cross-examination 117, 118,
        168
    previous convictions 107–8,
        115–17
    principle in law 114
    prosecution witnesses
      imputations against
          118–20, 123
      references elicited from
          123–5
    voluntary disclosure 123–4
  cross-examination on 112–14,
      117, 118, 120–2
  in examination-in-chief 221–3
  good 108–14
    cross-examination of
        prosecution witnesses
        110
    directions to jury 108–9
    facts proved in support of
        110–11
    guilty plea and 109–10

Character – *continued*
  value as evidence 108
  improper references to 123–5
  relative, advantages of admission
    222–3
Character witnesses 144–5
  in criminal cases 214, 215,
    221–3
  value 110–11
Children
  adult attendants 134–5
  competency as witnesses 132–5
  corroboration 141
  hearsay evidence 41
  sexual cases 8, 134
  television links 298–300
  of tender years 132
  treatment by advocates 134–5
  unsworn evidence 132
  videotaped evidence 133–4,
    135, 180–1, 300–3
Chronology of events 199
  in opening speech 203–4
Civil cases
  burden of proof 6–7
  conduct of hearing 202–5
  hearsay 34–5
  preparation 199–206
    pre-trial review 198–9
    written witness statements
      198–9
Closing speeches
  attack on weight of evidence
    14
  avoiding misstatement of
    evidence 227
  in civil cases 210–11
  content 226–7
  in criminal cases 214, 220
  for defence 226–7
  style 224
Co-defendants
  application for separate trials
    85
  confessions of, and confessions
    made in response to 85–6
  confessions implicating 83–5

Co-defendants – *continued*
  defendant as defence witness
    129
  defendant as prosecution witness
    129–30
  effect of defendant's evidence
    223
  evidence given against 122–3
  see also Accomplices
Codes of Practice (under Police and
    Criminal Evidence Act 1984,
    s.66) 63, 76–7
  A: power to stop and search 76
  B: searching of premises and
    seizure of property 76
  C: detention, treatment and
    questioning by police 64,
    66, 76
    checking compliance with 68
    recognising breaches
      (checklist) 79–83
    text 236–84
  D: identification of persons by
    police officers 76, 179–80
  E: tape-recording of interviews
    64, 76, 78
Collateral issues 193–4
Commonwealth citizens 253–4
Community opinion of defendant
  111
Computer records 56, 59–61
Confessions 63–87, 232–4
  admissibility 14–16, 63, 64–5,
    69–75
    statutory provisions 69–70
  burden and standard of proof
    70–1
  by mentally handicapped persons
    73, 234
  changes in law (1984) 64
  circumstances excluding 65
  Code of Practice C 64, 76
  concept of voluntariness 69
  conditions under which obtained
    67–8
  cross-examination of police
    officers 67–8

Confessions – *continued*
  definition 63–4
  editing 84, 85, 86–7
  exculpatory and incriminating
    parts 90–1
  implicating co-defendant 83–5
    cross-examination 84–5
  inadmissible 20
  language 68
  methods prior to 1984 64
  obtained by oppression 71–2,
    74, 78
  in response to co-defendant's
    confession 85–6
  revealing previous bad character
    86–7
  standard of proof 70–1
  taking instructions 67–8
  to 'person in authority' 69, 70
  totality of circumstances 72–3
  unfair 77–8
  unreliable 72–5
  weight 63
    challenges 83
  written record 68
  see also Tape-recorded interviews
Confidential information *see*
  Privilege
Copies 47–8
Corroboration 140, 141–2
  'dangerous' witnesses 141
  required as matter of law 142
  warning 141–2
Credibility, hearsay evidence
  45–6, 306
Criminal cases
  burden of proof 3–6
  closing speeches 214, 220
  conduct 212
  disclosure by defence 217–18
  forms of address 213
  gathering evidence 214–18
  incompetence of witnesses
    128–30
  practice run with client 223
  preparation 212–13
  reference to relevant law 227

Criminal cases – *continued*
  see also Hearsay in criminal
    cases
Cross-examination
  by opponent 208
  on character 18, 112–14, 120–2
  in civil cases 208–10
  conduct 167
  on credibility of witness 186–7
  in criminal cases 205–10
  danger of too many questions
    220
  of expert witnesses 148, 153,
    154–5
  hearsay evidence 45, 47, 305
  on matters not in examination-in-
    chief 183, 184
  memory-refreshing documents
    173, 174, 184–6
  phases 219–20
  of police officers 67–8
  preparation 218–21
  previous inconsistent statements
    187–9
  purposes 182
  reducing aggression 219
  relating to type of witness
    218–19
  rule of evidence 182–9
  technique 183, 208–10, 218–21
  witness's liability 168
Custody officer 237, 240, 241, 255
  property of detainee 245–6
Custody record 239–40
  action taken on request for
    solicitor 66–7

Damages claims 201–2
Deception in obtaining
  evidence 18
Defendants
  competency as witnesses 136
    in criminal cases 128–30
  evidence-in-chief 221–3
  limited burden of proof 5–6
  not obliged to give evidence
    221

Defendants – *continued*
  spouses as witnesses 130–2,
    136–9, 235–6
Denials 89–90
Detained persons
  charging 270–2
  Commonwealth citizens 253–4
  foreign nationals 253–4, 283–4
  medical treatment 256
  medication 257
  normal procedure 240–2
  property of 245–6
  rights 244–5
    delay in allowing rights
      275–8
  special groups 242–3
  terrorism offences 277–8
  treatment 256–8
Detention
  conditions 254–6
  extensions 269
  in hospital 268–9
  incommunicado 246–8
  property of detainee 245–6
  reviews 269
  rights, informing of whereabouts
    246–8
  see also Code of Practice C
Disclosure
  by defence in criminal cases
    217–18
  civil procedure 105
  criminal procedure 102–5
  defence statement 102–5
  failure to comply with provisions
    102–5
Divorced spouses, competency as
    witnesses 131
Documentary evidence 2
  business records 50, 55–7,
    295–6
  computer produced 56, 59–61
  criminal cases 55–7, 214–15
  hearsay 297–8, 303–8
    civil cases 42
    criminal cases 55–7
  preparation 199, 200

Documentary evidence – *continued*
  prepared for criminal proceedings
    58
  presentation 194–6
  production in court 204
  public authority records 50
  see also Records
Documents
  copies 204
  definition 47
Dress in court 202–3
  magistrates' courts 213
Duty solicitors 66

Editing, confessions 84, 85, 86–7
Entrapment 19
Evidence
  admissibility *see* Admissibility
  County Court Rules 308
  defence access to prosecution
    evidence 215
  definition 1
  disputed, avoidance in opening
    speeches 15
  exclusionary discretion 17–19
  expert *see* Expert evidence
  mixed statements 90–21
  of one witness, to prove case
    140, 141
  presentation 2–3, 167–97
  relevance 1, 2, 9–12
    definition 9–10
    demonstration after admission
      10
  rule 2
  Rules of Supreme Court
    309–11
  secondary 13
    on confessions 14
  television links 298–300
  unfairly/illegally obtained 2,
    19–20
    exclusion 20, 234
  unsworn, of children 132
  videotaped 133–4, 135, 180–1,
    300–3
  see also Confessions;

Evidence – *continued*
   Documentary evidence;
   Hearsay; Oral evidence;
   Proofs of evidence; Real
   evidence; Weight of
   evidence
Examination-in-chief 169–82
  Brown's rules 205–8
  conduct 167
  leading questions 205
  preparing defendant 221–3
  unfavourable/hostile witnesses
    176–9
  videotaped interviews with
    children 180–1
  written witness statements
    181–2
Excited utterances 35–7
  admissibility 174–5
Exclusionary discretion 17–19
Exhibits
  availability to defence 216
  preparation by defence 217
  unbroken chain of possession
    196, 217
  see also Documentary evidence;
    Real evidence
Expert evidence 146–55, 308–11
  admissibility 152–3
  advocate's understanding 148,
    201
  disclosure 309–10
  from opposing side 149
  meeting of experts 310
  pre-trial disclosure 149, 150–2
  preparation 147–50
  presentation 153–5
    oral 147
  restrictions 308, 309
Expert witnesses 143–4
  competency 144
  in criminal cases 215, 217
  cross-examination 144, 148,
    153, 154–5
  qualifications 143–4

False statements 90

Finality on collateral issues 193–4
Foreign nationals 253–4, 283–4
Forms of address 213

Guilty plea, previous good character
  and 109–10

Hearsay
  first-hand 294–5
  impeachment of maker of
    statement 189–90
  memory-refreshing documents
    174
  multiple 42
Hearsay at common law 24–38
  confusion in interpretation 24–5
  distinguishing from direct
    evidence 27–30
    examples 30–4
  explanation 25–7
  fallacies 25
  rule 25–6
    exceptions 34–5
    excited utterances 35–7
Hearsay in civil cases 39–52
  abolition of rule 41–2
  adducing evidence, notice of
    proposal 304–5
  admissibility 39, 40–1, 51–2,
    304
  admissions 51–2
  agency 52
  children 41
  Civil Evidence Act 41–50,
    304–8
  common law exceptions 49
  competence 45–6, 306
  computer produced documents
    56, 59–61
  copies use 47–8
  credibility 45–6, 306
  cross-examination 45, 47, 305
  documentary 42
  multiple hearsay 42
  notice 43, 44–5
  oral 41–2, 48
  previous statements 306–7

Hearsay in civil cases – *continued*
procedural safeguards 42–6
public authority records 50
reasons for not calling witness in
person 43
weight of evidence 40, 46–7,
305–6
witness
called 48–9
impeachment 49
not called 43
Hearsay in criminal cases 53–62
admissibility 53–7
business documents 55–7,
295–6
confessions 54
documents prepared for
proceedings 58, 297–8
first-hand hearsay 294–5
judicial discretion to exclude
57–8
notice 61
statements 53–5
weight of evidence 61
witnesses in fear 55
Hearsay witnesses 40–1
Hostile witnesses
examination-in-chief 176–8
handling in court 206–7
leave from bench to treat as
171, 177–8
use of leading questions 171

Identification 175, 179–80
of defendant, out of court
179–80
fleeting glances 179
parades 179, 180
of persons by police officers
(Code of Practice D) 74
Impeachment of witnesses 49,
177, 189–90
Impertinent witnesses 205–6
Interpreters 267–8
Interviews 78
Interviews at police stations
261–9

Interviews at police stations –
continued
deaf persons 267, 289
foreign languages 267
interpreters 267–8
police actions 264–6
presence of solicitors 65–7, 78,
230–2, 248–53, 276–7
records 66, 262–3
regulation of conduct 67–8
rights 243–5
delay in allowing rights
275–8
special restrictions 268–9
speech handicaps 267
terrorism offences 277–8
urgent 278
voluntary attendance 243
see also Detained persons;
Tape-recorded interviews
Intimate searches 274–5

Judges' Rules 75–6
Judicial discretion
on admission of character
evidence 120–2
on admission or exclusion of
evidence 17–19
Judicial notice, of facts beyond
dispute 21
Juveniles
charging 271
interviews 263–4, 278,
280–3

Law books, availability in court
201
Leading questions 169–71
in cross-examination 183
not admissible in examination-in-
chief 169, 208
permissible types 171
ways to circumvent 171
Legal professional privilege
evidence 161
furtherance of crime or fraud
161–2

Legal professional privilege –
  continued
  lawyer-client communications
    159–60
  third party communications
    160–1
Local knowledge of judges 20–2

Marital information, as compellable
    evidence 132
Matrimonial cases, standard of
    proof 8
Memory-refreshing documents
  contemporaneity 31–2, 171,
    172
  cross-examination on 173, 174,
    184–6
  hearsay 174
  referred to before trial 171
  replacement of lost documents
    173
  rules of evidence 171–4
  verifiability 171, 172
Mentally handicapped persons
  charging 271
  competency as witnesses 135
  confessions of 73
  detention 239, 245
  interviews 263–4, 278
Mixed statements 90–21

Negligence actions, burden of proof
    6
Nervousness
  advocates 198
  witnesses 206
No case to answer submissions
    221, 225–6
Notice
  hearsay in civil cases 43, 44–5
  hearsay in criminal cases 61

Objections
  to admissibility 12–17
  advantages to limiting 207
  reactions to 2
  resisting unexpected attacks 16

Ogden Tables 40
Opening speeches
  avoidance of disputed evidence
    15
  in civil cases 203–4
  not usually made for defence
    225
  for prosecution 224–5
  purpose 224–5
  style 224–5
Opinion evidence 146
Oppression 66, 69, 71–2, 74, 78
Oral evidence 2, 127
  of expert witnesses 147
  hearsay 41–2, 48
  if supplier of written evidence
    unavailable 41–2

Personal knowledge, of judges
    20–2
Persuasiveness of evidence 2
  weighed against prejudicial
    effects 17–18
  see also Evidence: weight
Plaintiffs, burden of proof 6–7
Pleadings 204
Police officers
  cross-examination on confessions
    67–8
  notebooks 58, 171, 172–3,
    184–5
  see also Codes of Practice;
    Interviews at police stations
Previous consistent statements 11
  admissibility at common law
    174–6
  defendant's shield against cross-
    examination 112–13
  fabrication rebuttal 175–6
  rules of evidence 26–7, 174–6
Previous convictions 107–8
  of prosecution witnesses 216
  refuting good character 111
  restrictions on disclosure 124
Previous inconsistent statements
    306–7
  cross-examination 187–9

Prima facie cases 4–5
Privilege 150, 156–65
  consequence of claim 158
  duty to claim 158
  general principles 156–8
  legal professional
    evidence 161
    furtherance of crime or fraud
      161–2
    lawyer-client communications
      159–60
    third party communications
      160–1
  original communication or
    document 157–8
  self-incrimination 162–4
  waiver 157–8
  without-prejudice
    communications 164
Proofs of evidence
  preparation 200
  see also Burden of proof;
    Standard of proof
Property, seizure by police (Code of
  Practice B) 76
Public authority records, hearsay in
  civil cases 50

Re-examination
  conduct 168
  of matters raised in cross-
    examination 183, 191–2
  rules of evidence 191–4
Real evidence 2, 217
  presentation 194–6
  proving authenticity 196
Rebuttal evidence 5
  admissibility 192–3
  rules of evidence 191–4
  of suggestion of fabricated
    evidence 175–6
Recalling witnesses 183
Recent complaint evidence 175
Records
  admissibility in civil cases
    55–7
  computer-produced 56, 59–61

Records – *continued*
  of interviews at police
    stations 58
  see also Business records;
    Documentary hearsay; Tape-
    recorded interviews
Relevance of evidence 9–12
Reluctant witnesses 139
  summonses 200
Res gestae rule *see* Excited
  utterances
Review officer 269

Searches of persons
  intimate 273–4
  strip 274–5
Searching of premises by police
  Code of Practice B 76
  without warrant, to obtain
    evidence 19
Self-incrimination privilege
  162–4
Self-serving statements
  rules of evidence 26–7
  weight of evidence 174–6
Separated spouses, competency as
  witnesses 131
Sexual offences
  child witnesses 8, 134
  corroboration of complainant
    evidence 141
  evidence of recent complaints
    175
Silence 66, 91–102
  adverse inferences 92, 99–100,
    221
  at trial 98–100
  in court 221
  defence statement, failure to
    provide 102–5
  directions to jury 100
  facts expected to be mentioned
    92
  sole basis of conviction 101
  solicitor advice 93
  when questioned 92–8
Similar-fact evidence 116–17

Solicitors
  access to   65–7, 78, 230–2,
    248–53, 276–7
  presence at police interviews
    65–7, 78
Solicitors' clerks   67
Spent convictions, references to
    124–5
Spouses
  compellability as witnesses
    136–9, 235–6
  competency as witnesses
    130–2, 138–9, 235–6
  see also Cohabitees
Standard of proof   7–9
  beyond reasonable doubt   8–9
  child abuse   8
  civil cases   8
  confessions   70–1
  criminal cases   8–9
  matrimonial cases   8
  references in closing speeches
    226–7
Statements
  by persons since deceased   35
  definition   41
  original   42
  written by police officers
    279–80
  see also Confessions
Stop and search powers (Code of
    Practice A)   76–7
Strip searches   274–5
Summonses
  for reluctant witnesses   200
  serving on witnesses   138–9

Tape-recorded interviews   13, 68
  after the interview   293
  availability to defence counsel
    68, 216–17
  changing tapes   290
  Code of Practice E   64, 78,
    284–94
  commencement of interview
    287–9
  conclusion of interview   291–2

Tape-recorded interviews –
    continued
  deaf persons   267, 289
  failure of recording equipment
    291
  interviews to be recorded   285–7
  master tape   284–5
  objections and complaints by
    suspect   289–90
  removal of tapes from recorder
    291
  security of tapes   294
  taking breaks in interview
    290–1
Television links   298–300
Terrorism offence interviews
    277–8
Trade records *see* Business records
Trials within trials   13, 14, 15–16
Tribunals of fact   13
Tribunals of law   13
Turnbull guidelines   179

Unfavourable witnesses
  examination-in-chief   176–8
  handling in court   206
Unsworn statements
  children   132
  see also Evidence: unsworn

Videotaped evidence   133–4, 135,
    180–1, 300–3

Weight of evidence   9, 11–12, 14,
    61
  attacked in closing speeches   14
  confessions   63, 83
  corroboration   142
  of defendants in criminal cases
    129
  of expert witnesses   144
  hearsay   40, 46–7, 61, 305–6
  increased by corroboration   142
  of self-serving statements
    174–6
Without-prejudice communications
    164

Witness statements
  civil cases   204–5
  examination in chief   181–2
  preparation   198–9
Witnesses   127–45
  afraid to appear in court   55
  assessment of demeanour   218
  availability to both sides   216
  check on willingness to appear
      200
  compelled to attend court
      135–9
    procedure   138–9
    spouses   136–9, 235–6
  competency   127
    of children   132–5
    in criminal cases   229–30
    of defendant's spouse   130–2,
      235–6
    of experts   144
    of former spouses   131
    hearsay   40–1
    of mentally handicapped
      persons   135
  handling impertinence from
      205–6

Witnesses – *continued*
  incompetence
    in criminal cases   128–30
    general and specific   128
  intimidated   55
  liability to cross-examination
      168
  nervousness   206
  not always necessary to call
      139
  number called   139–42
  order called   140
  previous convictions   216
  questions from bench   168
  recalling   183
  reluctant   139, 200
  types to be called   143–5
  warrants to arrest   138–9
  written statements   181–2
  see also Character witnesses;
      Expert witnesses; Hostile
      witnesses; Percipient
      witnesses; Summonses;
      Unfavourable witnesses
Written statements   181–2, 198–9
  under caution   279–80